The Cotswolds Wrecking Crew

A Tale Of Motorcycle Gang Culture For The Social Media Generation

John Beaumont

Copyright ©, John Beaumont 2023

All rights reserved. No part of this book may be reproduced in any form or by any means, electronic or mechanical, including information storage and retrieval systems, without permission from the author or publisher.

Cover designed by Alan Guest.

This is a work of fiction. Unless otherwise indicated, all the names, characters, businesses, places, events and incidents in this book are either the product of the author's imagination or used in a fictitious manner.

For Al, Craig, Oli, and Phil…

Contents

Prologue 1
1. Motorcycle rebellion 9
2. Pretender 23
3. Group ride 40
4. Custom parts 55
5. The new prospect 69
6. Crew 85
7. Brands and reputations 97
8. Exclusive opportunity 116
9. Hooligans 133
10. Collaboration 147
11. Just business 161
12. Fame 179
13. Grand tour 194
14. Realisations 218
15. Bike show 233

Prologue

A group motorcycle ride is an expression of a common bond. It is a shared interest in being on two wheels, rolling thunder through beautiful hills. Five thumping, purring parallel twin motors cut through the sound of late autumn bird song, the geese flying south, flapping manically as we cruised by. The soft rushing of the wind blowing through the remaining leaves on the trees, overwhelmed by the different tones of each exhaust, the harmonious melodies ringing sweet in my ears. We blitzed through another countryside village, the bikes buzzing from the fast-revving engines, matching our own excitement. I spotted a farmer in the field to my left. He saw the line of Triumphs and gave us all a thumbs up whilst holding the straight line of his rumbling tractor, collecting the late harvest. I wondered if he could hear us over his own massive engine. The three riders in front of me carved apart the plodding line of cars on this B-road. I followed their line, no hesitation. I knew the rider behind me would do the same.

"Watch he's not going to pull out, mind!" warned Darren.

"Yeah, I see him," I replied. A quick bit of counter steer, gently nudging the left handlebar, my bike responded instantly. I twisted the throttle and accelerated out of any potential harm. This was now a well-rehearsed action. My bike was fitted with top of the range custom motorcycle parts, excellent brakes and quality rubber keeping me pinned to the road. The cars were moving aside, a mixture of fear and respect on the drivers' faces. We were snapping them out of their trances. They were oblivious to the fresh air, countryside smells, and if lucky, the sunshine piercing the grey clouds for a moment of bliss to warm your back.

"Yes, you are on a beautiful ribbon of tarmac. Wake up and enjoy it," I muttered to them, grinning.

"I think your exhaust woke up that last dawdling driver," said Justin.

The induction roar kicked in, 3000 rpms and climbing, into its peak power band, reaching the crescendo, sounding like a lion with an anti-social-behaviour order.

"Yeah mate," I replied back to him, "to think I would never have removed the baffles to let her rip without your advice."

Another quick right and then left corner came and went in a flash of exhaust smoke, the lush smell of Castrol oil in my nostrils making me feel as if I were at a racetrack. I kicked the bike up to fourth gear, grateful no cars interrupted my flow for these fast few seconds.

"Justin buddy, I'm still loving this chat setup. So clear! I still can't believe you got all this for free!"

"Yeah," interrupted Darren, laughing, "just don't ask him what he had to promise to do instead of paying for 'em!"

A cacophony of muffled laughter rang out through my headset.

"Such a soul-selling, skinny, bearded hipster teen wolf, you are Justin," added Tyrone.

We were riding a fast, easy straight section now. How lucky we were to be able to chat as if we were in the same vehicle... mostly. I ducked down, hugging the tank, out of the wind to try to hear the banter.

"You're one to talk!" retorted Justin.

That was better. Justin was always very quiet, I reflected.

Tyrone was not. "Yeah man, but when I get stuff, I get paid for it."

I shook my head, smirking. Up ahead our next steel cages to overtake came into view, such was the nature of these beautiful roads, often busy with tourists. The chatter stopped for a second. A bad decision could ruin our day. Drawing level with a car, I noticed a young boy sat on the back seat. He waved at me, his face a mixture of awe and exhilaration. I wondered if the young lad drew pictures of motorcycles at home or at school. The Triumph Bonneville and her silhouette was iconic, I mused.

The first Bonneville was built after 1959 to celebrate Triumph taking the land speed record at the Bonneville salt flats in Utah for motorcycles in its engine class. Triumphs were fast and they were cool. Marlon Brando rode a 1950 Thunderbird 6T in the biker gang movie, The Wild One. Steve McQueen rode a 1961 TR6 Trophy to escape the Nazis in the movie, The Great Escape. Even Fonzie rode one, a 1949 TR5 Scrambler, on the TV show Happy Days. Everyone wanted to be seen on a Triumph.

"Woah, easy mate!" came Justin's voice, sounding surprisingly loud and alarmed for once.

I was suddenly ripped away from my daydreaming. I focussed on the rear wheels of Justin and Henry, both riders in front of me, their bright red rear brake lights firmly on. Justin's warning was a bit late notice, but I calmly gave my own front brake a decent and measured squeeze. I pulled up next to them both. I trusted my brakes, having upgraded the font calliper from the stock 2-pot setup to a Pretech 6-pot calliper. The pads were sintered and much harder wearing than the originals too. Using the stock front brakes was like trying to stop a motorcycle with two blocks of wood. With this Bonneville only having a single brake disc upfront, I wanted the extra stopping power.

"What's up?" I asked, forgetting we had mics in our helmets.

"No need to shout old boy," replied Henry, "just checking, we're going to the Potting Shed pub, yeah? Can go straight there on this road or do a few more B-roads first?"

Henry was the lead rider and knew the Cotswold roads better than anyone.

"Yeah, just go straight there mate," replied Justin.

Before anyone else spoke, they both revved off from the junction as if drag-racing. I shook my head in amusement again and rolled on the throttle after them.

My Bonnie was older than theirs, and slower off the mark, but she would put up a strong fight at full tilt in the corners. She had been mine from when I bought her brand new. Triumph didn't even make my version of the Bonneville anymore, but were doing very well with their newer, water-cooled motorcycles. The future seemed bright for the brand, certainly if the five of us was any metric to go on. It was not always that way after the glory days of the 1960s. Triumph, based in Meriden, went out of business in 1983. The parallel twin engine was not able to compete with the faster, more reliable Japanese inline four motorcycles. A man by the name of John Bloor bought the company and relaunched it from Hinckley. From 2001, the so-called Hinckley Bonneville was designed as a rose-tinted nostalgia trip back to the era of the Meriden Bonneville and Triumph's glory days. It worked.

"Henry?" piped up Darren, interrupting more absent-minded musings. I had zoned out, enjoying the flow of the road.

"What?" he replied.

"How many of your London corporate mates have you paid for a posh and overpriced bacon sarnie at this pub then?"

"Um... none," he replied irritably. "We've all been here before, including you!" Henry paused waiting for the penny to drop for Darren. It was quiet so he continued. "I'm raising your standards you see, buddy. Good local ales, not cheap supermarket cider that you drink. Decent food menu, locally sourced artisanal fayre."

Another cackle of laughter came over the airways.

"Fuckin' 'ell," responded Darren.

I spotted some headlights up ahead. Riding towards us was another group, on very fast naked bikes. One, two, three nods of mutual respect as they flew by and then they were gone in a blur.

I tried to place the bikes. What were they, I wondered? Yamaha MT10, KTM Super Duke, and... a Triumph Speed Triple. Very nice indeed. An inline four, a v-twin, and a triple cylinder engine. These fast machines were not our style though. Triumph started making modern bikes in the 1990s from the new factory in Hinckley. Their naked Speed Triple, so called after riders would crash their race replicas, and then put their bikes back on the road without the fairing, was very exciting when it was first released in 1994. It had the power of a sports bike, but with upright handlebars. Three cylinders also meant the bike was smoother, and span up quicker than a twin, but did not need the high revs of an inline four to get into the main power band. This, combined with decent mid-range torque numbers, meant it was fast, nimble, and useable on the road, without needing to go to a track day to make it rip.

Passing more brown and green fields on both sides, we approached the little village of Malmesbury. A few Cotswold stone houses and farms provided the only distraction from the hedgerows and fields. We were almost there now and slowed down. I could hear the bird song returning, without the noise of engines and wind in my ears. As rebellious as the crew were, we respected local speed limits... mostly. I noticed an old man bent double with his walking stick just leaving the local village post office, trying to steady himself. He looked up and towards us, catching my eye. I gave him a nod. He suddenly stood straighter. He was staring at the motorcycles, intently. Like the young lad we passed earlier, this old man recognised the silhouettes of our steeds. His mouth dropped open and formed a grin. I wondered if he was recollecting an image of his younger self. Maybe this was him fifty years ago? I had seen similar scenes at most petrol station forecourts.

"Is that an old Triumph?" they would walk over to me and ask. "I used to own one of them when I was young," they would continue.

The conversations were always the same, and I enjoyed listening to the nostalgia from their past moments on two wheels.

From 2007 the Hinckley Bonneville was beefed-up to 865cc. With tighter emissions controls, the new range of bikes caught up with modern fuel injection systems. This involved a fuel pump, and the electronic software configuration to manage the ratio of fuel to air mixture that went into the engine, replacing the carburettors of old. Triumph kept the old-fashioned styling of the Meriden Bonnies, making the throttle bodies look like the old carburettors. The fuel pump under the tank meant that the shape of the tank had to be bigger, giving it a slightly bulbous look. To keep the Hinckley Bonnies looking proportionate, the whole silhouette was therefore bigger than its 1959 namesake.

To the young lad in the car, the old man on the cobbled pavement, and the many friendly old timers at the petrol stations, they didn't know all that, however. My bike was the true and iconic Bonneville to them. We turned into the pub car park. I hoped Henry captured these miles on his GoPro. I reckoned an Instagram video reel would look awesome rolling through the little villages of Cotswold stone cottages, five twins reverberating off the neat rows of houses. A slick video showing the chocolate-box, picture postcard scene, torn asunder by our collective booming thunder, and lightning-fast machines. Imagine the 'likes', I thought to myself, anticipating the edited footage to be posted to social media to come. We moved the bikes into a straight line, front wheels facing the same way, equal space between each bike. I killed the engine and took off my helmet. The others did the same.

"Why I love the crew is because we ride! We actually fucking ride a bike hard! No mincing about, to the point of nearly stacking it into an old lady's motor! Could happen to any of us! But it ain't fake, it's real. On the edge! Fire it up and ride the bastard!" blurted out Darren, a huge beaming grin on his face. He was wearing the latest Nexx G200 helmet today, with Barstow goggles that colour matched. He neatly placed it on his seat, the helmet colour complementing the green of his fuel tank. We fell about laughing. It was poetic in its raw truth and the bombastic delivery. I hadn't thought of Darren as a philosopher. I looked around. No one seemed to have noticed the swearing. Either that or the pub goers were too frightened of causing a scene with a group of bikers. We sat outside in the beer garden, jackets keeping the creeping colder weather out. The Potting Shed was very much a typically quaint and respectable Cotswold pub. We stood out from the tweed jackets worn by many of the usual patrons. Our attire was badass. I chuckled to myself. Badass? I sounded like my teenage nephew. Would I have said that a year ago? Most definitely not. I was hardly Marlon Brando's Wild One, a Triumph-riding outlaw called Johnny, in that iconic movie. Our names were the closest thing we had in common with each other. I looked around. Families were enjoying good times and tasty food. Justin and Henry were on their phones already, no doubt posting a story on Instagram. I was more interested in what was on the menu of light bites. A black pudding Scotch egg with mustard mayo or twice-baked double Gloucester soufflé with spinach? I could wash that down with a non-alcoholic ale. Wild One indeed, I thought. I got my phone out, wondering what the boys had posted, having tagged us all.

There was a new notification. "Out with the #CotswoldsWreckingCrew for a sunny autumnal blast."

It was all about getting the online engagement and amplifying these posts to our masses of followers. I thought about the Wild One movie again. Maybe Johnny would have been in fewer fights if he was on the Gram, if social media had been around back in the 1960s of course? There was a simple satisfaction posting photos of our motorcycles, chatting about some bike-related stories, and subsequently feeling the positive validation from all the likes and sweet, sweet dopamine hits. If it got ugly with any negative comments, we would never meet the anonymous online trolls anyway. If it got threatening, it was easy enough to block the aggressors. No fights and no trouble with the law.

"Sorry Johnny, you're on your own." I chuckled to myself at the silly comparison. We were a social media biker gang.

1. Motorcycle rebellion

"What is he up to now?" I looked out of the kitchen window. It was raining, yet for some reason Colin, my neighbour from two doors down, had decided to climb a ladder, using a toilet brush to clear out leaves from his roof guttering. I paused washing the dishes to take in the spectacle. "I hope that's not his actual toilet brush." He wasn't wearing any gloves.

After half an hour of grabbing a few handfuls of brown mulch and a few wobbles on the ladder, Colin gave up. I was relieved. If he fell and I saw it, I would have got soaked in the rain rushing to his aid. Also, the water in the kitchen sink was getting cold and I still had empty jars to wash for the recycling bin. Seeing his attempt at jousting with dead leaves in the wet was at least something a bit different for a boring, rainy Sunday. This was entertainment in my quiet little street. I splashed, wiped, and rinsed, whilst intermittently looking out the window. The pitter patter of the raindrops hitting the glass was my only distraction from this dull task now. I suddenly wanted Colin to go back outside and try another stunt. Maybe he could rig-up a tightrope on his roof, I wondered? I focused again on the sink in front of me. The jars were looking respectable for the recycles finally. I pulled out the plug and washed away the grotty water.

"Ugh, this is disgusting," I muttered under my breath.

"What was that dear?" Olivia, my wife of six years, had mastered the art of hearing me whinge about washing up the recycles. She didn't even look up.

"Such effort! The bin collectors will just chuck it in with the other rubbish anyway," I added sullenly.

"That's nice, dear," she replied.

The next day, pulling back the curtains, I was greeted by a rare sight. I turned away, blinded, not expecting this bright glow at this time of year. My eyes adjusted after a few minutes, and I allowed the sunshine to warm my face. It had felt so long. Too long. The only real evidence of yesterday's rain and wind were a few blown over recycling bins, and the dull grey-brown puddles that dotted the otherwise smooth tarmac drives. There was a pleasant mirror-like sheen on the still water. I'd have to wear sunglasses in the car on the way to work, I thought. Colin was outside, already moving his big green wheelie bin back into position, perpendicular to his car. Olivia was still asleep, so I went downstairs to make her tea in bed. Whilst the tea brewed, I leafed through the pile of unopened letters from last week. A junk flyer from Farm Foods was top of the pile. "No thank you", I said, throwing it into the paper recycles box. A bill for the water was next. "Yes, I know how much I pay, and I pay by Direct Debit, thank you". I sighed and added that to the pile for the shredder too. I reached for the next one without even glancing at it and ripped it open. "Dear Mr. Don Beaumont, as a valued customer we want to offer you the chance to—" I stopped reading aloud. If they didn't even know my first name, then I was not that valued. Another one for the shredder. The tea was a lovely golden colour now. Before pouring out the milk I grabbed another letter. The writing on it made me focus. It was from the DVLA, the Driving Vehicle Licensing Agency. It was a road tax reminder. It was dated three months ago. Why had I not seen this one earlier? I spilt the milk on the table, missing Olivia's mug of tea as a slight wave of panic coursed through my body. "Bugger!" I reached for the kitchen roll and dabbed away, before carefully opening the foreboding envelope.

"Dear Mr. John Beaumont…" it began. Well at least the DVLA had the correct name for my 2014 Triumph Bonneville T100.

"Your vehicle tax runs out on 5 November 2021," the letter continued. I held my breath, waiting for the large fine. I turned the paper over. That was it. I sighed with relief. I hadn't ridden my bike for about a year and so had clearly not remembered this important date. My dear old Bonneville was under an old sheet in the garage. I stared at the cup of tea. That description was wrong. Neglected was a more accurate word that described the bike currently. I should re-tax it, I thought. I had got away with evading the law so far, but more importantly, I felt guilty at the current abandonment of the bike. Surely this riding season we would ride again, and she would be my dear old Bonneville once more. I had thought this before, last year, and the year before that, but the bike remained under the sheet. How many years had passed since I first bought it?

My 2014 Bonneville T100 'black' was my pride and joy. There it was, shiny and new, pride of place on the forecourt at the local dealership. The marketing jargon emphatically stated that this was the 'meaner Bonneville', with Triumph's decision to black out parts that traditionally were manufactured with a shiny chrome finish. The sales hype worked on me. The mean Bonnie was the bike I had to own. I was certain that when riding the bike home for that first time, Colin and the other residents of Tivoli Avenue would look at me in a different light, beyond the quiet, sensible neighbour who helped keep the streets clear of litter, and who donated to the local Scout group. The reality of motorcycling on UK roads soon hit me, often with rain and bugs, in the face. Our weather is mostly grey, damp, and cold with only a few weeks of solid sunshine a year. Our roads are blighted with potholes and diesel patches from the large, slow heavy goods vehicles that clogged them up. In addition, Cheltenham is rural, and that meant mud from neighbouring fields spilling onto what otherwise should be some epic tarmac for the rubber to grip. My vision of cruising the Cotswolds rural vistas, the warm evening summer sun glowing on my smiling face, taking in the golden views of freshly bound hay, looking forward to a crisp, refreshing cider, whilst returning glances from admiring farm girls, never came to pass. My first few years of riding mainly involved trying not to be killed by impatient and bad drivers. Even surviving a ride out, I would often arrive grubby from mud and rain. My kit was heavy, cumbersome, and did not really fit in with a lads' night out at a pub after work. I would have to strip out of my waterproof over-trousers, remove my heavy armoured jacket, and find somewhere to leave my helmet, where it was also safe from being kicked or stood on by progressively drunk revellers. I could not drink anything alcoholic either. Motorcycles were dangerous enough without being several pints into an evening and then riding home. Bikers also have notoriously bad hair, known as helmet hair. The motorcycle therefore was not the ideal vehicle to casually meet cool people in Cheltenham's more trendy bars. My non-motorcycling friends still admired the bike however because they didn't know any better. They would repeat back what I must have told them when I first bought the Bonneville, or Bonnie as the bike had become known.

"John, you own a Triumph Bonneville! It's so cool man!" they would say, often after a few too many beers. This was mainly down to my bike being pleasing to the eye, with its silhouette stuck in the 1960s, when motorcycles looked like motorcycles and not jet skis. My Bonneville harked back to the original bikes of the 1960s in only a faint way, however. I did not tell my friends this. Other bikers knew it, but my friends were not other bikers. My Bonneville was not the fire-breathing icon of rebellion that the classic Bonneville was. The Hinckley Triumphs are made in Thailand these days. Triumph's headquarters and main research and development still happens in the UK, but the marketing nonsense likes to sell them based on this former British heritage and lineage. The reality was that my Bonneville was not a motorcycle that should whip up superlatives. The engine was adequate but boring. The suspension was old fashioned, with only preload that could be adjusted on the rear shocks. The front forks had no adjustability. There was only one single disc for the front and rear brakes. This was not much to stop a heavy bike in an emergency stop. There was no ABS too, so if I grabbed a handful of front brake, it was likely I would lock up the wheel and crash it. There was no lock on the fuel cap. There was no space to secure luggage. As the weeks and months passed riding my Bonnie, I realised all of this. It became effort. 67 bhp was not a lot of power, certainly not for a bike of this weight. The motorcycle would cruise easily at 80 mph on the motorway, but without a windscreen, it was just noisy, and pushed back my neck and head after a few hours. There were lighter, faster, and more efficient bikes out there. Bonnie was a pretender. A fake. After a few years, she was parked in the garage one winter and then when the next spring arrived, she didn't come out again. Reflecting back on these memories was bittersweet and they made me feel sad. I couldn't place why that was. Was it that my imagined vision of what being on two wheels should be like didn't come to pass? Was it that the reality hit me that really, I was not cool, and no motorcycle, whether from a British company trading on its heritage, such as Triumph, or a slick, sexy, modern sports bike from Ducati, would make any difference? I was thirty-eight years old now, not far off turning forty. Was this some midlife crisis thing? I wrestled with these thoughts as I dutifully went online to the DVLA website to pay my road tax. Maybe I should just let Bonnie go, I thought. Someone else could enjoy riding her, surely? Why was I even referring to my bike, an inanimate object, a machine built on a production line, as a 'she'? I was thinking about Bonnie as I might think about a person. Like I was in a relationship that was neglected. The idea of someone else owning Bonnie, possibly riding her in the winter, with muddy, salty roads, letting her rust in the garage, and not cleaning her, stirred feelings of anger, of jealousy, and of remorse. I had a decision to make. "How long do I want to tax Bonnie?" I read aloud the question to myself. The cold, functionary website offered a simple choice; 6 months... or 12 months? I found myself clicking the 12 months button after what felt like an eternity. "One hundred and fifty pounds!" I said loudly. The transaction was done.

"Thank you for using DVLA vehicle licensing online," read the automated email. "Your application for vehicle tax has been successful."

That was it then. That confirmation message was like a formal renewal of marriage vows. It was binding. Bonnie and I were legally able to ride on our great British roads again. I rummaged through my motorcycle folder. Old receipts for my biker jacket, gloves, helmet, as well as previous service work, filled the folder to the brim. Where was my last MOT certificate, I wondered? I had to check she was legally mechanically sound too. I could not be in trouble with the law twice in one morning.

"Did you go all the way to China to make me my tea?" asked Olivia, stood halfway down the stairs.

"Your tea! Sorry!" I looked over at the mug of now tepid brown water. I had meant to pour in the milk after cleaning up my earlier mess. "I got distracted. Let me make you another cup," I reached for the fridge door.

"What have you been doing?" Olivia noticed the piles of opened envelopes.

"My damn bike tax expired three months ago. I never realised. I had to renew it quickly." I left out the details of my inner dilemma on purpose.

"Oh. Ok. Well, next year make sure you remember. I don't know why you just don't sell it?"

There was a pause. "It," Olivia had said. The word jarred. Bonnie was a "she," I thought to myself.

"Um, well I thought I might see how this year's riding season goes and sell her next year if I definitely don't do more than a few hundred, maybe a thousand miles this year."

I refilled the kettle to hurriedly make a fresh brew, tipping away the cold, sad, dark liquid of my first attempt.

"Whatever. You say that every year. I'm going to jump in the shower, just leave my tea on the bedside table please. Don't forget the milk this time... in the mug, please." Olivia smiled sardonically and walked back upstairs. I wondered if she was right. She often was.

"Did you see those hoodies round here last night? Bloody youths out and about snooping in Brian's garden." Colin walked towards me from over the road. "Wrenched open his shed and nicked his tools, they did! Made off with a power drill and his toolbox. Brian nearly had a heart attack, but he chased them!"

I was about to get in the car. "Oh, um, no I haven't seen anyone coming or going. Poor Brian, I hope he's alright?" Brian and Colin were good at winding each other up on gossip they heard about the neighbourhood. The perks of being retired and having time on your hands, I thought.

"Yes, well Brian was a little shaken up, and he's lucky he wasn't stabbed! Bloody youths have no respect! They'd stab you for an old rusty hammer as much as look at you!" He paused to catch his breath.

"Sorry, Colin, I'm running late for work. Can we talk about it later please?" I wanted to be more sympathetic, but two cups of tea and the bike tax dilemma had taken up too much of my time this morning. Colin just stared me, his cheeks now a dark red, flushed with anger. "I hope the police catch them." I tried a more sympathetic approach, hoping to bring down Colin's blood pressure. "Was Brian able to give them any descriptions of the unruly youths?"

"Unruly is barely the word for it! Dangerous degenerates they are! Need to be locked up and throw away the key! Good riddance!" Colin raised his voice further. He was forgetting he was in Tivoli Avenue. Neighbours did not raise their voices here. "Yes, Brian got a look at their clothes. Was two of them. Those baggy jeans that look like they're hanging off their backsides. Scruffy. Just hoodies otherwise. Had some pattern on the back. Braap and Burn written on them, whatever that means. Probably some imported American nonsense, brainwashing our children!" He paused, possibly waiting for a nod of agreement from me.

"Braap and Burn, eh?" I repeated back to him, rubbing my chin. "Never heard of them. Is that some kind of gang name?"

"Yes, that's what Brian told me. He also said there were cartoon drawings on the hoodies. One was of a skull wearing a motorcycle helmet with a snake slithering through the eye sockets. The other one was of a tiger wearing a bike helmet with a lightning bolt in its mouth."

That was some impressive detail to remember in the heat of the moment, I thought. "Well, I'll certainly keep an eye out for them and spread the word to lock doors and windows. I really have to go now." I wondered if it was just teenagers out for kicks in our boring neighbourhood.

It was another boring Monday in the office. Not much moved quickly in the land of green policy for Cheltenham Borough Council. Driving home, my thoughts drifted back to the morning. I was looking forward to digging out that MOT certificate. Ideally, she would be roadworthy before I went for a ride again after such a long time. Saying I did not have much mechanical skill was an understatement. I could put air in the tyres and oil the chain. Beyond that, the local mechanic at the local garage made easy money out of me each year, only needing to do the bare minimum to keep Bonnie on the road. I also reflected on the descriptions of those thieves. I wondered if they belonged to a biker gang, remembering the patch designs on the hoodies that Colin had mentioned. I didn't take that thought much more seriously. Biker gangs were a throwback to the 1960s, and were mainly rooted in America, with the Hells Angels. I locked the car and walked into the house. Olivia was not back from work herself yet. As I put the kettle on, waiting for it to boil, I remembered reading a biography of the group, written by one of their founders.

The life and times of Sonny Barger and the Hells Angels Motorcycle Club had whisked me off to a world of motorcycle rebellion last summer, whilst sipping some cold ciders in the garden, as a treat for keeping the grass in our front and rear lawns neat. Barger was in the US Army in the 1950s, and like many soldiers after they left the military, he tried to find something exciting and meaningful to replace the thrill and sense of belonging that Army life provided for him. The main Angels groups, or Chapters, were in California. Their coveted patch, known as the death's head, a skull with wings, became iconic and was to be feared and respected in equal measure. These ex-soldiers, with nothing to do or no place to go, often got into trouble with the law. The Angels became a place of belonging and brotherhood for these young men. Even if Angels were sent to prison, their brothers waited for them on the other side. Whole families became part of this legacy. Over the decades from the 1960s to the 1990s, loud custom motorcycles, tales of gunrunning, drugs, fights, and police investigations became the stuff of world-wide intrigue, and cemented the negative biker gang culture idea that still persists today.

The tea was perfect. I even treated myself to a biscuit. I chuckled to myself. I was a million miles away from our own rebellious biker stereotype, here in the UK, of the cafe racer. I dunked my Hobnob.

In the 1950s young men raced from one cafe to another, reaching breakneck speeds, earning the rider the respect of becoming a tonne up boy for reaching 100 mph. The Ace Cafe in London was one such racing destination. It opened in 1938 and today is probably one of the most well-known places of genuine cafe racer heritage. Racing in and out of there is inconceivable these days, however, as the cafe is situated on the congested London North Circular Road. The venue still attracts all sort of motorcyclists, young and old, as a sort of pilgrimage that a biker should make at least once. Sipping my tea, I reflected that I had not visited the Ace Cafe yet, but then again, I barely classed myself as a biker at the moment. I grimaced, wondering if they sold Hobnobs there?

Saturday arrived. I opened the garage door and was greeted by a gloomy darkness. As my eyes adjusted and the dust cleared, I could see white sheets draped over furniture long forgotten, half used paint tins with lids ajar, and crusty old brushes scattered on shelves of rusty tools not returned to the toolbox. Was I really this scruffy, I contemplated? I brushed some old cobwebs out of my face and sneezed. A ray of light crept through the one small, mildew covered window at the back wall, as if a sign from the heavens guiding me further into the darkness. The light settled on one old bed sheet draped over the shape of a front wheel, handlebars, sloping lower towards the back wheel. Bonnie was under there. Eagerly, I whipped the sheet off. Dust, dead spiders, and dry winter leaves were thrown into the air. I turned my head away, closed my eyes and then sneezed again. Wiping away tears, I saw the glint of the chromed headlight bucket, and the glass of the front headlight, the thin ray of heaven-sent light reflecting brightly off of it. My eyes adjusted further, and the smooth, glossy black fuel tank captured my vision next. I focused on the chromed tank badges on the side of the fuel tank, designed to remind me that this motorcycle was a Triumph motorcycle. I smiled at the sight. I ran my hand over the seat. The leather was soft. I looked at the engine cooling fins. Some carbon had settled on the once brushed metal. That was a shame. The carbon dulled the silver of the engine, the centrepiece of the bike. Some black paint below the fins was flaking off too. I'd have to fix that. I looked towards the rear of the bike. The classic spoked wheels had rust spots on them where water had managed to seep under the chrome and onto the steel. Damn, I thought, annoyed at myself suddenly at the neglect. I crouched lower to inspect the bottom of the bike, brushing away some cobwebs, gingerly. I didn't think there would be any big spiders or rats in here, but I was cautious. Both the front and rear brake discs were rusty. That was ok. It was only surface rust that some road miles would fix, when the brake pads pressed against the discs. I wheeled Bonnie out of the garage and onto the driveway. In the clear light of day, even a grey February day as it was today, she didn't look too bad. The wheels felt like they were rubbing on something though as I walked the bike outside. Likely that was the brake pads having some grime on them. Again, hopefully a good ride out would remedy that. At least pulling on the front brake lever, the calliper gripped the disc and the bike stopped to a halt. At walking speed. At road speeds I'd have to take it steady. Start slow. I was nervous. The next big test was to see if she started up. I turned the key. The fuel pump reluctantly whined into life with an ear-piercing squeak. The front and rear lights were on, and the speedometer clock showed me the time. Half past ten in the morning it told me. I looked at my watch. Yes, it was. I then pulled out the choke so the engine would run at higher rpms initially to help her start from cold. Technically this was not a real choke, but a slow start switch that Triumph had fitted to these Hinckley Bonnies to again give the impression of having to go through a start-up ritual of a classic 1960s Bonneville. A real choke was designed to restrict the air flow into an engine so the fuel-air mixture would be richer in the carburettor and help the engine start in low temperatures. This switch was really a gimmick and shouldn't have been needed. I actually liked the ritual, even though it was pretend. I thumbed the electric start button. Bonnie didn't have a kick-start.

"Nnng-nnng-nnng-nnng", complained Bonnie, but she didn't start.

"Come on girl!" I hoped the battery had enough juice to make the engine turn over. This time I gave her a few revs to help. I began to sweat, even on this cold morning. I thumbed the electric start once more and prayed to the spot from where the light in the garage had come through the window earlier.

"Nnng-nnng-brrrr-brrrr-VAROOM!" Bonnie reluctantly spluttered and spat but she was alive! I gave her a few more revs to stop the engine from cutting out. Easy now, I thought. The spluttering lessened and the steady thrum of the parallel twin engine became rhythmic music to my ears. I let her idle for a few minutes, for the engine to warm up, and checked that the indicators worked. Left, front and back. Check. Right, front and back, the same. I smiled and clapped my hands together in excitement. The brake lights were good too. I didn't want to switch the engine off for fear she might not start again but I had to go back inside the house and get changed into my biking gear. A bright orange light suddenly appeared on the clock face. That was the low fuel light. I had no idea how much fuel was in the tank. Likely a lot would have evaporated as Bonnie was left in the garage for so long. Triumph for some reason decided not to fit a fuel gauge to the Hinckley Bonneville.

I pulled into the petrol station, parked up next to the pump, put Bonnie in neutral and turned the engine off. I swung my right leg over the seat and removed my gloves, left then right. I unfastened my helmet and placed it on the seat next to the gloves, ruffling my flattened helmet hair. I looked around with a big grin on my face. Busy parents were rushing to fill up cars before their kids in the rear seats started getting grumpy. Labourers in white vans were leaving the shop with pasties and newspapers tucked under their arms. Bonnie was a thirsty girl, as I stood at the pump for a good five minutes waiting for her to be fully sated. I let her have the premium fuel too. I juggled my helmet, gloves, and wallet at the till, fumbling to pay. I suddenly recalled all of the faffery that went with simple tasks when on two wheels. I quickly removed those negative thoughts from my mind as I returned to the bike. I paused halfway across the forecourt. An old man was standing next to Bonnie and staring at her. No, he wasn't staring, he was examining the motorcycle as if he hadn't seen anything like it before, or maybe he had, but decades earlier. I walked over to him, and he looked up at me, recognising the sight of a leather jacket, matted hair, and clunky heavy biker boots. He started talking first without introduction.

"I used to have one of those back in the sixties." He paused and smiled. "A Triumph Bonneville eh! Beautiful bike. Took me all over the country back then, before..." he stared back at the shop. I followed his gaze and understood that he was looking at his wife, just finishing paying for their car fuel. I looked back at the old man.

"Yes, yes, it's a Bonnie alright but not a real, I mean, a classic one. This is a 2014 model." I paused to let that information sink in.

"Oh." His expression was confused.

"Yes, it looks like the original bikes of old but it's completely fuel injected. These throttle bodies look like carburettors." I pointed down to the part. "And it's completely easy to start with an electric push start. No need to kick it into life."

He was silent as he watched me prod and flick at switches. I needed this old fella to give the bike, and me, his seal of approval.

"Well, I never! It looks just like my old Bonnie from 1965! Amazing! I bet this one doesn't leak oil like she did though!"

We both laughed.

"No, thankfully not."

"George, come on! Stop gawping at that bike! There's a queue of cars waiting!"

The old timer was summoned back to the here and now. He looked at me with a serious expression. "Don't sell her, lad. You'll regret it, and you'll never have the experience of owning a Bonneville again." He whispered as if imparting some secret wisdom onto me.

I nodded back at him, understanding the implied meaning in those words. "I won't. I promise."

2. Pretender

I remembered an old video from a few years ago, the contents of which had fired up my interest in modern classic motorcycles shortly before buying Bonnie. The video was made by BMW to promote their new modern classic motorcycle, built to tap into a different market for them. The BMW R nineT oozed cool. It boasted a 1170cc air-cooled boxer twin engine that stuck out each side of the bike. Originally these types of engines were designed for aircraft back in the 1920s. It looked awesome and kept its silhouette throughout the decades since, with many iterations that improved power and performance. Bringing this engine to the modern R nineT was genius. The bike also used a shaft drive to turn the back wheel, which meant less maintenance and less mess, as there was no faffing around with oiling and adjusting a chain every few hundred miles. Perfect for the armchair mechanic. The bike had modern upside-down forks, proper brakes that actually stopped you, and claimed the power of over a hundred horses. All of this premium bike came at a price however, and it was therefore much more expensive than Triumph's offerings in their own modern classic line-up at the time. My 2014 Bonnie was essentially the same machine that Triumph had been building since the mid-2000s, but the R nineT was a brand-new machine. I could not afford such a bike, but I admired the German engineering from afar. Bonnie was my mild mannered, charming English rose, a girl next door... who spent her formative years in Thailand, noting the Hinckley Bonneville's production location. She looked splendid outside any quintessentially English village pub, with gentlefolk playing cricket in whites on the green next door. She was the plucky underdog. She'd never win anything, but my god, she gave it a go! The BMW on the other hand was the proud, confident, more powerful, faster, and very much more efficient machine. The motorcycle was 'vorsprung durch technik' for hipsters with a bit of money in their pockets. It was a slick offering and BMW had clearly done their research. They recruited custom motorcycle designers and builders from California, France, and Germany to market the machine. Potential customers working in online marketing, digital concept management, and dentistry were helpless to resist. BMW sold hundreds and hundreds of these bikes, also offering fresh 'factory custom' modification options. The motorcycles could be as unique as the new owner, straight from the showroom floor, without the customer picking up a wrench or getting oil on their precious hands. Olivia was in the shower. I clicked play again.

The sound of a ratchet tightening a nut on a bike frame, lazy shadows shrouding the yet to be revealed BMW, welcomed me to my escape. A voiceover confirmed that the designers had put all their soul into designing and building this bike. The camera constantly switched to shots of heavily tattooed forearms and long, bushy beards. I wanted to be in that dusty shed, in that quiet desert location, obviously where the R nineT idea was conceived, researched, and built. Only a cynic would think that it was really designed in a slick, corporate office in Munich by committee. I sipped my tea, getting into the commercial. The BMW suits had invited a few super cool custom bike designers to test ride the new bike too. One guy was wearing a T-shirt with his own name on it. That was some big ego, I thought. The level of beard was epic. More ratchet noise, louder now too. The custom biker guests rolled up to the shed as the R nineT was rolled outside, in slow motion. Mouths dropped open. The cool dudes loved it. The low growl of the boxer twin engine sounded great after a twist of the throttle. Then, saddled up, they all rode out together, spinning the back wheels and spitting out dust and small stones into the camera. I laughed, wondering if

BMW added the damaged camera lenses to the video production expenses. "Traction control must have been switched off", I said aloud, and dunked a biscuit into my tea. Rock music started up. I wanted to be part of that crew, all wearing open face helmets, with cheesy grins and beards flapping in the wind. I wondered if I should try to grow a beard. The voice overs evangelising the virtues of cool motorcycles came thick and fast. The bike was described as beautiful because of its simplicity. I wondered if BMW's finance package would be quite as straightforward. Heavy rhythmic bass guitar provided the soundtrack, thudding between soundbites. I was nodding along, lost in the sales pitch, dropping crumbs on my lap. There was some chatter about freedom, and expression, fear and adrenaline. That was a nod to the factory custom parts, and how much they would hurt your wallet, I reckoned.

"John, could you bring up a toilet roll, there are none left in the bathroom!" shouted Olivia from upstairs suddenly.

That was the end of my ride out with the cool hipster custom bike guys in the desert. Maybe I would not be leaving a trail of dust as I headed into the wilderness with just my wits and my machine to keep me going for my next adventure with Bonnie, but I was inspired to ride once more. I stared at the garage through the kitchen window and thought of fish and chips. A plan formed in my mind. A car driver might nip down the road to the nearest local chippy. For the biker, give him a fish and he'll eat for a day, but give him a motorcycle and he'll ride hundreds of miles for his fish and chip supper. We enjoyed the adventure that awaited us, and we took the long way on purpose. I remembered one such route that I rode a few years ago to Cheddar Gorge.

Living in the middle of town, it was always a slow grind getting onto the enjoyable roads. Bonnie started up fine now, thanks to the modern engineering of fuel injection, but the air-cooled engine was still old technology, and when a bike's engine of this sort is cold, in slow-moving traffic, it's not much fun. You cannot trust car drivers when on a motorcycle either. Everything bigger than you can kill you. The prudent biker rides as if any accident is his fault, even if it is the fault of the other road user. If I failed to anticipate the actions of others, then the potential of death was too high a stake. This might all sound a bit dramatic to the non-biker, but that's because they've not experienced the near misses of several hundred kilos of steel nearly hitting you. As I rode past the hospital, I heard a loud beeping sound. I jolted at the noise, surprised. I was not adhering to my own advice. The bike jolted to an ungracious stop. "Bollocks," I muttered to myself, as I stalled the bike. I was out of practice and the engine was stuttering. Bonnie's fuel mapping in its stock form was not good. I waved a hand to gesture at the car driver, owning my mistake. Easing out and feathering the clutch, I got going again. I navigated the smaller roads and junctions, but it was already becoming a chore. My left clutch hand was already hurting. I was clearly not bike fit. Thankfully though I was soon on the straight, free-flowing A46 towards Brockworth. I surged past some slower cars, seeing there was plenty of room. I made a mental note to watch for hidden side junctions too, then in third gear, once my way was clear, overtaking the plodding cars was so easy. "Yeeha!" I shouted into the wind. I wasn't riding quickly, but on the Bonneville, the rush always felt quick on these roads. You didn't really need to ride much faster. The tarmac was mostly smooth, and more importantly, today it was dry. I had confidence in my stock Metzeler tyres. They were never going to win me any points on a race circuit, but the rubber lasted ages and was, apparently, just as grippy in the wet as in the dry. I ascended the winding road, past Cranham, higher and higher, with a glorious view of Cheltenham appearing on my right. I rushed past half a dozen more cars, grinning.

Approaching Painswick, there were green hills and barren trees on both sides of the road. I looked forward to spring returning soon and seeing these trees on this road in full blossom. Entering the village, the traffic signs slowed me to a set of traffic lights. This was such a small Cotswolds village that the main street was only wide enough for one direction of traffic in places. Wall to wall Cotswold stone houses lined the road. As the lights turned green, I wondered who lived here. The tourists on the pavements must have been wondering the same thing as they craned their necks looking into front room windows, suddenly turning away from the picturesque buildings, towards the sound of my engine, the only distraction from the beautiful architecture. Out the other side of the village, I was back up to fun speeds and heading towards Stroud, skirting past it in a few blips of my throttle. I followed the A46 into Nailsworth, with cafe culture pouring out onto the pavements. I imagined the customers sipping their espressos watching me with envy as I cruised past. Bonnie certainly looked at home with this backdrop. I liked to think that fifty years ago, the genuine Meriden Bonnies also rode this same road, much to the delight of the locals back then. The road wound uphill again, with the visibility of some tight corners hidden by Cotswold stone walls. Take it easy, I thought to myself. Experience told me that an annoying cyclist could be holding up traffic ahead. Once I was able to see clearly again, then it would be time to open the throttle. The air was fresh, with a slight whiff of natural manure on the fields. You really did use all your senses on a motorcycle, I reflected. Soon enough the sun crept out through the clouds, and I felt its warm glow on my face and my back, even under the heavy leather jacket. The road was open now, with clear visibility all around as I crested the hill. I pushed Bonnie into fifth gear, her top gear, and just twisted the throttle. 70... 80...85... 90 mph. My eyes were streaming, and my head was buzzing. "Yeah girl, go, go!" I shouted at Bonnie, giving her encouragement. She responded instantly, when suddenly I felt a wobble that nearly threw me onto the other side of the road. "Woah!" I yelled, grabbing the handlebars more tightly and reining the bike back to the correct side of the road. I must have hit a bump with the front wheel. That was fast enough for now, I thought. This part of the road was quick all the way to the crossroads at Old Sodbury.

I stopped at the red traffic lights in front of the Cross Hands Hotel. With the engine just idling now, purring away like a contented kitten now that Bonnie was warm, I could hear my own breath. I was breathing loudly, and my heart was hammering quickly. We were in tune with each other. The next goal was to arrive in the city of Bath and navigate the best route through to the other side. I let the satnav manage this bit. I didn't know Bath at all, but I took advantage of the handy bus lanes which allowed motorcycles to ride past the slow-moving traffic. I joined the A39 on the Bristol road, the stop-start nature of this segment frustrating me. My hand ached again. "Damn heavy clutch lever," I grumbled. Once past the Bristol-bound traffic, the road opened beautifully. Had I continued on this road, I would have rolled into the cathedral city of Wells. It was a gloriously fast road, with low hedgerows allowing views of the endless rolling fields on either side of you. I was looking for a right-hand turn onto the B3135. A quick left-right segment past the village of Farmington Gurney took me on the A37, just for a few minutes, before getting back on the A39, crossing through Chewton Mendip. I spotted the junction up ahead, an old-fashioned white metal sign, the lichen growing on it giving it a timeless patina. "That would be good for a photo with Bonnie parked in front of it," I said to myself, grinning and patting the fuel tank. The road sign hadn't been changed for decades. The B3135 had fast stretches and tight, technical corners that rewarded you as you eventually rolled into Cheddar. The drama of the sheer towers of rock that meant craning your neck up, and up, and up, just to try to see the top was your treat for surviving this road. I would be there soon, I thought, and banged up to fourth gear. I was in attack mode. I turned right, hitting 60 mph in a few seconds. Lights up ahead on the other side of the road meant another biker. I nodded in greeting and respect. It was possibly a Honda Fireblade, an older one, but we passed each other too quickly for me to really tell. I saw him nod back at me. A top-down sports car drove towards me next, a smug looking man and woman sat in the front. This stretch of tarmac was not just for the two-wheeled thrill seekers. I gave them a wave. The nod was reserved just for fellow bikers. Closing in on the gorge, the walls of limestone began their looming presence. The very welcome sunshine on this cold morning disappeared as I was suddenly enveloped in shadow. I felt it get colder instantly too, another trait of being on two wheels. I slowed down, knowing that some stray goats on the road, or boulders tumbling down, could end my two-wheeled adventure instantly. The rocky towers hung right over the road, limiting visibility to just the immediate few feet in front of me. There were no goats on the road but a few standing on high boulders, grazing absentmindedly today. My neck was stiff from the long, fast stretches of road and the vibrations of the bike started to take their toll. It was too much to try to look up too far at them.

"Give it some beans!" came an echoey voice from somewhere.

I looked up and right, niggling my neck, and noticed climbers taking on some of the sheer vertical rock faces. They're brave, I thought to myself.

"VAROOM-ROOM-ROOOOOM!" I twisted the throttle, Bonnie and I acknowledging their request.

"Woohoo!" shouted back the climber, clapping, the sound booming around the gorge along with my engine. The road continued past the famous caves, with queues of tourists outside. "We've arrived," I said to Bonnie, giving her another loving pat.

I spotted a few bikes parked outside some shops, and without thinking twice, parked up next to them. As I glided in, I noticed a couple of older chaps in full leathers break from their conversation to watch me. "Don't stall it," I said to myself. Nothing would have been more embarrassing than that. They were riding bigger and faster bikes than Bonnie, a Honda VFR1200F sports tourer and a Suzuki Bandit 1200, both of which made a hundred horses in power, and both of which made their power via very smooth four cylinder engines, albeit in different configurations. I switched the engine off, flung my right leg over the seat, and gave the chaps a knowing nod. They nodded back and resumed their conversation. I assumed they would have at least smiled at Bonnie's beauty or asked where I travelled from this morning. The sun managed to creep through again, birds were chirping, and there was a very light breeze. It felt like Spring was around the corner, finally. The fish and chip shop was just over the road. There was no queue. I stomped over in my big biker boots, feeling like I had really earned this lunch after three hours of riding some great, twisty roads. My belly was rumbling.

"Cod and chips please... and a bottle of water, thanks."

"Where have you come from today, then?" asked the woman behind the counter. I smiled at her interest. This was my chance to tell her of my epic adventure. "Well, I started in Cheltenham—"

"You should have just come down the motorway. Nice and easy," she interrupted, shovelling a large portion of golden, crispy chips onto a tray.

"But that's not the point of the journey on a motorcycle," I began to protest.

She didn't even look up, instead telling me what I had to pay. The two chaps on their Japanese bikes were now in the queue behind me. I doubted they were planning on regaling her about their journey.

I found a nice grassy bank near a stream to sit and enjoy what I had ridden these 70 miles to find. I kicked off my heavy boots and let the cool breeze dry my slightly sweaty feet. "Ahh lovely," I sighed happily. To give the chip lady her due, these were golden, slightly crispy on the outside and fluffy on the inside. The fish was as white as fresh snow, flaky, and chunky. The batter had a satisfying crunch to it. Perfect. I reviewed the photos I took on the ride over. Most were only worthy of the bin, but I kept two. A selfie with helmet hair and Bonnie over my right shoulder, and one of just Bonnie against a Cotswold dry stone wall. I edited them with a simple iPhone camera filter in lieu of any photographic artistry and talent on my part. I wanted to share my trip with friends and family on Facebook. My status updated, I lay down on my jacket, belly full of tasty food. I peered up through gnarled branches and watched the grey clouds moving quickly, every now and then revealing the sunshine, warming me nicely. Had I not had to ride the same, winding, long route home again, I could have fallen asleep there, the soothing water from the stream burbling away. I wanted to spend longer in this idyllic spot. A solution entered my mind. I reckon I'll take the motorway home, I mused, the irony not lost on me.

I parked the bike in the garage and shut the door, weary after a long day. I hoped Olivia would welcome me back, interested in the roads I explored today.

"Good ride out? Bins need emptying. They smell," she stated as I opened the front door.

That was not quite the hero's welcome I was hoping for. After my chores, I checked how my post was doing on Facebook. Only six likes! That must have been an old number. I refreshed the app. The number did not move but there were a few comments. One was from my mum.

"Looks like you're having fun, son. Ride safe. Love you x."

My dear old mother was not my target audience. I scrolled down.

"Dead man walking," wrote one of my mates. He didn't ride and the comment typified a common view of the non-biker, who always seemed to claim to know someone who knew someone else who had died in a bike crash. I moved on. There was one other comment remaining.

"Midlife crisis, eh John!" it read, with a laughing face emoji. That comment itself had ten likes. Well, that wasn't fair, I thought. I wanted to write some snarky comments back, such as a few quotes on the virtues of motorcycling, how it was good for the soul, and something about freedom machines or similar. Posting that as a reply just didn't seem right though. I knew how it felt to be on two wheels, but that was because I had experienced the buzz for real. My Facebook friends and family had not. I needed a new audience.

Two years ago, I bought an oil painting that depicted a 1960s Meriden Bonneville on a golden beach, with small fishing boats in the background, on a glorious sunny day. The caption for the painting read, Bonnie Days. The image summed up the simplicity of escaping to quiet, beautiful locations, to be free. I wanted to experience those days and I needed a like-minded community who shared in this vision. I turned to Instagram, posting the same two photos from Cheddar Gorge. I made my account public as I didn't know anyone there in that community. This was the start of a new adventure. #bonneville and #triumph. Let's see what happens in the morning, I thought to myself. I slept well that night.

By Sunday afternoon I had thirty likes and ten followers. I didn't know any of them, but they liked my content, all two photos of it, and they wanted to follow me and my motorcycle. I followed them back, assuming this was the etiquette of Instagram. They were all bikers and, hardly surprising, they all rode Triumph Bonneville variants, Scramblers, Thruxtons, and Bobbers. They were all the newer liquid-cooled Bonnies too, whereas my Bonnie was now becoming an older lady, even for a 2014 bike, with her air-cooled engine parts. Emissions regulations made it impossible for manufacturers to continue building motorcycles in this manner, using the surrounding air and metal fins on the engine casing to dissipate heat to stop it from overheating. The future was water-cooling, like it or not. Even modern classics had to adapt. To give Triumph their credit, from 2016 and the release of their new 900cc and 1200cc Bonneville variants, the bikes looked gorgeous, had more premium parts than the air-cooled generation, and amazingly, managed to hide the water pipes out of the way. The radiator was fixed under the headlight, at the front of the frame, but it was not ugly, and it did not ruin that classic Bonneville silhouette.

I scrolled through pages and pages of gorgeous Triumph motorcycles. I followed some. I liked some. I ignored many. I made a note of a few more common hashtags. Some of the language baffled me. I scrolled to a photo showing off an aftermarket exhaust as the focus of the photo.

The caption read, "New zorst who dis?"

I had no idea what that meant. The post had over 500 likes though. Curious to learn, I read some of the comments.

"Sick!" stated the first one. The same sentiment was expressed another seven times. It seemed to be the most popular feedback.

"Was someone ill?" I chuckled to myself. I noticed that the flame emoji was used all the time too. I assumed that writing the word, hot, was too much effort. I rubbed my forehead and moved on, noticing a brand-new, very clean and shiny Thruxton. Gorgeous, thought. I scrolled through the photos and stopped to admire a photo of the lovely bike parked in front of a nice looking cafe.

"Take no shit, give no fucks!" the owner of the bike had written. There was a chap sat outside the cafe next to the bike, who I assumed was the rider. He was sipping an espresso, wearing dark sunglasses and not looking at the camera. The scene appeared to be at odds with the caption. I checked out his bio.

"Dentist in the Oxford area," it read. The bike looked immaculately clean. I wondered if this guy even rode that lovely machine more than twice a year. I grimaced at the irony in my musings. Next, I came across another air-cooled Bonnie like mine, albeit with chrome engine casing and a cherry red and cream white tank. This I knew was a 2012 model. I liked some of the photos and read a few of the comments.

"Looking good bro," was a common remark. Compliments were mixed with the flame, the fist, and the lightning bolt emojis. I had much to learn. I found upon @MotozModz, a custom motorcycle parts page that showcased an array of old and new Bonnevilles, all of which looked stripped back and improved, showing off gorgeous aftermarket parts that the company manufactured and sold. "CNC-machined billet aluminium," I read out loud, scratching my chin. I was looking at indicator brackets and fender eliminator kits suitable for Bonnie. "Very nice," I said to myself, nodding. The page was a seemingly endless makeover list for pimping out my metal steed. There were no instructions though so I wondered how I would fit these parts. I turned to YouTube.

After a few searches for installing specific Motoz Modz parts, I discovered Gary's Garage. Gary's video editing was simple. I doubted he even had a proper camera.

"Alright, welcome back... I've um, just nipped out for a ciggy, and realised that I striped an old rusty bolt from the engine case..." he explained, no preamble needed.

I couldn't see his face, and cigarette smoke was not helping to show off the issue in the bad light of his garage.

"You can solve this by drilling out the old bolt..." he continued.

I paused the video, struggling to follow what he was doing, Gary's unsteady hand shaking an old camera phone. I wondered how much more trembling there might have been without his cigarettes to calm him down. He put the camera on the floor finally in order to point to the problem area. I searched some more and found another video, this time for the parts I wanted. I made notes, paused Gary's video, rewound it, and watched again to check I had written down sufficient steps. I had tools in my garage, but they were hardly specialist. Gary made it look so simple and carefree. I was sweating just after putting pen to paper. Hopefully I had the correct mix of wrench sockets, for the Motoz Modz aftermarket indicators. After an hour or so of revision, my first custom parts were ordered. I was ready.

I went back to my Instagram page and saw that I had gained another four followers. The dopamine hits kept coming as the Gram recommended more content for me to follow.

"Oooh that's nice!" I said aloud, nearly wolf whistling at the bike on the screen. It was a gorgeous Triumph Speed Twin dripping with custom parts. Even the fuel tank had a lovely, personalised paint job. The bike's colour theme was gold, grey, and black. It looked sexy and was framed against a rusty ladder propped up against a red brick wall in what looked like a trendy Brooklyn backstreet. Every photo was beautifully taken. All the shots were high resolution with professional depth of field. Surely this was not taken on a phone, I wondered? I didn't think my iPhone could achieve such results. @KickAzTriumph was the account name. "One hundred thousand followers!" I blurted out, suddenly. This was the first Triumph Bonneville related account I had found with such numbers. The photos themselves had thousands of likes. I scrolled to one of the rider straddling the bike, wearing sunglasses, a baseball cap, and T-shirt. For some reason he was looking away from the camera, over his right shoulder. This photo had 6000 likes and dozens of comments.

"Get ready to ride!" he had written. It was hardly insightful, but I assumed he knew what he was doing. I followed him, hoping some of his followers would find my little page.

"Nice Speed Twin. Did you change the tyres from the stock Pirelli Rossi 3s? I heard the new 2021 model was going to come with Metzeler Racetec RR K3s, for a sportier feel," I commented on his most recent photo.

The next few days passed. A niggle irked me. @KickAzTriumph had not followed me back, nor had he liked my comment, after I had taken an active interest in the modifications to his bike. He must have been online since, as he had uploaded another four photos. Trying to ignore that, my Motoz Modz parts arrived. My journey into the world of the #custombonneville, #custommotorcycle, #modernclassic had begun. Using the old socket wrench that I had knocking about the garage was surprisingly easy. I was reasonably intelligent, could read and follow my scribbled Gary's Garage notes, and I was methodical. If I could source funding for the local Borough Council's green initiatives as my day job, then I could unscrew some nuts, reroute some wires, and plug the correct connectors into the wiring loom. I did not need to be a qualified electrician for this. Motoz Modz made this fun and accessible with their plug and play and bolt-on parts. I made a mental note to remind myself to tag those guys in my photos, #motozmodz and #motozmodzcustoms. After an hour or so, the new indicators were installed. I stood back and admired Bonnie's new upgrade. Certainly, the parts were neater and more minimalist. I prodded at them, gently, admiring my handiwork. They were far better quality, being aluminium, compared to the big, dorky, plastic original indicators. I could get used to this #motolife, #builtnotbought philosophy.

"Hi John, I'm back. How's the man cave action going?" said Olivia, peering in through the open garage door, smiling.

"Yeah, really good. What do you think? She looks good, eh?"

"Um... yeah. What did you change again? It looks the same as before."

I followed her gaze. Her eyes were desperate to find the thing that I had modified, I could tell. "Come on, Olivia. Here, look! The indicators... they're much smaller and neater than the original ones." I held up the old indicators, waving them around. They stuck out like dog's bollocks.

"Ah yes, I see it! How clever. I never would have noticed the difference. Yes, they do look much better... now that I know what I'm looking at."

That reaction was good enough for me.

Within an hour the photo of my new modification had received twenty likes.

"@MotozModz has tagged you in a post," came a new notification too. I could not help but smile.

My creative work had been used in an advert by Motoz Modz via their own page. "Our bullet indicators blinging-up this T100 Black. In stock now. We ship from Birmingham daily."

The Motoz Modz version of my photo had already received over 400 likes. I had also gained another nine followers, just from being tagged. "So, this is how the game is played," I said to myself. I returned to the Motoz Modz website.

I was sure that I dreamt of CNC-machined aluminium parts that night. I told Olivia of my plans, at least in part. I was scarce on details about how much money I intended to spend. If she asked, I divided the true price by three. I could live with this little lie. I ordered some more parts.

The fender eliminator kit/tail tidy, a speedometer/tachometer lay flat bracket, and a front fender/mud guard, all arrived a few days later. I told Olivia that I was given a small merit award at work for a recent bit of policy-writing genius. I made up some story how I had impressed my boss by modifying the existing household recycling chastisement stickers that the Council used when residents mixed glass with plastics. I returned to Gary's Garage.

"You need to disconnect the rear indicators first before taking off the old tail tidy... now, let me put the camera down... I crimp some bullet connectors to this wire extension on my bike, as the stuff you get with the kit ain't long enough..."

My notebook was already in hand. Olivia wondered why I was being so nice when I suggested she go shopping again or spend time with her mum. She knew really, I had an agenda to get back in the garage and spend more time #wrenching as Bonnie was becoming more #shedbuilt. I was becoming one of those annoying people who actually said "hashtag" out loud. The customary photo was chosen, and the likes came thick and fast. Bonnie was really starting to look great.

A day or two later I checked for feedback. I scrolled past the usual emojis in an automated blur. I yawned. Was this need for online validation wearing off already, I wondered? Skipping past a comment involving a banana, water drops, and a winky face, I paused on one comment containing some actual human dialogue.

"Really love this Bonnie, mate," it read.

I checked this person's page. He had posted some decent photos of a beautiful Street Twin. The bike looked brand new, with a gorgeous cherry red fuel tank. He had a good eye for a photo, and whatever filter he was using made the cherry red pop vibrantly. I looked at his bio. Henry was his name. He lived in Bath. He was a new rider.

"Works in the city," I said aloud, reading his page description, "and a top hat," I added, noting an emoji he used. Maybe he was a banker poser or something, I mused, now having seen my fair share of professionals with money claiming to be real bikers. This guy had spent time commenting on my photo, so I decided to give him the benefit of the doubt and gave him a follow.

The following day I had a direct message, or DM notification. It was from Henry.

"I love your bike, really neat. I was talking to another guy I know on Insta, and we were wondering if you wanted to go for a ride at some point soon? You're local and we ride the same roads. Let me know."

Well, that was just awesome. "Olivia, guess what?! Some guy from Instagram messaged me and liked my photos and wants to meet up for local ride!" I could not take the grin off my face.

3. Group ride

"Hey chaps, I figured I'd set up a group chat for tomorrow's ride so we can talk plans," wrote Henry.

I had given him my phone number and the next day I received a random invitation to a WhatsApp group. SW Ride Outs it was called. I assumed the SW stood for Southwest.

"Justin is calling it the first ride out for the SWMC," he added.

I deduced that MC stood for motorcycle group. The thought that this could be the start of an actual motorcycle club excited me, a proper sense of belonging on two wheels at last. I quickly checked out Justin's name on Instagram after he presented his page via a link in the chat. He was a bearded, well-groomed fella. In most photos he was looking away from the camera, mostly over his right shoulder. He wore sunglasses in every photo, even when it was not sunny. He never smiled either. I laughed to myself. He could have stepped right out of that BMW R nineT commercial. I read his account bio.

"Open to collaboration, digital creator," it read, with an emoji of a camera. He already had over three thousand followers and was thus an Instagram veteran in my eyes. I had no idea what any of that meant but hoped I could learn from him.

More messages from Henry ensued. "At the moment the plan is to start in Bath, then over the M4, to Cirencester, then over to Stow-on-the-Wold. Potentially some detours depending on time/weather/general feel for the group. See where the ride takes us!"

No pressure then, I thought to myself. I had to ensure I gave off the right vibe for the group. It was about time I introduced myself.

"Hi gang, that all sounds great. Looking forward to it, cheers, John". I hoped this struck an easy, casual, tone of the care-free biker.

"Nice one," replied another account in the group chat. "I'm Tyrone." He didn't mention his Instagram details.

"Was thinking maybe midday? Give us plenty of time to stop on the route for catch-ups, detours, cheeky Gram opportunities. Crescent sounds great." Henry set out the itinerary for the ride.

"I'm keen to set-off as early as possible. I have to help my mum with my nan. She's just very old and I want some of the afternoon left for myself, but I don't want to change the whole plan for everyone!" interjected another addition to the group. "Sebastian btw," he added.

I was glad I was not the first person to start making excuses. First impressions mattered.

"I don't mind setting off a bit earlier if we need to," replied Justin.

"Yeah, I'm flexible too but generally I do like a lazy morning," added Henry.

"Come on, Henry you can sleep in on Monday!"

I enjoyed watching the conversation play out. They didn't need me adding any additional complications to the plan.

"No way!! I'll be up and dressed nice and early," added Sebastian.

This was my opportunity to maintain my aura of being the cool, laid back one of the group. "I'm easy." I noticed that Tyrone had little to say too. Maybe laid back was his vibe, I wondered.

"Oh, btw I need to post some photos I took from about a month ago. Do you know those old petrol pumps up in Wiltshire?" asked Sebastian, changing the subject.

"On the A36?" Tyrone responded, some part of the conversation finally peaking his interest.

"Think so, yeah. Got some nice snaps from there of the bike. These ones." Sebastian posted a series of photos. Some rusty, old-fashioned petrol pumps, not in use anymore, but presented a throwback image to old American fuel pumps long-abandoned in the middle of nowhere. The patina and filter Sebastian used made the scene look very post-apocalyptic. Sebastian's bike was parked next to the pumps. It was another Triumph Street Twin, exactly the same as Henry's bike, although Sebastian's steed looked completely stock without any modifications. In place of cool custom parts were practical accessories. I noted a windscreen and tail rack, with an ugly fluorescent yellow and black rucksack strapped to it. I was no artist, but it did not complement the lovely cherry red fuel tank, nor the rusty patina of the old petrol pumps.

"These are cool, where are they from?" asked Justin, referring to the old pumps.

"Ahh that's in Steeple Ashton," interjected Tyrone.

"That's it! I couldn't remember the place. I have the worst memory for place names. I just ride and ride and just come across random things—"

"I often go out and find nice dogging spots with Henry on my bike," quipped Tyrone.

I burst out laughing at Tyrone's comment. I posted a laughing face emoji to show my appreciation. There was no reply from Sebastian.

"So, does anyone know of any good photo spots on route? Or dogging spots... keen to get the plan sorted, guys," said Henry.

"There's always Cotswolds airport. They've got some cool stuff over there... and there's Sudeley Castle, although that might be shut," suggested Justin. "Also, Bourton-on-the-Water... and Tetbury market, all pretty places for a park-up shot of the bikes."

"Yeah, but it will be very busy," responded Sebastian.

"That's ok. People can admire the raw British heritage rolling into town." Justin added the sunglasses and Union flag emojis.

"Heritage? #madeinthailand," remarked Tyrone.

My ride heading south to meet the guys at Bath Royal Crescent was bliss. I had not experienced riding with a group before. A pack of motorcycles, all Triumph modern classic motorcycles, would look so cool. Finally, the group agreed to meet at eleven, to satisfy Sebastian's need to start early, and Henry's desire for a lie-in. The route was my familiar A46 jaunt, via Stroud and up over the hill past Nailsworth, Petty France, and Old Sodbury. I trusted the satnav again to help me meander my way into Bath, this time telling it to take a right turn onto Goose Lane, just past the Tollgate to avoid the city centre. The route was pleasant, and the sun broke through the clouds every now and then to make this a typical spring day for the beginning of March, right on cue. The blossom was starting to appear too. Lansdown was picturesque, riding past the golf course, and then slowing down as a long, steep hill greeted me. I cruised past old stone houses and schools. I looked around, one hand on my thigh, casual and relaxed, the other hand just keeping the handlebars straight. This was a very affluent area, I thought to myself. Being a lazy Sunday, this part of Bath was just waking up. Families were rushing around their cars in their big driveways to my left and right, no doubt getting ready for wholesome activities for the day ahead. I nodded to one and all, enjoying the feeling of rolling into an unfamiliar town, like a loner cowboy riding into a dusty Midwest town seeking adventure and fortune. My brakes were struggling to slow me down to the required speed limit, so I shifted down to second gear, using the engine braking to knock off another 10 mph. "I should upgrade these damn brakes," I said aloud, at that moment happening to the catch the eye of a beleaguered looking father, carrying two bicycles and trying to shove them into his SUV. I grinned at him, glad that Bonnie's front brake upgrade issue was all I had to worry about right now. Turning right onto the crescent, over the cobbles, I spotted a lone, bearded biker waiting there. He was wearing sunglasses, even though there was only thick cloud above us. A gorgeous Bonneville T120, standing regal, was next to him, the vista of the Royal Crescent, the perfect backdrop. He saw me coming and already had his camera phone out. He filmed me as I rolled in next to him. He also had a leather strap over his shoulder. A camera was dangling from it. Normal people just carried a backpack, I thought to myself. Then again, this was probably what all the influencers did. I nearly stalled the bike, focusing too much on what Justin was doing. He would have captured that in digital high-definition infamy for all eternity. I pulled in the clutch just at the last moment and coasted to a stop, trying to look as cool and nonchalant as possible for the camera man. I reversed up next to his T120, waddling backwards and looking over my shoulder, to get the angle right, and then killed the engine. "Hi Justin, how's it going? That's a lovely machine!" I swung my leg over Bonnie and removed my helmet. Justin didn't reply. He cooly passed his eye over my motorcycle, taking his time to inspect her. I couldn't see his expression behind his trendy sunglasses.

After what seemed an age, he replied, his voice quiet. "Good. I've done some modifications since I got her a couple years ago. She is a 2016 model. I've ridden all over Europe on her." He was still staring at my bike. "I love these old, air-cooled Bonnies. I see some Motoz Modz parts there too?"

It was refreshing to hear someone I had never met before say something in the very same language as me. I grinned at the compliments. We were supposed to also meet Henry and Tyrone at the crescent, and then meet Sebastian at a lay-by outside of Bath, near the M4 motorway. Whilst waiting, I learned that Justin lived in the middle of town. He owned another bike too.

He put his phone in front of my face. "Here's the CB... a CB450... mid-seventies. This was taken outside my townhouse when I bought her. She's so loud, it's ridiculous. I need to rebuild the baffles in the exhaust."

The photo looked so classically stylish, with a Polaroid filter, to make it look like it was actually taken when the CB would have been a new bike. Justin was ten years younger than me and was super skinny. Maybe it was true that very thin people just looked really good in photos, I wondered? His gear helped too. He was rocking a classic leather jacket with shoulder epaulettes, silver buckles, buttons, and zips.

He caught me checking out his apparel. "It's from a company called Boda Skins. They contacted me one day and said did I want one. I said yeah why not. It's not a certified biking jacket, no armour or anything, but the leather is good quality and heavy. I reckon it'll be alright for a few photos on the road."

Did I hear this guy right that he was given a quality leather jacket... for free?! I wanted to ask more questions about this, but the low rumble of an engine, a parallel twin engine, caught my attention. I turned around and saw a set of two wheels speeding towards us. The rider must have been aware of this new attention as he revved his machine more, the lovely low purr from the exhaust reverberating off the classic Bath stone walls. It was amusing to think these gorgeous buildings used to all belong to landed gentry. Well, the three lads with our Bonnevilles were the lords of this manor on this Sunday morning. At least until we rode off. The newcomer parked up next to me, the three bikes striking the same pose at the same angle in a row. This was Henry's cherry red Street Twin. His helmet visor was one of those bubble visors, styled like an astronaut helmet. The visor was not a flip-up one either. Metal poppers held it in place. I recognised the helmet brand, having spotted them online previously. "Nice Street Twin mate and loving the Biltwell helmet with that mirror visor." He was rocking a short cafe racer wax jacket, from Merlin. It looked very dirty, and I reckoned it was well-used. I was concerned about his footwear though. It seemed like he was wearing his work shoes. They were scuffed, but once probably looked very expensive. I remembered the top-hat emoji from his Instagram account.

"Why are you wearing school shoes?" Justin asked him. I was not the only one visually interrogating his gear. I looked down at myself, suddenly self-conscious. I had proper riding gear, but it was just functional, and did not look cool compared to these lads.

Henry shot Justin an annoyed look, ignoring his comment, and then turned to me, smiling. "I like the mods you've done there. Motoz Modz, I see. I have the same indicators." He pointed to his bike. "Sorry I'm late, but I did warn you in the group chat."

"It's ok. Have you heard from Tyrone?" asked Justin.

"Yeah, he can't make it. Got a new tattoo yesterday on his arm and it's giving him some pain."

I wouldn't get to meet Tyrone today then. It was just Sebastian left now. "Shall we head off? I don't know these roads nor this lay-by, so I'll follow you boys."

"Yeah sure, follow me, I know it, happy to ride at the front," responded Henry.

I was glad Henry wanted to be the point guy in our group ride. I was confident in my ability to ride well, but I never liked the idea of holding people up, or constantly looking in my mirrors to check if others were still there or stuck behind a car somewhere. The engines either side of me fired up. Justin's T120 had some slash-cut pipes which sounded fearsome, the burble a very low bass compared to my pipes.

"I need some of those zorsts, they sound sick as fuck!" remarked Henry, beaming at the thunder emanating from Justin's exhausts.

They weren't my style. I knew I wanted to turn Bonnie into a lighter weight, fast, cafe racer. That would mean clip-ons, rear set foot pegs, and for the exhaust, upward-swept cones, actually quite similar to the Triumph Thruxton. A company called Arrow sold some lightweight aftermarket pipes I had looked at, but they were not cheap. I had been on the fence whether or not to buy them before, but now seeing these boys, I knew it had to be done.

Turning out of the crescent, the three of us turned heads as the rumbling steeds bounced along the cobbled streets, tourists jumping to the side with surprise. We headed out of Bath via the way I came in, going up the long, steep, Lansdown Hill. The previously frantic driveways were all empty now. Henry was standing on his pegs and swerving left and right, making his cherry red machine dance. His astronaut helmet was bobbing side to side. Justin just sat behind him, motionless. I was at the back of the convoy, enjoying the scene of two great looking Triumphs in front of me. The pace wasn't particularly fast, but they cut through the town quicker than I would have done normally. I guessed they just knew the local roads. I was cautious of cars poking out of junctions and not seeing us, but Henry just blitzed on through, seemingly without a care in the world. We got to the lay-by after about fifteen minutes. Sebastian was already waiting there. Thankfully his gear looked just as plain and boring as my gear did. Did I also see a hi-vis vest strapped down to his luggage rack? We pulled in next to him. I saw Henry give a nod to Sebastian, which he returned. I thumbed my indicator right, ready to get back on the road, barely even slowing down to first gear, such was the slick sign language between the two of them. Suddenly

Sebastian leaned in to talk to me and Justin. I tapped the rear brake and pulled in the clutch, stopping to listen to him.

"So, is there an order that we ride in?" he asked us, his voice shaking.

I didn't know what he meant by that. I looked at Justin for any semblance of understanding. "No, you can ride how you want." Justin was poker-faced as he spoke.

"Yeah, it's a chill one," added Henry, overhearing Sebastian's question. "First time together, just see how we do and get used to each other. I'm happy to go at the front though as I know a great route."

"Ok, just I've ridden with other guys before who get really aggressive and protective about having a place in the group and I didn't like it, so I left and haven't really ridden in a pack since," said Sebastian.

The engines, loudly growling in unison, sounded like a pack of lions eager to get hunting. "Don't worry," I said with a forced smile. "We'll take it steady. I can ride at the back and ensure we're all together, and no one gets left behind."

Sebastian turned his gaze to me and smiled.

Finally, the hunt could commence. We pulled onto the A46 towards Nailsworth but turned right on the A433 towards Westonbirt instead. The roads were open and fast, and we were blessed with there not being many cars on the road for a Sunday. Henry led us at a quick pace and was not shy about overtaking either. Justin was steady and followed him, waiting his turn safely, and then chased after him ferociously, the low bass burble of the slash-cuts killing any semblance of a quiet Sunday ride. We were heading towards Tetbury, skirting Cirencester on the ring road, before riding the fast A429 in the heart of the Cotswolds through Bourton-on-the-Water. We would stop in Stow-on-the-Wold for a brew. The trees were starting to turn green now that winter was leaving us, and the smell of new flowers starting to bloom was pleasant in my nostrils. I lapped up the cool, fresh air hitting my face and grinned as we raced through Westonbirt. This little village was famous for its arboretum, the colours of the trees amazing through all the seasons. This place would be full of creamy whites, pinks, and the bright brilliant green of spring very soon, I reflected as we stormed past. I did not know the roads but did not need to worry as Henry never missed a beat. Each road sign seemingly unread, riding too quickly to take in the directions and names of villages, it did not matter. If there was a junction to take, then he knew it. This guy was a homing pigeon on two fast wheels. Cirencester was the only frustrating bit of the ride. It was busy with shoppers now, and we had to wait our turn at the many roundabouts on the town's outskirts. I pulled up next to Sebastian. "This is great isn't it!" I hoped he could hear me above the din of the engines. A car driver to my left wound up his window to block out the noise. He shot me a dirty look. I found his distaste oddly pleasing.

"What? I can't hear you?!" Sebastian shouted back, gesturing at his ears manically.

Before I could repeat myself, we were off again, pushing past the remaining ring road traffic.

It wasn't long before we arrived to Bourton. We slowed the pace down again, soaking up the vibe of the pretty little Cotswold stone shops and cottages. The place was busy with tourists, as predicted, but we were happy to coast along with the flow of traffic, catching our reflections in shop windows, looking cool. Riding out the other side of Bourton, the road signs gave us permission to go at it again, 30 mph… 40 mph… national speed limit, then a big twist of the throttle. "Nice pace, Henry," I said to myself, my voice disappearing into the wind behind me, just like the speed limit. Justin followed his lines, in and out of corners, like they were both on rails. I was in third gear, nearing peak power at just over 3500 rpms. "You can't lose me, chaps... I'm right here." I grinned, keeping my head low, eyes pinned to Justin's smooth lines. I moved my left foot to shift up to fourth gear for more power. "Shit!! Blimey, that was close!" I yelled to myself, suddenly grabbing a bit of front brake, adrenaline surging for a moment. Luckily the block of wood that passed for a brake calliper and pads slowed the front wheel with just enough bite. "Phew, that was close!" I exhaled heavily with relief. I had nearly ridden into the back of Sebastian. For some reason he had not accelerated off with the other two as I assumed he would do, following Justin. I wasn't watching him, my eyes were focussed on the two pace setters. Sebastian's posture did not change. Had he not seen me in his mirrors even? I didn't want to overtake him, having previously said I'd ride at the back. I shifted gear down again, the engine braking making Bonnie whine, a sound that reflected my own frustration. "Come on! Get a move on, go, go!!" I shouted into my helmet. These roads were epic, and I did not want to miss the opportunity of enjoying every curve. I checked my right hand mirror, thumbed the indicator the same direction, and looked over my shoulder for a life-saver check. I gave the old girl a twist and pulled past Sebastian. I was in hot pursuit. Henry and Justin were way ahead. 80... 90... 95 mph, Bonnie was shaking now, the front wheel wobbling. The wind was pushing my head back. I dared not look down at the speedometer as my eyes were locked on Justin's rear wheel once again. I was gaining and it was awesome. I might have even hit 100 mph, the coveted tonne. The lads finally slowed as we started hitting the traffic waiting to turn into Stow. My heart was thumping. I pulled up next to Justin. He looked at me and gave me a nod. I couldn't see his eyes through his sunglasses.

"That was awesome!" I yelled to him. "Really nice pace!"

He nodded again and we rode off, filtering through the slow-moving cars as best we could. Another set of lights and Sebastian caught up with me.

He leant in. "I'm so sorry if I'm not going quick enough." The din of the engines was loud, but I heard him fine.

"Don't worry, it's a relaxed ride. No pressure remember. Everyone rides at their own pace. No point being silly and dangerous." I forced a smile.

We continued into a quaint little town square, full of parked tourist coaches surrounding a little village green. A van was already selling Mr. Whippy ice creams, trying to capitalise on the arrival of the early sunny weather. Henry led us to a gap where the four of us parked up in the now obligatory formation, bikes all parallel to each other. He had eyed up an old cottage, creeping ivy tendrils crawling all over the random mosaic of stonework on the front wall. I nodded towards him, giving him a sign of my approval for the backdrop. Flower boxes had already been placed on the windows. They were fresh and new as if the owner also had the same optimism for warmer weather ahead. Justin whipped his camera around. I guessed this was a well-rehearsed routine. He adjusted some settings and started clicking.

It was early evening by the time I was finally back home. I hadn't had a chance to see how the community had received Justin's photos on the Gram yet. I assumed he would have posted them by now. I checked my phone. There were numerous messages in the SW Ride Outs group, however the group name had changed.

"SWMC... so we are now a motorcycle club," I said to myself. I opened the messages, eager to read them.

"John, you went home you wimp!" Henry's opening shot made me laugh. I peeled off from the group when everyone else headed south towards Bath. Being from Cheltenham, it made sense to take a road westwards given the opportunity. I beeped at them and waved as I took the right slip road to the A436, a fun and quiet road I had ridden previously on my own.

"Nice day for it, sorry I couldn't make it!" typed Tyrone, online now too.

"Next time, Tyrone! Hope the new tattoo isn't giving you too much pain!" I replied.

"Awesome ride guys, let's make this a habit!" added Justin. "I'll dump a load of photos in here later on. Feel free to use any you want."

I visited the Gram. There were dozens of likes already, and eight new followers. I saw a notification for a repost. It was @MotozModz again. The guy who ran this must really like my bike now, I thought. I checked it out.

"Cotswolds Wrecking Crew in full effect. Not sure if they actually wrecked anything. Follow @MotozModz. We ship daily worldwide from Birmingham."

I laughed. Their social media team was very witty with the captions. There were already many likes and comments. The guys were all tagged too. Motoz Modz added #cotswoldswreckingcrew to their post.

"Well, that's the name of the motorcycle club sorted then," I wrote in the group, and added the link to the @MotozModz post. "You can't be in the CWC unless you have at least five Motoz Modz custom parts on your bikes!"

"I'm out then!" replied Henry, with a laughing face emoji.

A kiss from Olivia pulled me away from my new online world briefly. She was off to bed. "Don't be late!" she said and walked upstairs. The group was in full flow now discussing bike parts.

"Think I've hooked you up with an exhaust, Henry," said Tyrone.

"How did you manage that?" asked Justin.

"Maurice from Motoz Modz asked me if I wanted to test some new zorst tips, but I've got different plans for mine over the coming months. I suggested Henry test pilot them as he's local."

"Wait, wait, wait... rewind. Who is Maurice and how are you getting free stuff?" I tried to hide the slight jealousy in my question.

"Maurice usually wings bits my way as I ride all year round, so the parts can be tested in all weathers... salt, grit, and other shit. As a bonus he usually gets some free promo on Insta via @motosofthegram. I write a few words and that."

I quickly opened the Gram. The page had over 300k followers.

I read the bio. "Motorcycle news, lifestyle, products, brought to you, the community fuelled by gasoline and our insatiable passion for two-wheels. DM to collaborate." I checked out some of the random posts. There were hundreds of them, from all over the world too. Everyone tagged this page, with an array of different motorcycling products from different companies taking centre stage in gloriously well-produced, browsable photos. I gave the page a follow.

"Awesome, he needs some new tips, my bike was drowning his out yesterday," joked Justin, bringing my attention back to the group chat.

"Absolute legend Tyrone!" replied Henry.

"Yeah, you've got those brushed shorty tips from British Customs, right? These Motoz Modz ones are not headers or anything, but they are black, so it may be worth whipping yours off and getting some heat resistant satin black on it or whatever. BBQ paint. Will sound good with an x-pipe too."

Olivia was fast asleep, and I didn't wake her when I snuck into bed. I couldn't sleep. I crept back out of bed, went back downstairs, and turned on the laptop. That night I ordered some lifestyle oriented biking gear, now having seen the standard that the Crew... the

Cotswolds Wrecking Crew, was setting. I needed to at least look like I belonged with a bearded hipster model and a tattooed journalist influencer. I had work to do.

4. Custom parts

"John, another parcel arrived for you this morning. How much have you been spending recently?" Olivia's tone straddled a fine line between accusation and worry with a hint of disapproval.

I had little wiggle room here. "You mean the bike stuff? Oh great. That was quick. Um, not a lot. These things were on offer and the guys had a discount code." That was the best I could do in reply to Olivia's perfectly fair and reasonable question.

"Oh ok." She paused, staring at me. I started to sweat. "It's just I have been answering the door to lots of deliveries recently, heavy boxes, all for you. We're supposed to be saving our money for things to do together, and I've barely seen you the past few weeks."

I swallowed hard. I couldn't tell her exactly how much I had spent as it was ridiculous. CNC-machined billet aluminium parts did not come cheap. Olivia would assume they were just lumps of metal.

"You're right, angel. I have been ignoring you of late. I'll do better. Why don't we plan a trip, and we can go somewhere nice next weekend together?" I held my breath. Her face softened. I pressed on. "I can afford the parts, don't worry. I have been doing really well at work recently and I won't buy lots more, I promise." Time seemed to stand still as I waited for Olivia's response.

"I don't want to be that wife who stops her husband doing his hobbies… but just remember what your priorities are, yeah?"

A few hours later, I unboxed my new gear. I had seen on the Gram that some moto influencers actually filmed themselves unboxing new items. These films were posted as a story reel. The first time I saw this, the guy had literally posted a five minute monologue.

"Hi guys, it's me again! Um, today, I'm um, totally stoked to show you um, this awesome new product from a company called..." it went on and on and on.

I thought he should have at least prepared a script. The reel showed one hand using a knife, cutting the tape of the box, whilst the other hand shakingly held the camera, to film the great reveal. For some reason I watched all five minutes of this, whilst brewing, and then drinking two mugs of tea. This particular would-be influencer, for that was written in his bio, used the Instagram moniker @AlwaysParallelTwinning. I smiled sardonically at the pun. The name worked though as I found myself on his page, checking out this bad story reel. His bio also said he was a digital creator and was open to collaboration. I thought about Justin, who had written the same thing. Thankfully Justin had not made video content opening boxes... so far. The new open face helmet from Hedon made me smile. It was made in England and lined with top quality brushed leather. I chose an old-fashioned cream white paint for the shell. I also bought a very expensive jacket from Belstaff. This leather was so soft, 1 mm bovine, waxed, and with D3O ghost armour. The style of this jacket was inspired by Steve McQueen when he used to race in the Mojave desert in California. I tried it on in front of the mirror, smiling to myself. I looked good. My existing black jeans went well with any colour. My tan gloves were in good condition and actually matched the new burnt cuero jacket. I turned to our group chat. The name still stated, SWMC. I changed it to CWC. I was making a statement, emboldened by my new gear, like a superhero who had just tried on his new, flashy, costume. I felt like I had superpowers. We were the Cotswolds Wrecking Crew now.

A few hours later I checked in again. No one had noticed the name change. There were some messages to read, however.

"Anyone fancy a ride out to Cheddar after work tonight or tomorrow? Weather looks great for it," asked Henry.

Sebastian was first to reply. "Sure."

"Yes, but I need to tighten my chain first. Won't take me long," responded Justin next.

This was shaping up nicely, I thought.

"Could meet at that viewing spot at Chew Valley Lake, where everyone parks off the road and takes pictures," he added.

"Could do mate. Only issue is I have a call with a company at like five. Piss take coz they're in LA so I can't do it any earlier and if that drags on, I might miss you lot. What time are you heading out?" asked Tyrone.

"I was thinking after five anyway. Perhaps even later if people want to have some dinner beforehand. Could then make it six or seven? Bit colder, getting dark, but probably quieter roads? Me and my girlfriend have a house viewing in Kingston Langley at four so wouldn't be home till five anyway," said Henry.

"Sick! You buying I assume?" Tyrone added a gif of someone throwing money.

"Yeah hopefully, if they accept our offer. It's four-bedrooms, Victorian, detached. All gated private entrance so plenty of room for a couple of garages on the gravel driveway. One dedicated to the bike, of course. You chaps can help with the design!"

Tyrone left a short voice note. "Bit of wedge then mate, tidy!"

Maybe with that much space, Henry could build a bike shed for each of us, and a personal valet to clean the machines too. It boded well if he was buying in the area.

"That's too late for me," said Sebastian. "By the time we've met, chatted, ridden, and got home it will be nine-ish. I finish work at four thirty, so I'll be on the road then."

We were nearly so close to a group consensus.

"What about, Sebastian, if I meet you after you finish work, then we can ride a bit and head to the Royal Crescent again, and meet the boys as they arrive, Henry after his house viewing and Tyrone after his conference call?"

"Yeah, ok then, meet at that M4 junction again?"

"Perfect."

I was looking forward to getting to know everyone a bit more this evening. The sun was out, and the evenings were only going to get lighter. I had not been to Chew Valley Lake before and so here was a chance for more roads to explore, and backgrounds for the obligatory photo for the Gram. I was wearing my new gear and it felt very comfortable right away. The open face helmet also granted me a much larger field of view which added to the sense of freedom on two wheels. I arrived a bit early and took off my jacket and sat in the shade. It really was a warm one for a March evening. I was content just watching the traffic whizz by, building towards rush hour. I knew the route now. I wondered what Lansdown would look like on a weekday evening rather than a lazy Sunday morning like the other day. A loud beeping caught my ear, bringing me back to the present. I looked up and saw someone shouting. Traffic was slowing and I reckoned a car driver must not have been paying attention. I was glad I was not heading into the town centre to get stuck in all that. I heard another beep, higher pitched and less aggressive. I looked to my left. There was Sebastian, indicating. He stopped his Street Twin next to Bonnie.

"Hi, Sorry I'm late. Bad day at work and my boss is a dick."

I tapped at my ear to signal that I couldn't hear him. "Kill the engine, mate. He nodded and turned off his bike. A large top-box was secured to the rear. That was new, I thought. Maybe this was the usual set-up for him on a weekday, I wondered? He got off the bike and grabbed a hi-vis vest and a half-eaten cheese and pickle sandwich from inside the box.

"He told me to do all these last minute tasks and I was like, I've to go now, can't they wait? And he was like, no they can't, so I had to stay." Sebastian chomped down, chewing at the stale bread furiously.

"No worries, mate," I responded. He was snorting, breathing heavily as he tried to swallow a large, congealed mouthful of dough. I put on my new jacket and helmet in an exaggerated manner, wondering if he might comment on the new look.

"Oh, also I need petrol, my light just came on." He licked his fingers and turned the key in the ignition again, checking his fuel gauge.

"Oh ok," I replied sullenly. He was still checking out his instruments. "When I came this way the other day, I didn't recall any petrol stations via Lansdown. It's all old buildings and residential places all the way to the Royal Crescent. Will you make it with what you have left in the tank?"

"I don't know, the light is on, and I don't want to risk it to be honest. I know of a petrol station on the way into town so we can go there. It's not far." He fired up his bike. I followed suit. I was now following Sebastian rather than leading him via my route. He led us south on the A46, where I had heard that near traffic collision miss earlier. It was slow going and Sebastian wasn't keen on pushing it, likely as he wanted to conserve fuel, but it meant overtaking opportunities were limited and traffic was building.

"I could be enjoying an easy countryside ride, but I'm stuck in this shit!" I cursed to myself. At the first opportunity I pulled up next to him at a set of lights. "Where's this petrol station then?" I shouted to ensure he heard me. I was hot, overestimating how many layers I needed to wear under my new jacket. The bike was hot too, queuing with the cars, without room for filtering. The air-cooling of the parallel twin engine was not so effective in stop-start slow traffic.

"I could have sworn there was one at the end of this road. I'm sure if we keep going, there will be one soon," he replied.

The lights changed to green before I could vent my frustrations further, and we inched forward. My clutch hand was starting to hurt, trying to ensure I didn't stall the bike. At last, I saw a garage up ahead. "There! Sebastian, there! Turn in, indicate left!" I shouted, gesturing with my left hand, pointing frantically. "Unbelievable!" I added, exasperated as Sebastian just rolled on past the forecourt. I had no clue where we were going, now entering the town centre. At last, after another ten minutes, weaving into town, Sebastian indicated to pull into a petrol station. Whilst he filled up at the pump I parked out of the way. I checked the satnav on my phone and saw that we were firmly in one-way traffic congestion, and on the wrong side of town for the Royal Crescent. "Damn it! Fuck sake!" I cursed. A woman filling up near me looked up, startled. "Sorry," I mouthed at her. Sebastian walked over to me before collecting his bike.

"I didn't stop at that petrol station back there, as I wanted the loyalty points from this garage." He turned back towards his own steed without even waiting for a response.

"Fuck this!" I muttered loudly. The woman stared at me again. I set the location in my phone to where we needed to go and waved for Sebastian to follow me. I wished I had been less polite at the beginning and just took the lead. My lack of confidence in leading a group ride had brought me to this. Turning round the way we came was hell. The roads were narrow and often cobbled, with room for a cycle lane and a car but not for filtering on a motorbike. I didn't know the roads either and so the navigation software always chucked me down the smallest lane, either full of tourists or lorries unloading in front of shops at closing time. It was time for some radical filtering, including waddling, and pulling in the mirrors. A few times car drivers gestured at me to fuck off, dare I touch the sacred paint of their steel cages, the vehicles going nowhere.

"I can't fit through those gaps!" whined Sebastian at another set of lights.

"Yes, you can! If my Bonnie can squeeze through, your Street Twin can too!" In truth I had no idea if my handlebars were narrower than his, but I was not taking prisoners now. I reckoned the others were at the crescent by now and this minor bit of anti-social behaviour came with the territory of being in a biker gang. I weaved my way to the front of another queue of cars, half on and half off the pavement. A man in a wheelchair suddenly faced me. His face was pale, scared that my steel horse, angry and hot at not being allowed to let rip, was facing him down. I had to get off the curb. I gave the old girl some throttle, a bit obnoxious, but it felt satisfying to get some speed up, feeling some air against my sweaty brow. I got out of his way, spinning the back wheel on the cobbles but wrestling Bonnie enough to avoid running into him, the poor fella now spinning the wheels of his own mode of transport to put distance between us too. I mounted the curb again and got ahead of the queue. Finally, I pulled round to the crescent. The others were already there, chatting away. I did not wait for Sebastian, but he arrived just as I was taking off my helmet. I parked next to Tyrone's all-black Street Twin. I noticed he had a high exhaust fitted to it, akin to a Street Scrambler. His bike looked mean. It spoke hooligan to me, just how I felt right now having thrashed my way through the commuters and tourists of Bath's pretty, yet crowded, city centre.

"Where did you get to?" asked Henry.

I wanted to rage about how the past couple of hours had unfolded but Sebastian was now standing next to me.

"I had to get petrol and I got us lost in town. I don't come into Bath often and I hate it." Sebastian responded to the question instead.

Henry nodded, wincing. "Nice jacket, dude!" he said, turning to look at me. Tyrone and Justin were deep in conversation themselves. There were a few people milling around, likely catching up after work, or just passing through before heading home. It was a pleasant antidote to what I had just suffered.

"How are you getting on with those K-60s?" asked Justin, pointing to Tyrone's wheels. I tuned into their discussion, assuming it was about tyres.

"Yeah man they're sick." Tyrone was wearing a little beanie hat and white trainers, a pristine, trendy pair of Vans. What was it with the crew's inability to wear proper footwear, I wondered?

"I want some TKC-80s, but they handle like dog shit. They look the nuts though. These are much better." He gave his front wheel a gentle kick. "The centre is solid, so the bike doesn't wallow around. Last longer too."

"Where did you get your tyres fitted," asked Sebastian.

"Just did it myself... with some KY jelly." He looked Sebastian in the eye, grinning.

"You still talking about the tyres?" quipped Henry, seemingly pleased with his wit. I noticed some people sitting on the grass, enjoying the views in front of this spectacular eighteenth century building. We would make quite the cacophony when we fired up the engines later.

"I want to change my engine cases, but I'm concerned about messing it up if I do it myself," revealed Justin.

"Yeah, good idea. Easy job but smashing the bearings is an absolute ball ache. I just broke a bearing on mine," responded Tyrone.

I glanced at his Street Twin again. His gearbox cover, below the cylinder cores, was a lovely matte black, horizontally ribbed panel of sleek metallic art. I nodded in appreciation.

"Told Maurice at Motoz Modz about it so he's developing a tool," he added.

Was there nothing that Motoz Modz did not make, I wondered? I looked over at Sebastian's Street Twin. Nothing had been changed. His was the untouched virgin to Tyrone's sexed-up vixen.

Justin offered a solution. "If you freeze them first it works well."

"Did that and heated the cavities. But really it needs a press or lathe," came Tyrone response. "But I just work with the tools I have… fuck all!"

I chuckled at that knowingly, thinking about my own limited garage and the online mechanical ramblings of Gary's Garage.

"Talking about fitting ribbed ones eh, chaps? You sure this is chat about engine cases?" Henry was grinning like a fool.

The laughs came quick and easy for the next twenty minutes or so before we decided to do some riding together. The sun was getting lower, and the air was becoming cooler. We fell into the same riding order as our first ride out, Henry at the front, me at the rear, and with the addition of Tyrone this time, he just floated in the middle of the pack. I loved seeing the four bikes ahead of me, just cruising out of town. Henry knew the streets well and at junctions with traffic lights we blitzed through them on amber, barely avoiding a red light each time. I hoped there were no police nearby. We crossed the A39 and A38, then rode northwest up Valley Lane to skim the lake's northern peak, before riding south and down its western side. Before long the road opened up to a long stretch on the B3114 and the boys took off before pulling in suddenly to Herons Green Bay Parking. There was beautiful, clear water on both sides of us. Chew Valley Lake was like a mirror this evening. With no wind, the still water reflected the sunshine and any clouds in the sky in perfect symmetry. I leant on the fence around the lake, resting my head on my arms, and looked out over the water. I saw several swans chilling out in the distance. It was quiet here. Justin was already rearranging motorcycle gloves and helmets, crouching down, stepping left and then left some more, snapping away. He had his camera in a satchel today. I noticed a tripod folded up too.

An almighty high pitched engine wail made us all look up the road. Someone was gunning their bike. The revs sounded insane. I heard engine braking as the wail became a burble, and the bike slowed down. The rider was heading straight for us. Justin's pack with camera gear, a bag of lenses, and the tripod was on the floor. The rider stopped just next to it, nearly riding over it.

"Hey, watch it!" shouted Sebastian.

The rider looked over at him and gave his bike some more revs, hitting the limiter and sending the once peaceful swans scarpering away in fear, heavy wings flapping frantically, disturbing the once mirror sheen of the water.

"What a nob," said Tyrone. "Fucking Gixxer bro!" He shook his head. I cast my eye over the bike too. It was a 1000cc GSXR, a mid-90s bike possibly.

"What a cliche, eh!" I said. The Gixxer was notorious as a cheap super bike of choice, often ridden too fast on normal roads, in a reckless way. I saw the Gixxer bro lean in towards Sebastian.

"The chops on you to have a go at me!" His voice was muffled behind his helmet. Sebastian's face went white as a sheet. The rider was a fat lad but was tall with it. I reckoned he was no stranger to throwing his weight around.

"Could you just move out the way please, mate." I stepped in to give Sebastian some back-up. "We're trying to take a few photos of the Triumphs and then we'll be on our way. You could park anywhere else." I gestured to the large, open, and empty car park around me.

Gixxer bro laughed. "What a bunch of poser cuckolds!" He gave his bike more revs.

I stood my ground and waited for his next move.

"What if I don't?" he continued with a threatening look.

"Well, there are five of us and only one of you." My statement of the basic maths was obvious. I wanted him to realise that, but I still did not want any trouble. Fighting was not my scene. He looked around at the others, possibly sizing up each of the crew. No one else said a word. His gaze returned to me. I didn't look away from his face. Then, suddenly, he kicked his gear lever down, stomping on it hard, and hit the rev limiter once more. Any remaining swans were long gone now, squawking angrily in mid-flight.

"Fuck you, benders!" he said, as he sped off. I watched him disappear down the road. He nearly lost control of the bike on some gravel about a hundred meters away from us. Thankfully he regained control. Fishing him out of the lake was the last thing I wanted to do. I let out a long breath and looked at the others.

"What a nob," reiterated Tyrone.

Henry brought along an old GoPro camera to capture some footage of the ride.

"Um, John, could you wear this please?" he asked, holding out a chest harness rig. I looked at it having no idea how to attach it. It might as well have been a sports bra. Tyrone walked over, noticing my confusion.

"I've reviewed dozens of those things. I tell people not to bother buying them, certainly if you're as short as Henry, no taller than a fat child with a thumb for a head." He grabbed Henry in a bearhug, laughing.

Henry squirmed and tried to break free. "Ahh, get off! If I wanted to be touched, I would have let that Gixxer guy do it."

Within minutes, Tyrone had fitted the harness to me as if I was being prepped for a deadly bungy jump.

"At least we'll get some footage above the handlebars now," quipped Justin, observing Tyrone tighten and adjust the straps. We hit the road again, this time with Tyrone at the front. Every now and then he stood on the pegs and wiggled his backside in our faces. Other moments, he stretched out on his seat in a superman pose, as if flying. I was shaking my head and laughing to myself. He was leading us on a merry jig via a mesh of unfathomable B-roads that you either had to know or be prepared to enjoy getting lost riding them. They all looked the same to me, with gravel, mud, and very tall, unkempt hedge rows that encroached any remainder of smooth tarmac. It was a fast and bumpy one. I strapped in and focussed, following the lines of the rider in front of me, peering through his dust trail, scanning for the next stone or pothole that might send Bonnie off the road. My bike did not have ABS and it certainly did not have traction control.

I noticed Justin, who followed Henry, swerve blindly into the wrong side of the road several times, his head also ducking and dodging left and right. It looked like he was having a fit. Suddenly I heard a pinging sound on my visor. "What the hell was that?!" It caught me by surprise. There was another sound, louder this time. I looked ahead towards Henry. His rear tyre was spitting out stones and gravel backwards and flinging them up into our path. Only two had hit me so far, but I was a few bikes back in the pack. Poor Justin must have been getting a shotgun barrage to the face. As if trying to avoid Henry's friendly fire flak wasn't bad enough, these roads were also the main routes used by tractors going about their evening business, with farmers leaving the fields to head home after a busy day. God only knew what they must have thought seeing the five us of buzzing around their giant machines, like annoying insects dancing around their mechanical monsters, as we attempted to overtake, riding blind, as we passed through a cloud of dust. I prayed that nothing made of metal was heading in the opposite direction. I just hugged the back wheel of the rider in front of me and went if he went. It was frustratingly slow going, but the instant adrenaline rush, once committed to the overtake, was exhilarating. We all got through unscathed and before long I recognised the road. We pulled into a layby to take a breather.

"Fucking hell, Henry, your tyres mate! You're ruining the paint on my tank!" I had not heard Justin raise his voice before.

"Just ride further back. I don't understand it. I reckon your tyres are the same. It's just the gravel on the road," retorted Henry.

"No, yours is far worse." I joined Justin with the charge levelled at Henry. I looked at his bike, trying to suss out the issue. "You've taken the chain guard off, and you don't have a rear-fender? That's the issue!"

"I'm waiting for Motoz Modz to send me a free one. Sorry chaps." Henry shrugged.

"Mate, just buy one. You're minted!" said Tyrone.

"You're such a hypocrite, you get free stuff all the time!" Henry was not going down without a fight. We all started laughing.

"Such little cuckolds, all of us. That Gixxer asshole was right!" added Tyrone, grinning, before thumbing his engine back into life. We all followed suit.

The claustrophobic hedgerow-lined roads gave way to the open and quick B3135. The road I made my pilgrimage to only a month previously. The boys opened up the throttle now, with Henry at the front. Justin had learned his lesson and was holding back. Our sudden surge in speed was like hares being released, the gates lifted, the greyhounds in full chase. Even Sebastian was keeping pace this evening.

"Let's see what you got," I said to myself, watching his rear light, and grinning. He was my hare now. He was going to get caught. I followed his lines, sweeping left and right, through tight corners and longer sweeping bends. I was in that trance that all bikers searched for, just the zen of enjoying a pure ribbon of tarmac, the machine and rider turning in as one. All of sudden on a fairly tight right-hander Sebastian veered off the road and onto the grass verge towards a ditch. I was right on him and so all I could do was hold out my left hand in an instinctive gesture, and then I was gone. I didn't stop, and the others hadn't seen the episode either, being too far ahead. I managed a glance over my shoulder. He seemed ok. He just sat there, parked in the grass. The bike was still upright thankfully. I raced to catch the others, flashing my lights and beeping whilst waving at them to slow down. They got the message. Soon afterwards, Sebastian caught up with us again. I gave him a thumbs up. He replied with the same gesture. We rode on as if nothing had happened.

5. The new prospect

Up early, curtains still pulled, I was already downstairs and brewing tea for the both of us. Olivia was still asleep. I was looking forward to a lazy day with her and I owed her that in truth, having spent the past few evenings out with the crew. I sipped my tea. It was too hot still, so I decided to wait a bit before taking Olivia's mug to her and waking her up. This was my time. My window of quiet. I checked the Gram. There were lots of notifications. It looked like Justin had uploaded some of his shots from Chew Valley Lake. Damn they looked good, I thought! He had captured my Bonnie on the third photo in. I reposted that one to my story. The bike shone radiantly in the low, hazy sunshine, the pristine mirror that was the lake, providing the perfect backdrop, casting sun rays onto the chromed headlight. I was pleased I could see some swans in the background too. I laughed to myself. There were swans before Gixxer bro turned up. We showed him, I reflected. I felt like I was in a real biker gang just then. I read one of Justin's comments.

"Five parallel twins roared out of town and into the rural Somerset heartland last night. The golden hour sun giving our steeds the perfect patina. Our ASBO exhausts brought out the outlaw in us."

I liked it. It was naff, but I had learned that these sentiments got the likes. Justin had used my account name in his comments.

"What has he written here then?" I asked myself, attempting to sip my tea again. It was cooling down slowly.

"Took on a Gixxer bro and won too. He had a litre bike but, on these roads, the Triumphs ruled. Better to ride a modern classic fast rather than a sports bike slow!"

I nearly spat out my tea. I re-read it to check Justin's version of events. That was not quite what happened, I thought, and the wording was open to interpretation. There were several comments underneath that comment, written by random followers.

"That's rude man! Great shots!"

I liked that one. I assumed rude was like sick. There were half a dozen routine flame emojis and fist emojis. Lazy, but an emoji was still a comment and an acknowledgment of liking Justin's work. I kept scrolling.

"No way you beat down someone on a litre bike?? Your Triumphs are basically tractors lol. Keep dreaming. See you at the track!"

Had he assumed that I had beat a Gixxer in a race, I wondered? I sighed. This was the trouble with writing your thoughts online without extra context, I supposed. I skimmed more comments.

"You come down to Bristol again and I'll show you pricks how to ride! #gixxer #gsxr #pwned." There were a few others. Justin's vague words had snowballed into insults too. Our simple ride-out had seemingly triggered an entire sports bike community somehow. I chose to ignore it. Let them argue if I was some badass Triumph Bonneville rider who smoked a litre bike. I saw that @MotozModz had reposted some of the photos and used #cotswoldswreckingcrew again too. It seemed that Maurice, if indeed it was he who ran the social media side of the business, was spreading the word and promoting us amongst this community. I should thank him later, I thought. In fact, I wanted some clip-on bars for my project to turn Bonnie into a cafe racer. I saw that Motoz Modz made some and wondered if Maurice might be able to do some discount for me. After all, even Henry was on the scrounge for that free chain guard. I could only ask. I sipped my tea. I told myself it was still too warm for Olivia. She could sleep another five or ten minutes while I wrote my message.

I hadn't checked my phone for a few hours, it was actually refreshing. When I got some time to myself again later in the day, there were already dozens of messages to catch-up on.

"Blimmin' heck, Olivia, do these guys not have a life outside of their bikes?" I asked rhetorically. She rolled her eyes and left me to it. I started scrolling.

"Fuck me Justin, you should have had a GoPro on. You lot missed me nearly getting my head taken off by a pheasant last night."

"That's the main concern I have with my open face lid. A friend of mine got hit by an owl once."

"Pheasant tastes nicer, mate."

I could imagine Tyrone stopping, scooping up the fresh roadkill and taking it home for dinner.

"I would love to see an owl though. Aren't they rare?"

"Not sure you'd see much with it hitting you at 60 mph!"

"Only 60?"

I chuckled to myself reading the back and forth between the two of them. Skimming the messages further, I saw that Henry had added a photo, taken from his GoPro video footage. I was excited to see what my body cam had captured.

"Sebastian in the bushes!" captioned Henry in his message with the image.

"What happened there??" asked Tyrone.

"Sebastian went off road, remember? Were you high or something? How did you not know? Anyway, it's going in the bloopers section," added Henry.

"Been there myself," replied Tyrone. "Have you got it on video?! Get it on here now!"

I was also intrigued to see it play out on video. I kept scrolling. There it was, in glorious High Definition. The camera position on my chest was the perfect height, showing my handlebars and gloves in frame, and most importantly, a lovely view of the bikes in front of me.

"Noooo!" Sebastian appeared online. "My gears seized, and I was coasting and wasn't at the right angle to get round the corner so went onto the grass, then back on the road when I got it into gear. You only see me go onto the grass, so it looks like I've had some tragic accident. Regardless, you all just left me to die in a ditch! What if I had come off and broke something??"

I was laughing. Olivia tutted at me and put her finger to her lips, telling me to be quiet.

"Get the video up on the Gram!" urged Tyrone.

"Yeah I'm sure it will be hilarious, but not for me!"

"Listen, everyone's been there, Sebastian. Part and parcel of life on two wheels." Tyrone was not letting it go. "Did you drop the bike?"

"I've done green-laning, so I didn't panic and lose control. I put it down a gear." Sebastian started to retell the incident. "And released the clutch slowly to get me back on the road."

I could see he was still typing, one short message after another. "If I had kept coasting on the road, I would have hit a gravel patch and the bike would have gone from under me—"

"Anyway, someone get the video online before I forget about it haha," interrupted Tyrone. There was a pause.

"Fuck you!" wrote Sebastian, suddenly.

Another day and another opportunity for a ride out. Henry, true to form, put out the call and we responded. We were riding to Sudeley Castle, deep in the Cotswolds. The boys headed north to meet me in the village of Nailsworth, on the A46. We rode together on tiny B-roads, including the twisty B4070, via Stroud, and Birdlip, winding our way northwards before bursting forth onto the bigger A436. We skirted east of Cheltenham town, and then slowed it down again for the final leg of B-roads that descended towards the castle. I was glad for a shorter ride today as I was getting used to my new clip-ons. Maurice had really delivered for me and responded to my DM better than I ever expected.

"Why don't I just send you some?"

For a moment I paused my reply, wondering what the catch was. I was no Instagram influencer, and my photos were very amateur. I doubted any content that I might have to create would be good enough, if that was my part of the deal for a freebie. "Thanks so much. Are you sure?" I eventually said.

"Yeah, no worries. You've bought lots from me recently, and these are new. There aren't any photos with the clip-ons for the AC twins yet. I could do with a few and get you opinion of the bars."

I smiled at the simplicity of the deal. I could see why @MotozModz had a good following online and people always tagged the products.

"Besides, no doubt the bearded Justin will take some photos for any professional shots that I might use. Your crew gives me lots of entertainment for thinking up captions. No offense," he added.

I left him a laughing face emoji. Within a couple of days, the new bars arrived. They were a faff to install as I had to conjure a contortionist's magic act, fitting the bars around the forks whilst moving the brake and clutch cables without pinching any of them, nor loosening the brake bleed nozzle. Gary's Garage couldn't help me this time. I really was trailblazing on my own. No video tutorial content existed for the Motoz Modz clip-ons yet. I wondered if I should film my install but then I remembered that cringy @AlwaysParallelTwinning unboxing reel and decided against it. Thankfully I didn't need to remove the top triple clamp to loop the bars over the forks. The Motoz Modz clever design meant the bars clamped in two pieces around the forks and were held together firmly by four 8 mm anodised steel bolts per clip-on. I ensured Bonnie could still turn full lock, left and right, with the angle of the bars pulled back, and then I tightened it all up. She looked awesome. Low and aggressive.

On these B-roads, I felt every pothole and bump through the new bars, however. I was hunched a lot further forward and lower down than with the stock bars. This was the cafe racer position I was after, albeit I had not envisioned myself racing on these roads. A dirt bike, or quad bike, would have been preferable. I wondered if I needed some new shock absorbers next, to ease this new discomfort. That would cost more money. Olivia would kill me. I blocked the thought of more new parts out of my mind and focussed on the road ahead. There were also nasty patches of loose gravel that would wipe out my front wheel if I lost concentration. This castle felt like it was at the ass end of nowhere. We lined the bikes up and took the obligatory photos for the Gram.

"Coffee?" asked Justin.

Henry and I both nodded. It was only the three of us today. Tyrone said he would join us later if he had time.

"So, is it just me or does Sebastian not like Tyrone?" I asked the question and sipped my cappuccino as if discussing something as casual as the weather. I looked at the cup. There was a neat Sudeley Castle logo printed on it. I'd take a photo of that on the bike later and tag them. I wondered if #castles was too generic for a custom motorcycle page.

"Um yeah. I don't think Tyrone is that bothered with him either. Very different personalities and you know what Tyrone is like." Henry offered his opinion first.

"Yeah he doesn't give a fuck. Is always telling us that much too," added Justin.

There was silence for a bit. The other two had already gone to their phones. I looked around. It was a grey day. I watched some tourists milling around, posing for photos. A castle did make for a good backdrop.

"You want to make this stuff your full time work, yeah?" I asked him, bringing his bearded face up from his phone.

"Yeah I'd like to. You got to work a long time. May as well make it something you enjoy."

"Needs to pay the bills too, mate!" added Henry. "A free helmet, some gloves, and a jacket made from virgin skins won't keep the lights on at home, no matter how good you look wearing it. There's a reason models are skinny. They can't afford food."

I looked at Justin's camera, placed on the table next to our jumble of leather gloves, croissant crumbs, and empty cups.

He saw me looking at it. "It's a Sony A6000."

The camera type meant nothing to me. "You reckon you'll become as famous as that Speed Twin fella online? What's his name? @KickAzTriumph, from America. You follow him? He's got thousands and thousands of followers."

They both nodded in reply as if I had just stated that the Earth was round.

"What does he do? Just sells a few T-shirts he stands there wearing? I know nothing about his passion, interest, or knowledge about bikes. He could be a complete fraud. He's rude too! I commented on his photos, wanted to compare some technical notes, and gave him a follow. I got nothing back!" I found myself raising my voice.

The other two burst out laughing.

"That is the game my friend!" said Henry. "It's all nonsense, but it's cool nonsense. His bike looks the business. I'd kill to have the talent to modify mine like that and get all those endorsements. I mean, I have the money for the parts, but I'm not allowed to spend it on stuff like that."

I noticed a flicker of sadness appear on his face. He looked away suddenly.

"His photos are good, but most look the same. He's clearly figured out something with the algorithm and knows his best crowd pleasers as they get ten times more likes than some others. It depends on the brands he's wearing too. If he tags the right ones, they reshare his content, and that brings in the follows. There is a science to it," added Justin.

Henry looked back at me, laughing. "I love how you got upset because he didn't comment back or chuck your little account a follow. How many followers do you have now anyway? What is it, like twelve?"

Justin chuckled. I stuck my middle finger up at both of them.

Tyrone finally arrived to join us for a brew. He mentioned that some guy called Darren had messaged him about joining the crew. I was excited by this prospect. If our name and reputation was getting noticed, then that was really cool. I imagined he would have to go through a Sons of Anarchy biker gang initiation thing. We'd have prospects, the term they used for potential new members. Maybe we'd have them do menial jobs like clean the bikes and fetch coffee or whatever until we deemed them worthy.

"Guys, are you aware of @AlwaysParallelTwinning? I found him the other week. Rides a Bonnie like mine, albeit not a T100. Similar year though I think. He loves a good long story reel, documenting everything he does. Going to the supermarket and grabbing a coffee, going for a haircut... Can't believe people have the time or inclination to make such shit."

"Ah yes," replied Henry.

"Did you see the one earlier when he was complaining about getting a brand new, expensive DMD Racer open face helmet to review, but had to wear goggles with it? It's an open face and there's no visor!" chimed in Justin.

"Who's this matey?" asked Tyrone, talking with a mouthful of brioche. Justin showed him the profile on his phone.

"Ah yes. Gets his missus to follow him around everywhere, dragging a ton of photo gear around just to snap him posing away. He's worse than Justin for that." Tyrone winked at him.

Justin didn't even twitch at the remark.

"Jesus! What she sees in him I've no idea. His reviews are always click bait."

We all sat back, silent.

I folded my arms, smirking. "Please continue."

Tyrone brushed away the crumbs on his lap and wiped his mouth with his sleeve and launched in again. "He's starting to piss people off, going on about some raffle recently, when he's meant to be doing a simple gear review. The brands don't like that. People are onto him. Easy to hook in followers that way. 'Tag five mates and follow me for a chance to win this shit jacket...' and all that." He took a swig of coffee to wash down what was left of the brioche. "Trouble is, no one actually wins. Or it's not clear there was even a jacket to begin with. Easy to say, 'oh yeah this made-up prick won it. Sorry, raffle over'. Cheap move."

Tyrone's insight was interesting. I had engaged in a few of those posts myself. I had never won anything. I kept that quiet.

At home later, I saw some discussion about the crew's name.

"What about SWxS? Sort of like taking the southwest by storm?" Sebastian had started the debate.

"Too cheesy," replied Tyrone.

"Alright, marketing wanker."

"Look, what about playing on a SW colloquialism or something? Gurtgrumbles... some shit like that?"

"But then it starts to sound like some old man pub quiz name."

"Will resonate more with a local audience, and will mean fuck all to most others, so will make for a nice logo or whatever... and yeah, I didn't mean literally that, but something of that ilk maybe."

The two of them were taking this seriously. I read on.

"What about a play on machinery words?" chipped in Henry.

"Ooh good one! Yeah... baffle, cranks, piston, throttle, forks... work that into the name? It wouldn't need to be based on a location then," responded Sebastian.

"Crank my dirty piston and pull my baffle! How about that?" added Tyrone.

"Ha-ha fuck sake, Tyrone," wrote Henry.

I posted a laughing face emoji too.

"Well, it always seems I'm the guy getting the piss taken out of and ignored and so this is not for me. I'm out!"

Sebastian left the group. There was silence. No one wrote anything for a few minutes.

"Let's just stick with Cotswolds Wrecking Crew, yeah?" I wrote, trying to break the awkwardness. "Maurice loves it for the reposts of our photos, #cotswoldswreckingcrew is doing well, and it is the local area to us." I couldn't believe Sebastian just left like that. I wondered if we'd be able to get him back.

"Fine, yeah whatever. Don't give a fuck," said Tyrone. "Not sure what Sebastian's problem was."

There were no messages the next day. I kept checking whilst at work, but the usual banter was silent. I hoped this Darren guy would turn out to be cool too. Not that it was a rule to have five members in the CWC, but it was a comfortable number for a biker gang. A couple of nights later we met up at the pub for a drink, at Henry's local, The Potting Shed in Malmesbury. The ride south to get there was bliss. I left work early, already agreeing with Olivia that she would eat dinner on her own tonight. I hit the A435, blasting out of Cheltenham. Damn it felt good to feel that fast rush of air on my face again. The group chat politics had been weighing me down. I remembered it was all about the ride. #justgoforaride. Good advice, I told myself. I would use that hashtag later. I skirted Cirencester, riding past Kemble, on some lovely curvy roads, before rush-hour traffic clogged them up.

I got a round of drinks in and a few packets of crisps. We munched away and talked bikes.

"Boys, I'm upgrading my rear shocks. Quick Google search, and for around five hundred pounds I reckon I could get these YSS G series piggyback ones." I wanted their approval that the big cost would be worth it for some race performance quality. These shocks could be adjusted for pre-load, rebound damping and compression damping. Bonnie would feel like riding on air.

"Yeah sick. I might get the Fox ones. They look the nuts for my bike," said Tyrone, through mouthfuls of cheese and onion crisps.

"That'll be my pick too eventually. All black," added Henry. Fox had done a good deal with Triumph for the newer liquid-cooled bikes.

"Henry, just spray your current ones, mate. Bit of barbeque spray all over it." Tyrone offered his opinion and signalled to a waitress for more drinks.

"What? whole bike? Tyres and all?" asked Henry.

"Yes, all-weather the shit out of it!"

The waitress raised an eyebrow and took our order.

Justin was on his phone, sitting quietly, concentrating. "Look at this idiot!" He beckoned us to his screen. "Someone else who loves a bit of barbeque spray."

I leant in to have a look. There was an Instagram profile of a guy riding a Triumph Scrambler, all in black.

"Wow! I reckon you've found Batman there!" I said. The pub was filling up nicely, which meant it was now the end of the working day. I looked around. Men in suits with loosened ties were stood at the bar, looking very grateful for their first pint of the evening. We ate more crisps and added peanuts to our gourmet dinner.

"Check out this guy and his story!" Justin had found another biker of interest. "He reckons he's going on a ride out with us tomorrow or something? What's he talking about?"

I took a look. It seemed some guy was advertising a group ride with the Cotswolds Wrecking Crew and used our hashtag.

"Does he mean us, or has he used the wrong motorcycle club name? For another group ride I mean?" asked Tyrone.

"I recognise this guy. He follows me. He seems a bit of a wannabe. Rides with his dad who owns a sick Norton Commando. That's the real bike right there. That dude just rides one of those new Triumph Tridents." Justin filled in some of the blanks.

"We need to sort this out. He's saying he's doing a ride out with the CWC, who are the SW Triumph Club." Tyrone had found some more information, scrolling through more of the comments.

"He's confused. We're not the SW Triumph Club. Or he's using our name to generate more engagement," said Justin. "That post has far more likes than anything else he's ever posted."

I laughed and looked around, sipping my beer. A family was finishing a nice dinner, with young kids pestering their parents for some ice cream. If this was a scene from Sons of Anarchy, the bar would be full of drunks, playing pool, smoking, and discussing the best retribution for having their biker patch, their logo, tarnished. In our case, our hashtag and name had been misused. That surely called for revenge. Were we to now find this guy, kick in his front door, and smash up his motorcycle? Before my imagination went any further, Tyrone provided a more reasonable suggestion.

"We need a logo and other brand stuff for us, make it look pro and all. We should get a CWC page up. Then there won't be any more confusion. These wannabes will want to join us, but we are the only CWC members and founders. Fuck Sebastian. Maybe this Darren geezer will be alright too, but no one else."

I nodded. I liked the idea of a logo, a biker gang patch, and a proper home for the CWC on the Gram. I thought about the tradition for new prospects to pass an initiation test. "That Darren chap will have to tie Henry's little lace-up school shoes every time we stop. Make sure they don't get caught in his chain."

The others laughed.

Henry shook his head. "Well, he'll never pass that test, they're always coming undone."

"Seriously though, dude, just buy some proper biking boots! Leave your work shoes for the office. They look expensive too," added Justin.

Henry nodded and changed the subject. "I've called out that chap on Insta too by the way. Look at my comment. Told him he can't use our name."

I looked at my phone and read Henry's crafted words. It was a very polite response. No rival bikers were going to get beaten up this evening.

I ordered the shocks. After telling Olivia I'd stop the spending on the bike, I still did it.

"You promised!" shouted Olivia. "You've spent too much time with those lads… that bloody crew or whatever you call yourselves!"

I stood there and took the scolding. I was due it.

"And now you go and spend more money! We're supposed to be saving up for things for us! We might want to move house one day or have a nice holiday this year." Her voice softened, her tone turning to disappointment.

"I know, I'm so sorry. The money is ok. Trust me. Yes, I've been spending lots of time with them, but I'll stop going out as often. You know how it is, any new thing is exciting, and we chuck ourselves into it, to give it the best chance of working. Now we're established, I'll hang out less. I promise."

Olivia stared at me.

I had a window to make this right. "The lads have discussed a big day trip down to the north Devon coast on Saturday. This new guy, Darren, is meant to be going too. I'll say no to that, and we'll go away ourselves, for a nice long weekend. What do you reckon?"

"I would like that." Olivia sighed and sat down on the sofa. "Thing is, John, I get this is your hobby, that you've been missing riding your bike after many years, and I do enjoy seeing you happy. But when I'm stuck here with nothing to do, that's no fun for me. It's fine if my sister is in town, or I can see friends, but they are all married and have family lives too, you know? I never want to tell you how to spend your money, but you must also think of our future."

I apologised further. Olivia was right. I went online to book a weekend away. The crew would ride without me next weekend.

I never got my phone out once, and that meant a whole two days without social media, without likes and follows, and without motorcycle related gossip. Sunday night came around too quickly again, and as I was ironing some shirts ready for work, I finally thought it safe to check my messages again. I wanted to see how the ride to north Devon went. I saw a new phone number had been added to the group.

"Great to meet you today Darren!" wrote Henry.

That was a very quick and painless initiation, I thought to myself. I hoped the crew made him buy them all a round of beers when they stopped in the village of Lynmouth at least. It was a good sign if they liked him enough to invite him to the group after one ride out. I continued reading.

"Another awesome addition to the crew… and a sweet bike!" added Justin.

I wondered what bike he rode. Surely it had to be a Triumph.

"Get your photos on here!" demanded Tyrone.

"Cheers boys, I'm fucking knackered! Great day out, looking forward to the next one!" replied the new prospect. He posted half a dozen photos of the day. It looked a blast. The weather looked hot too. Tyrone was wearing a hoodie and white trainers again. The others looked warm in their proper motorcycling jackets, as if the April sunshine had taken them by surprise. Red cheeks, ruffled sweaty hair, but big smiles all round. I saw Darren rode a very clean, mean, and green Street Scrambler. I welcomed him to the CWC and asked where they had ridden.

"We did the valley road up to Wheddon Cross, Somerset, it was awesome!" he replied straight away.

"Those pics look sick. Did you Lightroom them up?" asked Tyrone.

"Can't beat a good Lightroom pre-set! My photos are shite without it!"

I assumed Lightroom was an app that Darren had used. I'd check that out later.

"I have fly guts everywhere…" he added for good humour.

"So many bugs in my beard!" chipped in Justin.

The start of the better spring weather meant it would be time for bug splat everywhere. That was still a lot better than cold, wind and rain. I was looking forward to it.

6. Crew

It was a bright yet cool Sunday morning. I took advantage of the quiet roads. Sundays at this early hour meant normal people were enjoying a cup of tea in bed or lazily waking up to brunch in their pyjamas. It was nine thirty and I'd already ridden the 10 miles to Painswick, along the now very familiar A46. Some Lyra-clad keen early risers were also making the most of the lack of cars on the road. I felt sorry for them as they struggled up the long and winding hills leaving Cheltenham. It looked a slog as I smugly twisted the throttle and ripped past a line of three cyclists, sweating away, creeping forward and upwards inches at a time. I arrived at the meeting point very quickly. Justin, Tyrone, and Henry were riding north towards me from Bath and then we were going to check out a new biker cafe in Gloucester. The cafe's Instagram page looked stylish. It did not seem to be the stereotypical, old fashioned, greasy spoon biker hangout that you might see on a busy layby. The artistic photos showed off flat whites and fresh croissants. There was not a rasher of bacon in sight. I was already thinking of the motorcycle photo opportunities to come. The cafe was called Piston Place Motor and Bean. It promised to be a good day.

It didn't take long for us to all rumble into this promised new holy land for our little crew. Henry took up his place at the front of the pack and somehow knew the best twisty B-roads to skirt around Cheltenham town and arrive to Gloucester with the minimum of fuss. There was ample parking for bikes, and we were far enough away from residential areas to rev our engines until content without getting a police ASBO for our unruly behaviour. Rolling to a stop, we parked next to three immaculate, chromed-out Harleys. They looked expensive and well-loved. The owners were sat on a bench outside, all leather waistcoats, grey beards, and dark sunglasses. They stared at us as we backed the bikes in together, choreographed, lined-up neatly. Our engines were left idling just to complete the ritual announcing that the Cotswolds Wrecking Crew had arrived. The burly older Harley riders went back to their coffees and their conversations. Finally, we killed our engines, and all was quiet again. I took off my helmet and smiled. We had parked in front of some large signage with the words, "Need coffee?" in bright neon letters.

"Perfect for a photo of the bikes," said Henry.

I was thinking the same thing. I looked back at the Harleys, next to us. "I would have thought those fellas would have parked here? It's the best spot." It was their loss. No #harleydavidson this morning, I thought to myself.

"They know what they're doing," said Justin, nodding towards the front door of Piston Place Motor and Bean. "The owners I mean. With that sign there."

We ordered our coffees and sat outside too.

"Chaps." Henry paused to ensure he had our attention. "I'm potentially exposing myself to ridicule here, but does anyone have any videos to help me improve my cornering?"

Justin was busy snapping those Harleys now, and a few other cool custom machines that had just arrived. I watched him. Standing up, down on one knee, shifting position, kneeling down again, camera up to his left eye. The clicking and whirring of his camera was audible over the general hubbub of conversations and intermittent exhaust notes. I then looked at Henry. He looked like he was holding his breath, waiting for an answer to his question.

"Do you know of any open spaces?" replied Tyrone finally.

I was waiting for a joke to be set up at Henry's expensive, but it never came.

"Car parks you mean?" Henry asked, exhaling loudly.

"Best thing to do, mate, is to get some small cones, find a big open space and practice figure of eights."

"Yeah sure thing. My cornering makes me tend to lose you guys on a ride. You all go flying through the twisties and I just don't have the same confidence going into them at speed."

"Neither do I. I just shut my eyes and hope for the best. Try that first." There was Tyrone's joke.

We all laughed.

"If you ever want to book a track day or something, give me a shout. I'd be well up for that. That would probably help too. Not on our twins though. Proper sports bikes," he added.

"Your cornering speed is fine, mate," I chipped in. I meant it. The pace that the crew set was plenty fast enough for me.

"Well, that Devon run the other weekend, with Darren..." He paused, looking at Tyrone, who nodded.

"He's a quick boy. Did some proper racing a few years back. Doesn't give a fuck. On the gas, kick up the dirt, and he's gone! On a 900 Scrambler too! Used to ride a CBR thou. Said he don't need a sports bike these days. Would kill himself." Tyrone looked at me, seeing he had my full attention. "Trust me, he don't need one!"

I hoped these tales of Darren's speed were exaggerated. Henry was a newer rider, and I had more experience, but still, the pace was already too quick for poor Sebastian. He was not crew material. I didn't want to lose anyone else because we might ride even faster.

"You've been riding a while though, Tyrone?" I asked.

"Yeah man. Been riding since I got off my old dear's tit. Live and breathe it. These days my back gives me pain, so mainly I do the bike stuff for work. Turn a few reviews, take a few photos like the bearded hipster over there." He nodded towards Justin who was now chatting to the woman behind the counter, just inside the open door to the cafe. She looked to be hanging off of his every word.

Tyrone continued. "Really though it's the words that I care about now. No one reads them though. Sad it is but likes and followers equals ad revenue and that means money in my pocket. I can't stand the print media stuff. The future is on the Gram and TikTok and all that social media shit."

"The photos of the night at the lake, looked like you were making some sweet pre-sets," said Henry.

"Oh, in the background? Nah mate. I've got a question series going on Motos of the Gram for a project I'm working on. I've got a few pre-sets. Tend to just make them on the fly usually. This is the thing with pre-sets. You can get one that applies a general look and feel to all of your photos but if you really want one to align you still have to go in and make changes to them all individually because inevitably the light setting is never the same on each photo. So, a copy-paste job never works."

That was good advice. I found myself nodding. Not that I really had a clue what Tyrone was talking about. Henry nodded too. I looked around. Piston Place Motor and Bean was filling up. I spotted a couple of Royal Enfield Interceptors. They were nice bikes. Royal Enfield had captured the market on that one. There were even a few sporty fully-faired bikes here. I smiled at the diversity of two-wheeled machines on offer. A love for caffeine and motorcycles was not just reserved for us custom modern classic boys. The vibes were positive here, and it was all real.

"On a typical day, how many pests do you get online?" I asked. "Fake accounts and trolls?"

"On Motos of the Gram? About fifteen. All in my DMs. Usually a few shit business enquiries." He put on a silly, mocking voice. "Review this gear. Review that gear!"

I laughed.

Tyrone continued. "Offering me money for trash Chinese knock-off products."

Justin walked over, interrupting Tyrone's lecture. "They've got some cool clothes in there, guys, go in and have a look."

We followed him inside and I introduced myself to the woman behind the coffee counter. Justin started snapping away at the Piston Place Motor and Bean T-shirts, sweatshirts, and other apparel hanging from modified old motorcycle parts, turned into clothes racks and hanging rails. Some of the metalwork must have taken some talent to shape and weld together. I introduced myself to Jane, the owner. As we talked, the other lads rifled through the clothes on display, holding them up to mirrors, and nodding appreciatively. Jane's husband, Jim, was a bike mechanic and custom bike builder. The custom clothes racks made sense now. I bought a trendy yet expensive T-shirt for Olivia that I thought she would like, so she might cross the boundary into this new part of my life I was getting into. I later found out that Justin got a T-shirt, a neck buff, and a hoodie... all for free.

I snuck upstairs when I got home without Olivia noticing, quickly removed the price tag from the Piston Place Motor and Bean T-shirt and wrapped it with some leftover Christmas paper I found under the bed. It would do.

"Tea, Olivia?" I asked, kissing her on the forehead, not breaking my stride. I had one arm hidden behind my back with my surprise for her.

"Yes please. Thanks. You're in a chipper mood I see. That coffee at that new biker cafe must have been good!" She cocked her head to the side and grinned, playfully. "John... what's that you're hiding?"

The gig was up. I smiled back. "Surprise! It's for you." I brought out the hurriedly wrapped gift from behind my back and gave it to her. "I got you a little something from there."

Olivia was not a woman to wear biker chick apparel normally. She looked at the wrapping paper and tutted.

"What?! I had to improvise!" I replied, reading her look.

She unwrapped the garment and held it aloft. "To be fair to you, John, this is a stylish T-shirt!" She nodded, examining it further. "This is something I will actually wear! Well done!" She kissed me on the lips.

"Well, you are the wife of a tough biker gang member. Our ladies need to look the part around here too."

Olivia sighed and rolled her eyes. "Is that tea ready yet?"

The YSS shocks arrived. It was time to test my wrenching ability once again.

"Welcome back. Today it's a shocks upgrade for the Bonneville," stated Gary, mumbling through his video introduction, a limp cigarette hanging from his mouth. I could barely see his new parts because of all the smoke in his workshop. "I received a lot of negative comments when I said I was going to fit these to this old bike. Like buying your granny Nike trainers, someone said."

That made me chuckle. I didn't care what people thought, and neither did Gary's Garage. The stock rear shocks were probably made from paper clips they were that bad. It was a short video for a straightforward job. At least it should have been.

"I can't loosen the stock bushings from my frame, lads. I'm trying to install the new YSS shocks now. Any ideas?" I waited for the jokes to start at my expensive. I would take those on the chin, providing someone in the crew was currently online and could actually give me some advice.

Justin was there. "I had to use vice grips to get my gear shift pedal off the other day. So much lock-tight! Try that."

I checked my toolbox, and rummaged through some old spanners, nearly dropping a claw hammer on my foot. I spotted what I needed hanging out with a random assortment of nails. I had the tool for the job.

I went back to the chat. "Yeah I think my issue is six years of rust, the natural pressure of sitting on the bike over bumps, and liberal use of lock-tight."

Justin gave me a thumbs up emoji. "My ribbed-for-your-pleasure engine cases are arriving in a couple days too."

"Nice. Sexy. Maurice is doing very well out of us. Glad it's not just me spending money!" As soon as I wrote that, I wondered if Justin was actually paying for his new parts or if this was another influencer deal with Maurice. The Motoz Modz ribs gave the Triumph Twins a sleeker and more modern look, extending the horizontal lines of the engine cooling fins across to the gearbox case, front sprocket covers, throttle body tops, and the fuse box side panels. A simple idea but it worked.

"Unreal! You jammy bugger!" Henry appeared online now too. He posted his own photo to the chat.

I laughed. It was a screen capture of a conversation between Maurice and Henry. I was never going to get these shocks installed with all these distractions. I scrolled on to read what Henry was typing next.

"He was giving me some nonsense for choosing slash-cut exhausts from his rivals! He said they repel women too!"

"Savage!" I replied.

Justin added a laughing face emoji.

Henry continued to type. "I said I'd happily test a free set of the Motoz Modz exhausts for him if he wanted to send me some. He said he'd only do that if I filmed a video putting my current exhausts in the bin. Drainpipes he called them!"

This time I added the laughing face emoji.

"Are you deliberately trying to boycott Maurice then, Henry?" asked Justin. "You've missed out on free exhausts there."

"No, not really. Just trying to set the bike modifications apart from others on the Gram. Pretty much every Street Twin is starting to look the same. Motoz Modz everywhere!"

I thought back to Sebastian's Street Twin. That felt a long time ago now. He hadn't changed a single thing on that bike. Ironically it probably stood out from the crowd now for that reason.

Henry posted another image. "Excuse the dodgy Paint drawing, but this is the plan roughly speaking. It will look sick with a grey helmet."

Henry's artwork depicted his bike, but with shorter mudguards, clip-on bars, and the cherry red tank replaced by a dark grey one, a red diagonal stripe running through it. No one commented for a few minutes.

"BBQ SPRAY." Tyrone's comment was timed to perfection. He added an image. It was Henry's drawing, but the bike was covered in black. I laughed. Henry and Justin posted several laughing face emojis too.

"I was going to chop down your seat too but then I couldn't be arsed," added Tyrone. "Since your missus ain't going to be riding on the back, sorting out a chop mod would be a priority if it were me. I know a good welder too. Chop it right back to the rear indicators he would."

Taking an angle grinder to the bikes was the next level in customisation. Bolt-on parts could be changed back again. I wondered if Gary's Garage did a series on chopping the sub-frame?

"Pippa won't join you for a ride out then Henry?" I asked.

"No, she hates bikes."

There was a pause. I thought about Olivia. She had never really been hugely enthusiastic towards Bonnie, but she had ridden pillion a few times. She tolerated it when the weather was nice.

"Good one, Tyrone. Yeah it would look awesome I suppose," added Henry a few minutes later.

"I like the red. It distinguishes your bike from ours, mate," chipped in Justin with some serious feedback.

"Fine, you win. I'll keep the cherry red."

"Cotswolds Wrecking Crew... wrecking wallets all over the Cotswolds!" quipped Justin.

I knew the truth of that more than anyone at the moment and loosened the bushings finally.

The new shocks felt stiff, assured, robust, and confidence inspiring. Another sporty addition to Bonnie's makeover was complete. I uploaded a photo to the Gram of my new work. More followers arrived. I noticed a new DM.

"Hi mate. Those clip-ons. Where are they from? Cheers." It was a message from some random account I didn't follow. Suddenly, another notification appeared as if by magic. "Sweet bike dude. Clip-ons worth it?"

Strangers wanted advice from me. I spent some time replying, giving my views of the modification. I was actually influencing! Another DM alert popped up.

"Hi sweetie, your profile is perfect for us. DM us to be brand ambassador for our new and exciting carbon neutral jewellery brand. 10% off when you buy your first order and tag us in your content."

I deleted the post.

One new follower account stood out, a community page called @BabsGoRide. This was a collective of women who rode together and raised awareness of women getting involved in motorcycling. They were centred in Birmingham, but riders seemingly came from all over the West Midlands. I smiled at the Brummie turn of phrase in the name. It seemed from their posts that they often rode south to the more northern Cotswolds towns such as Chipping Campden. Our motorcycling turf overlapped. I hadn't really thought much on the topic of male bikers or female bikers. If you rode a motorcycle, you were cool, regardless. Scrolling through the feed, these ladies looked badass. Whether it was big and fast bikes, or small and classic machines, this sisterhood celebrated it all. I followed a few of the personal accounts tagged via the Babs page.

I spotted a Street Twin that stood out and left a comment. "Nice bike. Love the custom tank."

The bike's fuel tank was covered in a detailed, intricate tapestry of 1960s inspired bright flowers.

"There you go, Henry," I said to myself, whilst liking a few more photos. "This is how you customise a tank properly." There was no barbeque spray in sight. The @BabsGoRide riders sold a charity calendar, I noticed.

"Sassy female riders and our sexy machines." I read the advert aloud. I was sure Olivia would get on board with that message. The calendar would look cool in my garage too. "Proceeds will raise money for the local hospital, who cared for Mildred after her heart attack and her final days." That was a noble cause. The group posted a range of photos of Mildred as a tribute. She was in her seventies and looked like she had lived a life of adventure on two wheels. I hoped I was still riding into my old age like her. I bought the calendar. "For the ride!" I commented on another photo on their page.

We met in Nailsworth. Summer felt like it was upon us as we sat outside in the beer garden of The Old Lodge pub, familiar shandies and non-alcoholic beers in hand. Darren ordered a proper pint. Whilst deciding whether I should join him for a real beer, Justin excitedly shoved his phone in our faces. "This will get so many votes in the next 24 hours." He had created an online poll.

"Ribs or no ribs?" I said, reading the words to his question on his small screen. "But you already received your free ribs from Motoz Modz, no?"

"Correct." He smirked and sipped his drink. "All about giving the followers the illusion of choice and get the engagement anyway." He wiped froth from his beard.

Tyrone shook his head and tutted.

"You could grill a steak on he!" said Darren, nodding appreciatively at Justin's photo accompanying the poll. He got his own phone out. There were now two devices thrust into my eyeline.

"Look at my grill mate, at home. Fucking lush! Last weekend. Check out those prawns!" Darren's barbeque set-up looked impressive, I had to admit. His whole garden looked a perfect set-up for the summer.

"Is that a hot tub I see in the corner?" I asked.

"Pan's not hot enough," replied Justin, viewing another one of Darren's photos. He fixated on a steak, proudly the centrepiece of the shot. "You fucked it before you even started."

We all laughed. I spat out some of my beer.

"Fuck off, it's perfect! Pan was hot as fuck!" Darren's voice was raised.

We laughed some more.

"You made carpaccio." Justin was relentless.

"Yeah, well what about this one?" Darren swiped to another photo of the heavily criticised meat.

Justin leaned in to get a proper look at Darren's camera. He stroked his beard, considering the image in front of him. We all waited, anticipating the critique to come. "Looks burnt."

I spilt some of my beer, laughing too hard.

"How can that be?! Wasn't hot enough a minute ago, apparently!!"

I was convulsing with laughter. A group sat at a table next to us looked over, slight worry on their faces.

"You should get a proper iron skillet for a good steak." Justin was not done. He sat back, cooly, and yawned. "You've not used any butter either."

Tyrone joined in the ribbing. "If you eat your steak well-done, I'm quitting the crew and riding off right now!"

Darren stood up, red faced. "Fuckin' 'ell lads!" What about this one then?!" He scrolled to another giant slab of meat. Darren was wearing a chef's apron, smiling in the photo, looking happy with his work. "This is a fresh Wagyu, cooked to—"

"Cold pan. Burned. No butter!" Justin cut him off.

We all lost it at that. Henry spat out some of his cola and I was crying with laughter now.

"Fuckin' 'ell!" repeated Darren, shaking his head.

We got another round of drinks in. All the outside tables were full with happy punters. Conversations about all sorts continued as another hour passed in the blink of eye. Darren showed us a video of his young daughter riding a small off-road bike in a field. The girl was bossing it.

"Get her hooked, mate!" enthused Justin.

"Got to keep her going. She has her old man's talent. Get oil in the blood!" added Henry.

I watched Darren's face. He looked so proud.

7. Brands and reputations

New hashtags encouraged more followers to flock to my page. #fortheride, #justgoforaride, and #irodetoday even widened the appeal of my motorcycling photos to cyclists and equestrian enthusiasts. I was nearly at a thousand. I was proud that this corner of the Internet was flooded with the #cotswoldswreckingcrew hashtag too. We owned this turf. #visitbath showed off our normal meetup spot, the Royal Crescent, but with glorious photos of our custom Bonnevilles, pride of place on those hallowed stone cobbles. I could not see any other motorcycles in any photos tagged at that location. Other biker gangs respected the crew too much to ride to the crescent and tag themselves on our patch for fear of our retribution. I chuckled to myself at that silly thought. However, other riders did reach out to us in the comments.

"Cool location. Where is that mate? I'll give you credit if I use that location too?" they would ask.

These followers were not asking for our permission to go there, but there was an etiquette to be followed. A tag to be added as a nod to the crew. Credit was owed for the finders of cool locations. We had fused eighteenth century beautiful Georgian architecture, with 1960s-style motorcycles, and blended it all together with the modern hipster cafe culture scene. It worked and others wanted some of that. It was a community, and it was bigger than I had ever imagined, once the follows and the likes and the recommendations from Instagram's algorithms all came together.

I found myself on Darren's page. Several scanned polaroid shots of a younger Darren racing bikes and lifting trophies. Not a bad way to spend your teens, I thought. Darren looked like Steve McQueen in the 1971 movie, On Any Sunday, riding hell for leather, pit crews and mechanics, bikes leaking oil. This was motorcycling with no filter. It was real. There were photos of him tagged at racetrack locations. Castle Combe, Donington Park, Mallory Park. A grinning Darren stood on a few podiums too. The current online mob I followed on the Gram would hand over their smartphones and flat whites in a heartbeat for this slice of genuine legacy. I felt like a fraud again suddenly. "No," I told myself. "You are riding Bonnie again. That is real. The crew is real. The Gram is about community." I nearly convinced myself. Scrolling further, the middle photos on his page were of Darren, his wife and his young daughter. There were no motorcycles. I scrolled to the most recent few snaps. Darren posing with his brand-new Triumph Scrambler. The last two photos included Tyrone, Henry, and Justin, arms folded and looking badass on the north Somerset coast, Minehead harbour providing a cool backdrop. The ride I missed. I poured out a mug of tea and grabbed the Sunday newspaper from the door mat. I could not have been any further away from McQueen's movies, or from Darren's former glory days. I headed upstairs back to bed where Olivia was now stirring. I passed her a biscuit and checked the crew's messages on my phone. Darren and Justin had gone for an early morning local blast.

"How's the caffeine? Seems a lot of effort just for a coffee," asked Henry.

"Good, man. I know you like your bed, but you should get up for the early morning rides. We had the roads to ourselves," replied Justin.

I was very much on Henry's side this morning. I yawned and checked the Gram. Justin had already posted a story including a photo of his cappuccino and an almond croissant with his T120 in the background. A grainy retro filter had been applied.

"John, your tea is getting cold," said Olivia, nudging me.

I took a sip and browsed on. "What time did you set off?" I asked.

"I met Darren McQueen at seven thirty. Was an epic blast, rode that top road to Stroud. He rides at like a million miles per hour!"

I laughed to myself how Justin and I had thought alike this morning.

"What's all this shite about me riding fast? I nearly hit you a few times. Seriously mate, the difference between your rear light and brake light is minimal! Dangerously faint!"

Justin's rear light was a modification. I couldn't remember if it was from Motoz Modz. For the #shedbuilt #custombonneville enthusiast, as we all were in the crew, our modifications were not always better than the original parts. Just so long as they improved the look of the bike, I thought.

"Like MotoGP that little stretch of road! So fast!" responded Justin, ignoring the jibe.

#ridefastdontdie came to my mind too.

"So enough about MotoGP," said Henry. " Anyone fancy a good laugh?" Four photos appeared in the group chat. They showed his old slash-cut exhausts. "Old ones off, the Motoz Modz pipes on. They don't bloody fit! Awkward!"

Had Maurice sent him some pipes after all, I wondered? There was another photo.

"Old pipes back on." Henry finished his saga with a facepalm emoji.

"Maybe they changed the dimensions of your bike? What year is it?" asked Justin.

"2018. No changes to the dimensions."

The crew was quiet. Whole minutes passed. I guessed everyone was wondering how to solve Henry's problem.

"Tell Maurice to sort his quality assurance out, I would!" came Darren's advice.

A flurry of laughing face emojis landed in the chat.

"Anyway lads, I'm annoyed that my most-liked photo ever has you fuckers in it!" he continued.

"Which one was that?" I asked.

Darren dropped the photo. It was the Minehead harbour snap. "At least I was the one who took it, so I won't get hounded by Henry for a photo credit tag."

It was the crying with laughter cat emojis that came thick and fast this time. I sipped my tea. It was cold.

June arrived and we were heading to Wales, into the valleys, and the land of song. Our Triumphs would be singing some fine, bass engine notes indeed. We were leaving our home turf of the Cotswolds and venturing to Brecon. The roads there were stunning. Fast, open, with views of dramatic mountains, majestic under the ever-changing shadows of fast-moving clouds. One minute it would be dark, gloomy rain, and then the next, glorious sunshine. I was looking forward to this. It was just Henry, Justin and me today. We met at Piston Place Motor and Bean. I rolled into the cafe at ten in the morning. Justin and Henry had already arrived. I coasted in slowly towards their steeds, already parked, side by side, in neat formation. They had grabbed the top spot again in front of the cafe's large sign. I reckoned they had already taken some posed photos. Justin must have heard me arriving, for he was already on one knee, camera up to his honed eye, snapping away. Previously I might have worried about stalling Bonnie, riding slowly and under pressure to look cool for the camera, but not anymore. I was more confident on the bike at all speeds than ever. I looked Justin in the eye and gave Bonnie a few blips of the throttle, clutch held in to avoid launching Bonnie into the cafe window. The other punters already here for their croissants and coffee looked around. Outside any other cafe, my enthusiastic twist might have been deemed anti-social behaviour, but here, the rich raspy bark of the exhaust drew nods of appreciation. I was still getting used to the new sound myself. I upgraded my stock pipes from the heavy, fully chromed peashooters, to some lightweight, brushed stainless steel up-swept zorsts from Arrow. The performance increases were minimal, but boy did they sound good! Gary's Garage showed me the way as usual. The main bit of advice from his video was to ensure the gaskets were fitted properly at the headers. That was where pressure, and thus power, could be lost if exhaust fumes were to escape at that connection.

"Alright, lads, good ride up?" I asked as I switched off the engine and removed my helmet.

"Yeah mate. I introduced Henry to MotoGP road up over the hill towards Nailsworth," replied Justin, a big cheeky grin on his bearded chops.

I laughed, wondering if Justin was being led astray by Darren.

"Why does he say no MotoGP and then do it anyway??" replied Henry, raising his arms in protest. Well, he had survived to tell the tale and I reckoned that fast stretch of the A46 would be good corning practice for him.

"Well, let's take it a bit steadier on these Welsh roads today, eh! I need a coffee." I nodded towards the door to the cafe.

Getting out of Gloucester was frustrating. We buzzed through double lanes of traffic and pushed to the front of the queuing cars at traffic lights. Some let us through, some beeped at us. I never understood that. If anything, being on two wheels meant we weren't another car taking up room. It didn't bother me though, as when riding with the crew, what other drivers thought of me didn't matter. I embraced this tiny bit of rebellion. We blitzed through roundabouts, often in the wrong lane, but could accelerate out of any trouble to dodge oncoming cars with ease. Finally, crossing over the River

Severn, the road opened up. The speed limit was 50 mph, but following Henry, he took no notice of the signs. The boy was off. He was overtaking at any opportunity.

"Steady on. Justin and I need to squeeze through too!" I said to myself, watching him overtake yet another car. He was four cars ahead now. Justin showed his experience, being more cautious on this road, yet still managing to pick his moment for a quick overtake. Out towards the villages of Churcham and Huntley I noticed him hold back a few times when he could have gone. I knew what Justin was thinking, as I was thinking the same. Junctions, petrol stations, and side roads. To be T-boned by a car pulling out, not noticing us, would have been the end of us. A few times I held my breath as Henry blitzed past a car without seemingly noticing this hidden danger. He did know a good route though. I wondered if he used #homingpigeon on his Instagram posts. He should do, I thought. My satnav was not turned on. There was no need for it with Henry up front.

We turned off from the A40 and onto the A4136 through Little London and Mitcheldean, the road becoming ever more twisty, leaving the towns and villages behind us. Traffic was still busy though, with tourists heading the same way as us, towards the Forest of Dean. We overtook it all, almost hypnotically, swinging the bikes outwards to have a look if clear, roaring past, and then swinging back to safety again. If the bike in front went for it, then it was clear for the bike following, albeit often a car or two behind. I loved riding at the back and seeing our little convoy make progress. The A4136 heading west through the Forest was a peach of a road. It was open and fast, with corner after corner of motorcycling heaven. We were surrounded by dense trees on both sides of our ribbon of tarmac. The air smelt pine fresh and breathing it in made me smile. Ribbons of sunlight streaked through to the road where the trees were less dense, as if signs from the motorcycling gods, encouraging us to ride faster and faster. After a few miles of glorious and addictive speed, the road tightened up and descended towards the picturesque market town of Monmouth. Traffic was backed up again heading over a tiny but quaint little stone bridge over the River Wye. Without a care in the world, we just filtered past. There wasn't much room but somehow we found the gaps, poking out between cars and waddling into position where we could. I got the sense that the frustrated, queuing tourists wanted to be angry at us, but our swagger and the engine noises stopped them. They had no idea that on another day, if with Olivia, it might have been me stuck in that queue in my very sensible car.

Justin straddled his T120 beside my T100, almost knocking off the right wing mirror of a stationary car. He moved his bike so the oncoming traffic on the bridge could get past, but he would be ready to go when it was our turn again. "Mate, your new Arrows sound great. When behind you, I get a blast to the face too. The angle of those cones is insane! Nice smell of Castrol oil too. Old school!" He had to shout to be heard.

I grinned. "Thanks mate, yeah I love them. Very happy I committed." I thought of Olivia, fleetingly, but pushed the guilt away.

"I reckon they would sound even better if you took the baffles out! Proper motorcycle outlaw!"

I hadn't considered that before. I nodded back to Justin and then our lane of traffic was moving again. I noticed the car driver behind him angrily stick up his middle finger.

Back on the A40 it was fast and open again. The Brecon Beacons appeared in front of us, somehow performing a magic trick, one second not being there, and then with Bonnie leaning into a corner, and riding out of the bend, there they were, looming and formidable, taking up the entirety of the foreground. We were lucky with the weather too. It was cloudy but there was no rain... yet. I twisted the throttle, getting side by side with Justin and held out my left hand for a fist bump. He replied in kind, the gesture saying more than words could at that moment. You really had to trust the biker next to you to get this close. Lots of bikers were here today. On this road the big sports bikes were out in force. A few passed us, screaming at unfathomably high revs, embarrassing our parallel twins and putting us pretenders firmly in our place. I wondered if any police might be out today. It was a good day to fill the coffers, courtesy of speed cameras. We passed a few fully faired beasts at a roadside layby burger van. I gave Bonnie the beans to get the induction roar of the engine going to let them know I was there. I nodded to them as I whizzed past. I could also go fast. They gave me a wave. I laughed with glee. Bikers were a tribe regardless of the type of two wheels they rode. That burger van was not serving the artisan vegan red velvet cake and Nduja sausage rolls sold at Piston Place Motor and Bean, but otherwise, these moments and gestures were universal. We arrived to the small town of Brecon. Henry tried to find somewhere to park, outside a cafe to have a rest finally. I looked at my trip counter. I had ridden 70 miles so far. I was glad Henry didn't faff around looking for a special backdrop for a photo. Today was about the ride. Now it was time for food. Seeing that burger van earlier, and riding fast all morning, concentration and adrenaline burning the calories like Bonnie had burned through fuel, made me hungry.

"Boys, Darren and I have been chatting online and we want to make a start on sticking a lot of our photos up on a Cotswolds Wrecking Crew page, as there are lots of photos just sat there on our phones. Start to build up a CWC collection of shots, that sort of thing."

I was finishing my coffee and looked up at Henry. I liked his idea but remembered Tyrone saying something similar months ago at the pub.

"Tyrone's always working and hasn't had the time. I like this plan, scrapbook vibe," added Justin as if reading my thoughts.

I gave the proposal my blessing too. This was awesome. Up until this point we were really five separate riders with separate styles on our Instagram profiles.

"The page can chronicle our adventures, mods done to the bikes, and give mechanical advice. That sort of thing," I added. "I've no idea how to create a brand though." As far as I was aware, only Tyrone had a professional page with @motosofthegram.

"Darren reckons he has a bit of creative flair with painting and crayons and stuff. Not professionally, just a hobby. Reckons it calms him down, he told me. Some therapy or something. He didn't go into it much," said Henry. The cafe door opened. A man and women stomped past us, the sound of huge plastic biker boots making our coffee mugs shake. They were wearing matching Gore Tex riding suits, head to toe. The man nodded, recognising fellow bikers. I nodded back. They looked prepared for a Tsunami in that gear. Maybe they knew something that we didn't, riding these Welsh roads. Justin and I looked at each other and he shrugged. I didn't know if he was wondering about the new arrivals too or Darren's need for his artistic release.

"He reckons he's been working on something. I've asked him to share it with the group," continued Henry.

I sipped more coffee in silence.

Justin wiped some cappuccino foam from his beard and leaned in. "I like the old school vibe of very detailed hand-drawn cartoons. Over the top, loud graphics, but shows off the rebel counterculture of two wheels." He was gesticulating excitedly. He had my full attention. "Very late sixties and early seventies California style. Has hints of that Easy Rider movie. No shits given, that sort of thing. Several brands are doing this now for the likes of us, wannabe Peter Fonda and Dennis Hopper, cocaine in your backpack, riding the American southwest, but really pushing a desk in a miserable grey suburb. Piston Place Motor and Bean are getting into it, but Braap and Burn do it best." Justin sat back and waited for our applause.

"Wow you really know the market!" I replied. A memory came flooding back. My neighbour, Colin, had mentioned that Braap and Burn brand a long time ago.

"Are we thinking T-shirts and hoodies like Braap and Burn then?" I asked.

Justin nodded.

I had ridden up to Builth Wells several years ago, more by accident than by choice. After retracing my steps, it was the B4520 that took me there. What a road it was too. It was a wide farm track that took you up, higher and higher over the hills. Once you reached the top, you were totally exposed. The Army used the surrounding area for training. Neatly formed forest blocks dotted the otherwise bleak terrain. This was not a road for flaky motorcycles with a penchant for breaking down. The wind howled a gale up there. Today, I realised the couple in the cafe had thought this through. They were prepared if they rode this way. We were less so. I prayed the rain would stay away as the lads wanted a photo to document this epic day on the Gram. This dramatic rugged landscape north of Brecon was the perfect backdrop. Henry was at the front again, but even he slowed down to take it all in. Entire hills would disappear behind cloud and then reappear again to play tricks on the mind, the winds ensuring our vista was constantly moving. I was being buffeted from left to right and could see Justin was suffering the same fate in front of me. He was so skinny, I was almost surprised the winds had not lifted him clean off his T120. We rode past hardy, scraggy sheep lining the sides of the roads. Even they were hunkering down. Some invaded our sacred tarmac, oblivious to the perils of the mechanical beasts that rode towards them. I did not fancy my chances if I hit one of them on this wilderness road today. I heard Justin's burbling exhaust boom towards Henry and then fly past him. His right arm was out, gesturing for us to pull in. I reckoned he had eyed a beauty spot that he wanted for the photo. We all stopped at the side of the road. I checked Google Maps. Pen-Y-Garreg was to be featured in Justin's craft today, splendid and mighty in the background of shots of our Triumphs. I went for a piss in the nature, taking in the vastness of the place, trying to gauge the direction of the wind cautiously. Justin was busy doing what he did best, snapping away this side and that, up and down, finding the right angle for the bikes.

Back at home in the group chat, Darren had come good. "The tint in that orange visor looks shit but not bad as a test." He posted a photo to the group. He had already sent designs to a printing company and got a cheap T-shirt made. The design was of a mean looking skull wearing a helmet in black, grey and orange. "That's direct to garment. Cost me a tenner. The solid colours look good though."

"You reckon any printing company might be able to do an orange visor properly?" I asked him. I was amazed that he could draw that well.

"If you had it properly screen printed maybe? But it's difficult to get right. Might rethink the design. The good thing about these is you can print as you go, so if you just want a few for us lot, you can without having to do a run of fifty or so."

"Maybe lose the visor then?" I tried to help out.

"That's the brand though. Very recognisable," chipped in Justin.

The crew did own a number of orange and tinted goggles and visors that were often shown off via their Gram photos. Tinted visors were not for me. If you had to ride at night, you wouldn't be able to see anything. I continued my encouragement for Darren's work. "I'd chuck in for a T-shirt, mate."

"Likewise," Justin added, following suit. "They look good. I wonder if you went darker on the orange overall it would print better?"

"Yeah you have to work with solid colours, can't use tones. I'll rethink it a bit when I get some time."

Justin had convinced me. I ordered a couple of Braap and Burn T-shirts from Piston Place Motor and Bean's online shop. I loved the designs. The first T-shirt depicted a lion's head, jaw open, holding a wrench in its teeth, with the quote, "Wild Wrenching Customs". The other, more understated, showed a skull wearing a helmet with two bony hands, fists grabbing handlebars. The words "hold fast" were tattooed on the bony skeletal knuckles. They arrived a few days later.

"You look ridiculous, like your ten year old nephew!" Olivia's first impression hit me in the gut. She had a point though. I doubted my work colleagues would allow me into the office wearing these T-shirts, even for casual Fridays.

"Look, I'm not saying I'll wear them out with you when we go to a restaurant, but whilst riding with the crew, this is the image."

Olivia shook her head and sighed. I smiled at her and handed her my phone. Tagging the brand of your riding gear was a guarantee to bring in the likes. I moved the recycle bins out of the way and covered up the tumble dryer and the lawn mower in the garage. I made sure that my new @BabsGoRide calendar was in view, and that the real star of the show, Bonnie, adorned with all of her Motoz Modz parts, was in frame. Olivia took some photos of my chest, getting a close up of the designs. I was sat on the bike, and then I stood behind the bike. I looked over my left shoulder and then over my right shoulder. I did not smile in any of the snaps.

Olivia started to laugh. "I'm sorry, but this is silly. You could at least smile!"

I grabbed the phone from her and gave her an infuriated look. That was Olivia's cue to leave me to it in the garage. To give her credit, there were three or four decent photos. I blew her a kiss and got to work editing them.

A few hours later, the photos had been reposted by Braap and Burn. I gained twenty new followers from people I would likely never meet, and fifty likes from all corners of the Internet. One of the women whom I had messaged the other day about her cool artwork on her Street Twin from the @BabsGoRide group DM'ed me and gave me a follow too. @LoudPipesLisa. I liked the name. It was creative, fun, and cheeky. A glance at her photos showed that she was always out at motorcycle festivals and parties. Most of the other Babs riders also tagged her in their photos.

"Nice T-shirts and sexy bike," she commented on my photos.

I gave the message a like.

I had a DM from Maurice too. "Nice Justin pose. Nailed the right shoulder look."

That got a like too. "Ha-ha, yeah I'm learning from the bearded hipster master there," I wrote back. Giddy with dopamine, I sent the photos to the crew for their appreciation. There was already a conversation in full flow.

"Have you got some sort of live dashboard?" Justin asked Tyrone.

I assumed this wasn't just chatter about car interiors, I thought to myself.

"Just like the stock market, to keep on top of trends and analytics?" he continued.

"Yeah man, I've got some nutty backend stuff. Not sure at what point you get access to it. Maybe at 100k followers. Dunno. Yeah it really is one big game, learning to read the mainstream," responded Tyrone.

This was way out of my league. I wondered if this was what all the pros did for engagement. Likely a good photo from inside one's garage was not enough on its own for engagement at these heady numbers. I looked out of the living room window, sad at the thought. A cat was sitting on the neighbour's fence, licking its paws before stretching and yawning lazily. I stared at it for a minute, wondering how our human lives had all become so complicated, desperate for this online validation. I returned to my phone and saw Tyrone had posted a screengrab of a graph. It showed hundreds of followers leaving his @motosofthegram motorcycle page.

"Woah, what happened there?" I asked him.

"Fucking Henry wasn't it. Always pesting to get his photo on my page for greater exposure to his lonely little account."

"Ha-ha what photo of mine did you repost then?" Henry was online too.

I wondered if he was as baffled as I was regarding talk of analytics. Tyrone added the photo to the group. It was Henry's Street Twin, with a Cotswold dry stone wall behind the bike, and the last of the winter leaves on the ground. He had zoomed-in the shot to focus on the cherry red tank. Henry's helmet and matching red leather gloves were perfectly placed on the slab leather seat. I thought it was a decent photo.

"So, I did the little attention seeker wannabe a favour. He makes me sick with all his ratty little photograph posts, giving it, 'I took that btw, tag me', or 'that's my photo btw, tag me', and 'what sexy beast took that, tag me'... absolute desperado!" Tyrone was spot on. I was dying laughing to myself.

"Ha, shit! Oops!" replied Henry.

"The followers were literally back up again within minutes though. The Gram is fickle as fuck," continued Tyrone.

"How many left then because of my bike?"

"Just over a hundred or so within twenty minutes. I always track initial engagement. Justin mate, you on the other hand... that series you did at Piston Place Motor and Bean, and the ones from Brecon, send them to me and I'll pass them to some contacts of mine at Triumph. I've a big set of reviews coming up with their new cafe racer jacket range, and I reckon I could get you in the photos. They love a skinny beard. I'm taking my Street Twin. They want more of the genuine biker fan stuff."

Justin replied with a single thank you emoji and a link with the full resolution shots he took.

"They look great, Justin!" I congratulated him. How did the photos of him and his T120 look so much better than those with Henry and me and our bikes? He was lucky he brought along his tripod for the day, otherwise he wouldn't have been in any photos. Any decent ones anyway. "Who's your favourite @BabsGoRide lass then, lads?" I asked, trying to draw at least some of the attention towards me and my Braap and Burn garage photo series. I posted the link to the Babs Instagram page to the chat. "I like this Lisa. Nice custom tank... nice pipes too." I flushed with embarrassment at my crass comment. I couldn't unsend it.

"She from Bath?" asked Tyrone.

"Nah mate, Birmingham," I replied.

"Ah well. Still... followed."

I had finally hooked Tyrone into talking about what I had been doing.

"I like this one," he added, and posted a link to the @BabsGoRide group. "Wouldn't might a bit of her, but that bike... Harley Davidson Street Bob! Fuck off! Hardly able son lol."

I clicked the link Tyrone sent to see which biker lass he was talking about. I started to sweat, my cheeks going an even darker shade of red. No one else in the group uttered a comment for a few minutes. I had to say something. "Mate, she's dead! She's the main reason they have been fundraising with that calendar!"

He had posted the link to the page belonging to Mildred, the veteran @BabsGoRide rider who died of a heart attack.

"Fuck. Off. OMG!" he replied.

"Jesus Christ, Tyrone!" added Henry.

"I don't read. I can't read!" Tyrone tried making his excuses. "I've been on the whiskey too, mind's fucked."

Darren appeared in the chat posting four crying with laughter emojis. "I've been sat on the sofa with the missus, and we've been creasing up with that. Which is very bad. But funny. Tyrone you utter twat!"

"And bad mouthing her bike too. She'll be turning in her grave," commented Justin next.

"Fucking hell lads, I'm such a tool!" Can we change the subject?"

Tyrone read my mind. I wanted to talk about anything else and forget I ever led him to the @BabsGoRide pages. At least it was only the crew who would read his comments.

"Justin, I've sent your photos to my Triumph contacts for this gear and bike review. Will let you know what they think," he added before going offline.

It was time to give Bonnie a thorough clean. Opening the garage door my eyes locked onto the @BabsGoRide calendar, pride of place over my tool chest. The garage was beginning to look legitmate now. I smirked and shook my head. "Tyrone you idiot," I said to myself, whilst turning the page from June to July. A photo of a young woman in a trendy oxblood leather jacket was straddling an awesome Triumph Rocket 3, Hedon Heroine helmet on her lap. The photographer had done an excellent job. She looked badass and the bike was an absolute beast. The new Rocket, with its 2500cc engine produced eye-watering levels of rip your arms off torque. The sun was starting to melt away the mid-morning white, fluffy clouds. The birds were chattering in the trees that were dotted along Tivoli avenue, in full song. A few neighbours were washing their cars. Colin was out too. I caught his eye and gave him a nod. He nodded back. Machines, whether two or four wheeled had to be kept clean. Whilst the bucket was filling up with water, I checked the group chat on my phone. There was a message from Justin. "Guys, I've been DMing Jane from Piston Place Motor and Bean. I've managed to sort out tickets to an exclusive invite only Royal Enfield bike test event at their cafe next week. Who's in?"

I dropped the sponge in the bucket and stared at the sky, letting my imagination run away with me. "Exclusive" and "invite only" rarely applied to me. This could take my online influencing adventure to the next level. I replied straight away. "Yes mate, 100%!"

I hadn't checked with Olivia but opportunities like this didn't come around that often. I was sure she would be fine with it. These motorcycles weren't Triumphs, but Royal Enfield were a cool brand too. I was excited to ride their modern classic 650cc Interceptor, or the more cafe racer inspired Continental GT. These machines were nice and easy for a beginner rider and perfect for British B-roads. I knew a small bit about the brand, I reflected.

Royal Enfield had come back to the motorcycling market at the peak of the renewed interest in modern classics and retro cool. They were slightly lower on power and torque than the Triumphs, but a lot cheaper relative to slight performance losses. They looked good too and the Interceptor had won many bike of the year plaudits for its style, simplicity, robustness, and price. For the image conscious motorcycle rider, authenticity mattered. Royal Enfield could boast being the oldest motorcycle brand in continuous production in the world, first selling bikes back in 1901.

Ignoring the bucket of water, I searched for #royalenfield on the Gram, quickly. As I suspected, the riders in the photos were like brothers from another mother. I was looking forward to meeting them via our own photos and their hashtags. I started splashing soapy, cold water over Bonnie. The phone pinged again. With a dry hand, I checked the message.

"Guys, I've fucked up," wrote Tyrone.

I could see he was still typing furiously as I read that message. I would never finish cleaning Bonnie with these distractions. Colin over the road had already headed back inside, his car gleaming on the driveway in the bright sunshine. Next message.

"I copied that message about that dead old dear to Triumph along with Justin's photos. I'm fucked."

I grabbed the side of the garage wall to steady myself, hand raised over my mouth in shock.

"Shit!" I exclaimed, staring down at a wet foot, tripping over the bucket of foamy water. I reread the message to check I had understood it correctly. My left sock was soaked. I needed to sit down. The bike cleaning could wait.

"Mate, I'm so sorry!" I wrote. The other lads had seen the messages and added their own words mirroring mine. They asked him what Triumph had thought of Tyrone's message and a half dozen other quick-fire questions. I could only watch the chat play out.

"They've dropped me from this clothing range review piece. Said I would never work with them again. Said I was unprofessional and had no place in bike journalism with values like that."

"But it was a mistake. A silly moment of juvenile behaviour... and you had a few drinks!" I tried to add hope to the situation. It was all I could do.

"Cancel culture nonsense," added Darren.

"Really, I'm fucked," reiterated Tyrone again.

8. Exclusive opportunity

Days passed without a single message. I didn't know if it was some unspoken sorrow or regret... or shame on the part of the crew regarding Tyrone's recent mistake. None of the lads had posted anything. Maybe we all felt we had to give him space to sort it all out. I messaged Justin separately. He had these tickets to the Piston Place Motor and Bean Royal Enfield event. He told me that everything was in order. We all needed this. A focus on the riding and on the motorcycles.

Two days before the big day Henry appeared online and posted a couple of videos. Justin was playing cameraman, his steady hand showcasing a beautiful, thatched cottage in frame. He panned left, revealing a single lane road that disappeared into the horizon. Cue the sound. "WHAAAAAAAA VROOOOM!" A lightning-quick bike zoomed from left to right in a blur. I could only really make out the headlight, an iconic cherry red fuel tank, and a rider, dressed in black. He was gripping on for dear life, his head nestled into the handlebars for some semblance of aerodynamics. Justin had done a decent job tracking Henry on the approach, the Twin's induction roar ascending to a crescendo as Henry approached the rev limiter, before backing off the gas, probably running out of road, or more likely, before hitting and ruining a pretty Cotswold stone wall. The second video was another run of the action. Before I could comment, Darren appeared online. "Fuck me, I bet they love you in that house!" He posted a gif of a fighter jet taking off.

"That's exactly how it felt!" replied Justin.

"To be fair, I'm really fit so they didn't mind. They invited us in for tea," added Henry.

I smiled, knowing that Henry would be loving this video of his hooligan antics. I rewatched the second video again. "I see you've finally fitted those free Motoz Modz slash-cuts!" I spotted the new addition whilst pausing the video halfway. "Maurice can finally make some money out of you."

Henry replied with a thumbs up. "Well, I am a ratty desperado, remember?"

I chuckled but then felt guilty once more. There was still no news nor chatter from Tyrone.

"Tower, this is Ghost Rider requesting a flyby," joked Darren, another fighter jet gif added to the chat.

"The edit is posted here, boys." Justin posted a link to a short Instagram reel. I gave it a like straightaway.

"He didn't even tag me?!" exclaimed Henry. "Always tag the creative! Isn't that the phrase?"

"Fucking hell, Henry, alright! I'll redo it," retorted Justin.

"Negative, Ghost Rider, I'm about to sit down for my dinner, ya thug!" Darren continued his Top Gun analogy. "I can just imagine the bloke in that gaff sat in his armchair chucking his dinner on his lap after you shot by!"

I laughed. The Cotswolds Wrecking Crew were back. Mostly.

It was a Friday morning in the office. My coffee had yet to kick in. I yawned and stared out the window. I was also ignoring a waste disposal efficiency report that I was due to write for my manager before the day was done. I had spreadsheets of data showing when the local recycling lorries visited their designated zones in one column and a second column that compared the figures against the non-recyclable waste disposal lorries. I was due to present on how inefficient the two collections were currently, and then give my recommendations for improving it all. I could barely keep my eyes open. I took my phone out my pocket to distract myself for a moment before getting started with this epic task. I smiled. There was some chatter from the crew.

"Lads, you can't go unless you book your bikes!" warned Justin.

"Apparently my email isn't valid. Is it a paid gig? I need all the work I can get! They got their bike press sorted?" added Tyrone.

"Yes! Welcome back lad!" I exclaimed, too loudly. I looked around. Two colleagues from sewage policy a few desks over shot me an evil glance. I ignored them and spun my chair around, facing away from them.

"No, it's free. We get to ride bikes, and they get our content. I'm not that famous yet! Don't know about journos," responded Justin.

"I'm riding the Continental GT at twelve. Splendid!" chipped in Henry.

I swore that none of these lads ever did any actual real work. I had not yet registered for any test rides. I wanted to check out the Continental GT like Henry. It had clip-ons like I had fitted to Bonnie. The GT's pegs were higher and set back a few inches to the rear, compared to the Interceptor. These rear set pegs provided a foot angle that differed to standard roadster pegs. It forced the rider into a more forward and aggressive stance, leaning over the clip-ons and getting the rider's head over the front wheel. This put the rider in tune with the bike's cornering and quickened handling too. This really provided scalpel-sharp precision on a spirited ride. I really wanted some rear-sets to complete the cafe racer look of Bonnie, so the GT was a great chance to check them out. I typed-in the website address for this event. I couldn't find what I was looking for so checked in with the group again.

"There is a little drop-down menu at the top of the page with the different bikes," replied Tyrone. "It's like a nineties website. Awful design. Shite colours too. No contrast."

I was so pleased he was back.

"I'm not gonna bike it up with you boys though. Will book a test ride, but gonna take the car. Too gutted to take my own Triumph still. Can't face it," he added.

He wasn't completely back to his old self then.

"My missus is away so I don't think I'll get there for twelve, sorry!" Darren had made it to the conversation finally. The plan was not turning out how I had hoped. I had no idea how many other riders, influencers and journalists, would be at this event either. I spied my manager walking round the corner. My phone pinged but thankfully he didn't hear it.

"Oh, fuck it, I booked the Continental GT too. She will just have to get her ass back home quickly!" wrote Darren minutes later.

"You beauty!" I said, too enthusiastically. I looked up. The sewage duo tutted, and my manager looked back round at me, raising an eyebrow. I smiled at him. "Just excited for this report, boss." I was wide awake now.

Sunday morning was here. Tyrone was already at Piston Place Motor and Bean by the time I arrived, and I was early myself. He was perched on the bonnet of his car, chatting enthusiastically to other lads and lasses, influencer sorts I guessed, all looking cool. There were tattoos on display everywhere. I spotted checked shirts, Dickies trousers and Red Wing boots in all corners of the car park. It was a day to be noticed. I pulled up to the normal photo spot but was too late for the usual prime location, even at this early hour. There were about a dozen or so motorcycles there already. I wondered if I had rolled in with the crew this morning, would we have challenged these tourists? This was our patch. I parked where I could and killed the engine. Today was about Royal Enfield motorcycles and not our Triumphs. I nodded at Tyrone. He nodded back. It was good to see him here. A sound of low, thumping thunder cut through the buzz of chatter. I looked around to the cafe entrance. Here they were! Darren, Justin, and Henry made quite the entrance, gliding in slowly, letting eyes focus on them as they blipped throttles and revved engines. I wished I was also part of the pack and cursed myself for being too efficient. They stopped dead, Justin nearly rear-ending Darren and losing his footing. He saved a fall though. I laughed. They didn't know where to park.

"Come on lads, get on with it," I said out loud, watching them awkwardly find any space to squeeze into. I walked over to Tyrone, gesturing for him to wind up his chat with his new pals and meet the crew with me.

"I hope one of you lot has sorted the admin. I haven't got any paperwork," he said.

Justin laughed, grooming his beard. "No shits given eh Tyrone!"

"'Fuckin' 'ell, Tyrone," exclaimed Darren, removing his helmet. "I printed a few spare disclaimers. Am I your dad, am I?" He gave Tyrone a hug and grinned.

"Henry was late to arrive as usual so we set off late. Made up for it though on MotoGP road. Hit the tonne I reckon." Justin was grinning with glee and staring at Henry.

"Why do they say no MotoGP then do it anyway!?" Henry looked like he had just walked off of a deadly quick roller coaster after thinking he had tickets for the teacups. I looked around at the other invited exclusive guests. I wondered if Jane had picked the would-be riders from a scan of Instagram accounts that followed Piston Place Motor and Bean on the Gram. I recognised a small group of the @BabsGoRide crew too. They had sorted their admin better than us lot, wearing a matching Babs patch logo sewn to their jackets and leather gilet vests. I walked the line of their bikes. A good mix of cruisers, adventure tourers, sports bikes, and a Triumph Street Twin, with a custom paint job on the tank, decorated with hippy flowers. My heart quickened suddenly. It was stupid but I found myself looking around for her, standing taller too in case she saw me first. There she was, just to the left of the group. I couldn't breathe. She was staring at me. I looked away instantly. I didn't know why. I looked back at her and smiled, sheepishly. She walked over to me. I was starting to sweat.

"Hi, John isn't it?"

"Hi, err, yes. That's me. It's good to meet you in person... err, Loud Pipes Lisa? Sorry, I don't know your name."

She laughed loudly and confidently. "It's Lisa."

I gulped and focussed on the machine. "I love the custom work on your Twin. Who painted that... paint then?"

Lisa laughed more. "Thanks, yeah I love it. So many boring Street Twins out there."

I thought of Sebastian and grinned.

"This little independent shop in the middle of Birmingham did it. I was so pleased. An artist called Ellie. So talented. She does hand-painted signage. It's her passion. I didn't want cheap transfers or spray paint. Too many bikes are covered in horrible barbeque spray. I wanted something really personal and unique, you know?"

"Ah yes, I hate barbeque paint. Very naff. You're from there aren't you?"

"Have you been stalking my page?"

"No, no!" My protest reply was too rushed. "I mean, it's written on your bio and the Babs motorcycle club are centred there. Are you involved with them lots? Seems a great group."

I hoped I saved it.

Lisa laughed. "Yes indeed we are. I help organise ride-outs. It's easy for me being in the middle of town." Lisa nodded in the direction of the crew. "That your gang over there?"

Justin was already snapping away, ducking and diving, finding the angles. Tyrone was talking to Jane, looking a bit serious. Darren and Henry were trying their hardest to make it look like they weren't staring at me and Lisa. They were giggling childishly.

"Yes, they're my crew." I was thankful that some semblance of confidence returned to my voice. "The Cotswolds Wrecking Crew. We've ridden together for several months now. It's great. So much fun. Top guys all of them."

"I know. I've been following your online antics." Lisa was still smiling at me. She held my gaze. "Well, enjoy the day on the Enfields. I'm looking forward to checking out the Interceptor."

"Yes, you too. I'm on the Continental GT. Should be a fun day!"

I walked back to the crew with a spring in my step. Get over yourself John, I told myself. It was just a bit of bike chat with a fellow rider.

"How were her pipes then, John?" asked Darren, his mouth stretched wide with a stupid grin.

"They looked quite loud from where I was standing," added Henry, with a smirk somehow bigger than Darren's.

"Yeah, yeah, funny one guys!" I walked towards the Enfields. It was time to focus on the ride.

An older chap, with a fantastic white bushy beard, wearing a hi-vis vest and a modular helmet stood on a bench to be seen and heard. I spotted a Royal Enfield badge sewn onto his chest. It was time for the pre-ride announcement. We huddled in, the hubbub of creative chatter fading to silence as the marshal spoke. He welcomed us to the test ride day before launching in with some rules.

"Do not overtake each other..." he spoke plainly, sounding almost bored. I was struggling to pay attention myself, thoughts of Lisa on my mind.

"Do not ride above sixty miles per hour on open roads, follow the speed limit at all times..." he continued. I looked around to see what group she might be in. I locked eyes with Tyrone. He was all smiles too, gazing at me. I shook my head, knowing instinctively that Darren had briefed him on events, no doubt exaggerated.

"No revving the engine excessively, no wheelies..." The marshal was still going through his list. I tuned back into the brief. How could anyone wheelie one of these heavy Twins with the limited power they offered anyway I wondered?

"Now I have the groups here," he revealed, waving some pieces of paper aloft, "erm, but you must have completed the consent form... in case of spills from too many thrills." The marshal looked around and paused, a smile on his face. No one laughed at his attempt at humour. The exclusive invite only crowd had already started talking amongst themselves again, ambling slowly to their bikes. I was with Darren and Tyrone. Lisa was not in our group.

We headed out like little ducklings all in a row following our bearded mother duck. It was a lovely day for it and hi-vis was not needed. The sun was out but it wasn't too hot. Escaping Gloucester was hell as it always was, but in a pack of six riders and following our Royal Enfield marshal, it took even longer. There were times at a roundabouts where the whole pack could have ridden through, but the marshal paused... and then paused longer. I stalled the bike once due to pre-empting that we would ride through, only to hit the brake as the rider in front didn't move.

"For fuck sake!" I said into my helmet. I wondered what Darren and Tyrone must have been thinking as they were behind me in the ride order. Once outside the hustle and bustle of town traffic, the road opened up. The green of the hedgerows lining the roads was bright and luscious. I could hear the birds chirping. Sparrows darted about as we breezed past field after field. I relaxed into the slow ebb and flow of the ride. One thing struck me straight away. This bike was quiet. Very quiet. I couldn't remember the last time I heard bird song whilst riding Bonnie. This actually felt quite pleasant, I had to admit to myself. The slow pace meant I never had to concentrate either. There would be no #ridefastdontdie overtakes, following Henry blindly into a corner. There was no Darren hooning it past me, with a #braaap exhaust note, less than a foot away from my right shoulder without any warning either. There was also no stress about potentially getting lost. I reckoned I could spot the marshal from the moon in his bright vest, a few bikes ahead of me. We were on the A38, heading towards the medieval market town of Tewkesbury. It was very much a photograph backdrop location for the crew on any other day. I had time to think of other stuff on this ride. Lisa appeared in my thoughts. I wanted to get to know her more, but only because she was cool, and we had a shared hobby. I told myself that. I didn't know if I believed it.

To give the marshal credit, he led us well. No one got lost nor left behind. We didn't head into Tewkesbury for a photo, but that was a good thing as traffic was getting busier again. This group would not be filtering past cars. I was getting a feel for the bike too. It steered and turned in quicker and easier than Bonnie. The Continental GT had a smaller front wheel than my classic nineteen inch wheel. The backend felt floaty though and I could not feel any precise connection with the road. That was likely due to the poor and basic stock rear suspension. Bonnie used to be like that once before I started turning her into a corner carving machine, once you managed to turn in that big front wheel of course. I also enjoyed the rear-sets on this bike once my feet had got used to finding the rear brake and gear lever positions.

"Sorry Olivia my love, I've got to get some of these," I told myself, the usual pang of guilt hitting me just after.

We meandered our way through a blur of left and right junctions on pleasant B-roads through little villages. Some of the houses we rode past had thatched roofs, their windows adorned with boxes of bright flowers. I had no idea where we were until I realised the marshal was leading us towards the little medieval town of Winchcombe. "Royal Enfield have done their research," I said aloud, into the wind. I hoped we would ride through this town as its timbered inns and centuries-old buildings were beautiful. This town was a favourite photo spot for the crew. I reckoned I knew where we were heading after this, likely to Broadway on the lovely and quick B4632. With long sweeping corners, and few hedgerows, you could see through the whole bend safely for a fast ride. In my opinion Broadway was one of the finest villages in the Gloucestershire area of the Cotswolds. Many groups of bikers made a pilgrimage here on any given Sunday for a quick pre-roast dinner blast. We knew it well. Thankfully the marshal increased his speed. It was not quite 60 mph, but it meant I could kick the Continental GT into its top gear, sixth gear. I wasn't used to this. Bonnie had five gears and that was fine. Six felt like overkill for this machine. It only had a 650cc engine and 47 bhp. It ran out of puff at higher revs, and I didn't feel the engine was straining in fifth gear, let alone requiring number six. A bright, flashing light caught my eye in my right rear-view mirror suddenly. I looked over my right shoulder. Two bikes went whizzing past me. The rear one gave me two fingers as the rider looked back at me, expression hidden behind the rider's dark visor. "Fuck sake lads," I muttered to myself. I recognised the visor. That was Tyrone. I smiled. The other rebel must have been Darren then. I could already hear the bollocking from the marshal when we stopped next. I looked ahead. They overtook the next rider in front of me too. I was laughing now. "Cotswolds Wrecking Crew!!" I shouted, my right fist pumping the air. The rider in front of me either agreed or he was not happy about being overtaken, his own fist shaking vigorously in the air. I reckoned it was the latter.

"BEEP, BEEP, BEEEEEP!!" came the sound from his horn a few seconds afterwards. Well, this rider was able to review the Enfield's horn at least, I chuckled to myself. Waiting at the junction to turn right into Broadway I caught up with the two hooligans, side by side. "Didn't you hear the rules?"

"Mate, me and Darren have been going mad back there. This is not what we expected. Can't get no feel for the bike like this," replied Tyrone.

"Gonna try and get her front wheel up in a bit through the town. Give something for the crowd like," added Darren.

Before I could reply, we all pulled out from the junction as a group and were cruising Broadway's picturesque high street. We all parked together in a gaggle outside the beautiful Lygon Arms hotel. The place was a picture postcard of an English hotel. Union flags were flying in the courtyard, the sun giving the red, white and blue a majestic look. We had ridden the Triumphs here a few times for photos at this very spot. Justin and Henry had come here one evening to do a photoshoot with Land Rover too. Both British icons. This was the perfect backdrop for photos of these Enfields too. I was glad for the chance to grab a coffee, stretch my legs, and compare notes so far.

Tyrone was talking into his phone, and gesturing with his left hand, no doubt making voice notes on what he thought of the bike so far. He looked focussed. Darren was in the queue for a coffee. I walked over to him, trying to catch his eye. He could get the brews in.

"Oi, watch it!" Someone pushed past me, seemingly oblivious I was stood there. He didn't turn around to acknowledge my annoyance. He was walking quickly towards Darren.

"You! What was that? No overtaking, remember! You could have got me killed! I nearly lost control of the bike, you complete hooligan!" He was right in Darren's face.

"Whatever mate just a bit of fun. Don't cry," he replied casually and turned away, focusing on the coffee menu. "John mate, you want an Americano or one of those fancy flat whites?"

The protester's face went from red to purple. Darren looked right past him, waiting for my answer. The angry man was wearing a tweed blazer, shirt and a cravat. It all clicked. I hadn't noticed his smart clothing attire previously as he was wearing a hi-vis jacket in front of me on the bike whilst on the road. "It's no wonder he's dressed like that for today," I scoffed quietly. He was carrying a camera tripod with him.

"My vibe is all off now thanks to your aggression!!" He pointed the tripod wildly at the alleged hooligan.

"What?" Darren turned to face him again. "What are you talking about, you melt!?"

The lad serving the coffee at the counter was enthralled, watching the conversation unfold. Blazer rider hesitated then finally found his words. "My followers are expecting live content soon, and this is a big gig for me. I wanted to set up in front of that hotel and do an Insta vlog about the bike, but I'm too triggered because of your mad riding earlier!"

Darren looked him up and down and shook his head. "Fuck me, look at the state of you, mincing about in that cravat. That jacket is too tight for you, mate. Those buttons are gonna pop off, pinging all over the place. Probably on the road. You'll be the one causing danger to the rest of us then! Vlog? Honestly, what kind of bike ride is this?!"

Blazer rider was trembling. I was ready intervene. If anything, I didn't want the top quality artisanal coffee he ordered for me to go flying everywhere. Blazer rider raised his camera tripod, looking like he was going to swing it at Darren.

"Woah, woah lads, calm down!" I positioned myself between the two of them, arms stretched out. "My mate just loves a spirited ride, that's all. He didn't mean any harm. If you go to your bike now, set-up for your live feed, you'll be able to say something to your followers, I'm sure. You have time." I pointed to the bearded marshal. He was easy to spot. I guessed that was the point. "That marshal bloke is still drinking his brew anyway," I added.

Blazer rider stared at me, pointing his tripod at my chest now. "If I can't get me words out, it's on you!" He about turned and walked away.

"Alright, you prick, you've said your piece!" shouted Darren, his words following Blazer rider all the way back to his bike. He quickened his pace and didn't look back at Darren.

"Calm down buddy," I said, hoping this would be the end of it. "What's all that about?"

He sipped his tea and handed me a flat white. We walked up the road a bit, away from the other riders.

"These fucking influencer soy boys, mate. Can't stand them. They're not proper bikers. I mean we barely went over forty today. Slow as fuck. That's not riding."

I laughed at the influencer comment. "Have you taken a look at who we ride with recently?" I pointed over towards Tyrone. He had finished talking into his phone and was now taking photos of his Royal Enfield in front of the flag poles.

Darren laughed finally. "Yeah and we can pack it in and all!"

"To be fair to Tyrone, this is actual work for him," I replied. I sipped the flat white. It was delicious, the rich espresso perfectly blended with the velvety foamy milk. Darren still had the teabag in his cup. It looked a sorry colour. "All this is not like your racing days I'm guessing then?"

He chuckled at my observation. "The biker meets I used to go to, even when I was a young lad on the back of my dad's bike, we would have filled that guy in."

I nodded and reckoned he was not joking. Our little corner of Instagram was a very self-obsessed place. We were both silent for a few minutes, just drinking our brews.

"Look mate, I'm forty now. I have a young daughter of my own who always wants my time. It's football training one day, or dance club the next. When I go out on the Scram, I want to make it count. Time to myself is limited and precious. You must get that too?"

I nodded again. "Yeah but it's just me and Olivia. No kids."

"Trust me mate, when they come along, you'll be lucky you don't end up selling that nice Bonneville cafe racer of yours. Then the back hurts more, and the neck, and the wrists, and before you know it, you can't ride a sports bike no more." He looked away, staring at nothing in particular.

"Are we still talking about me here?" I had never ridden, let alone owned a sports bike.

He looked at me seriously. "We're both ten years older than the other boys in the crew. I enjoy riding with them, reminds me of those days."

He did thrash his Scrambler around like a BMW S1000RR sports bike without doubt.

"There is a moment," he continued, "going above two hundred, that no one can describe unless he's been in that moment. It all slows down, life, worries... and your heart and the bike's engine are beating together in harmony. Nothing else matters."

I just gazed at him. I hadn't thought of Darren as a wordsmith. That was poignant, I thought.

"Come on, old man." I patted him on the back and walked towards the bikes. "Less of the philosophy. Let's go ride!"

Fuelled with caffeine and pastries, we set off again. Darren revved his engine so loudly that everyone looked at him. He was in a low gear and on the grass verge. His Enfield surged forward, narrowly missing a few families, as he drifted the heavy bike sideways. I thought he had it all under control, when suddenly the rear end swung violently from right to left and back again, mud and grass flicking up from the rear wheel like a jet ski in water. He lurched over the tank and over the bars as he tried to regain control. He wrestled the heavy bike onto the road finally. It all happened so quickly. Thankfully the marshal hadn't seen it. He was already halfway down the road leading some of the group. I saw Tyrone was laughing. He had his phone out. I hoped he caught that on camera.

We headed south now on the A44, then onto the A424, skirting Stow-on-the-Wold followed by Bourton-on-the-Water, another pair of beautiful Cotswolds towns. On a day like today the roads where busy and slow. Tourists and locals alike were enjoying a stroll and checking out the artisan goods for sale at boutique shops. I was grateful to the marshal leading us that we didn't turn off into the towns themselves. I actually wanted to enjoy the ride for what it was, and not stop for more photos. I took a few phone camera snaps back in Broadway, and realised how much I was missing Justin and his skills behind the lens. I knew he would have taken epic photos for their group, and Henry would be chomping at the bit to be the focus of them for his own Instagram page.

Keeping a steady pace, we hit the A436 heading back to Gloucester, westwards. This was a fast A-road, and I was grateful again for a chance to hit sixth gear and put the Continental GT through its paces. I wasn't sure if the marshal at the front had drunk too much coffee in Broadway, but he was breaking his own rules now. He started overtaking a few cars and that gave licence for the rest of us to follow suit. Good lad, I thought. Maybe he was on some sort of schedule and was running late for the next group to ride out. Blazer rider was being hesitant in front of me, so I dropped the bike down two gears, and hooned it past him. I checked my right mirror and saw two other sets of headlights behind me pull out and do the same. I smiled. The crew rides together. Tyrone and Darren were on my six. I heard beeping behind me. I hoped it was blazer rider venting again. The Continental GT was far better when allowed to open up and breathe a bit. It had enough overtaking poke on this road, quite busy with cars but straight, and therefore we had good visibility to plan such manoeuvres. If careful and keeping an eye out for junctions on the right, I was able to make good progress, weaving in and out. The road opened up further when we joined the A417 dual-carriageway, and the boys were having fun now. Two lanes, nice and quick, and space away from the cars, Tyrone rode beside me, one lane each. He was showboating, doing a superman impression on the bike, feet stretched out behind him on the seat and head resting on the bars. I could see Darren was trying to pop a wheelie, slowing down, then speeding up, but the Royal Enfield hog was too heavy and didn't have the torque to get the front wheel up under hard acceleration. He managed a couple of inches off the ground, and I could see from his body language he was laughing to himself. By the time we arrived back to Piston Place Motor and Bean the three of us were right behind the marshal. The others in the group arrived a few minutes later. We didn't overtake him, as we didn't want to push our luck, but I could tell he was an experienced rider and he cut a quick pace when he finally wanted to.

Shutting the garage door when I finally tucked Bonnie away, I gave her a little pat. "Nice to ride a different bike today, girl, but she wasn't a patch on you." Royal Enfield and Piston Place Motor and Bean hosted a top event.

"Good day today," wrote Henry.

"Still don't know how I actually kept hold of the bike on that grass... wahey!!" added Darren.

"Fuck yes!! Send it!!!" replied Tyrone.

Henry and Justin were intrigued and asked how our group was. Tyrone posted the raw phone footage of the tank slapper. That would be turned into a reel later, no doubt.

"Ave it!" responded Henry immediately. I didn't feel it was my place to mention blazer rider and the standoff outside the coffee shop. From their accounts of the day, Justin's and Henry's group was quite boring. I didn't want to ask about Lisa in their group either.

"Justin reckoned he took some great photos," said Henry.

"Think I must have bashed my ankle on that tank slapper! Fuck me, it hurt this evening after I got out the shower," added Darren an hour or so later.

"All worth it for the Gram," replied Justin.

"Never forget it," I added, chuckling to myself whilst thinking of Darren's rant about would-be influencers earlier in the day.

"Mate, we wrecked the shit out of that event!" he wrote back. I put my phone away.

"Yes we did," I whispered to myself.

9. Hooligans

"Notice the god-like sun shining down on my Scram because he knows it's the number one Scram! Just saying, who needs a twelve hundred anyway!?" boasted Darren whilst looking at Justin's Instagram account on his phone.

"You're currently winning the poll," said Justin.

Triumph's current Scrambler line came in two flavours. A 900cc Street Scrambler and a larger 1200cc Scrambler. The latter made about 30 bhp more than the street version, itself marketed as a more beginner friendly bike. If Triumph saw how Darren rode his Street Scram, they would have changed their marketing strategy. He was outgunning bikes with twice the power on these roads. Skill and experience always beat raw horsepower in my opinion.

"Is it wrong I voted for myself?" jested Darren, taking a sip of his beer. It was a Friday afternoon. Our local pub, the Potting Shed, already had a good buzz about it.

I raised my eyebrow and looked at him. He looked away quickly.

"Got to be done," replied Henry. "Great pics mate. Could you send them to me too, unedited?"

"Why, are you going to make them look worse?" retorted Justin.

I couldn't tell if he was joking or not. I looked at Henry. He didn't say anything and just sipped his diet cola. From what I remembered viewing earlier there was an online poll posted to Justin's story. They went for a ride out with some lads from up north somewhere. These riders followed the crew and wanted a chance to meet us and ride with us. I looked at the story. It looked like a great day. I was sad not to have been part of it. Cheddar Gorge was always going to be the destination of choice to show off to the northern riders.

"It was hard taking photos there though, wasn't it? Sun was a right pain. I struggled with the glare and making the shadows work," said Justin, filling the silence.

"Some proper bellends driving around too." Darren's thoughts were less artistic in articulation.

"What's the deal with the other two coming as the Ghostbusters?" asked Tyrone. He was looking at the posts now too on his phone. He also wasn't there for this ride. "Honestly, I get a bit busy with work after that Enfield ride, and you three cosy up with any other biker that flashes a bit of exhaust pipe at you."

Justin chuckled. "What are you talking about... Ghostbusters?"

We all peered at the tiny phone screen and started to laugh. The two guest riders were wearing matching all-in-one riding overalls, in white. I had seen these reviewed online. Some Dakar Rally vintage heritage celebration garments. Cheddar Gorge was a million miles from The Dakar, I mused. The Dakar Rally was an annual off-road rally across the toughest terrain. The talent and courage on display for that event was awe inspiring. Bikes, cars and trucks would race for days on end across deserts, with little sleep, big breakdowns, and hopefully few broken bones. I looked at the northern lads' Instagram accounts. "Absolute posers," I said, shaking my head. I looked straight at Darren again. He avoided looking me in the eye, instead staring into his beer glass. They had both reposted Justin's photos from Cheddar. I looked at the action shots from the day. The riders were standing up on the pegs, as if riding offroad. Their riding suits didn't have a speck of dust on them either. I thought they looked a bit contrived. I was glad they had used the #cotswoldswreckingcrew hashtag though. Etiquette was always required. I hoped they were both in a northern pub right now too, telling tales of how much they enjoyed hanging out with Darren, Justin, and Henry.

"How quick were these lads then?" asked Tyrone.

"Not as quick as Darren," quipped Henry, grinning at him.

"Yeah but I was a tool," he replied. "Could have been curtains if I'd gone down on that gravel!"

"Bit of an off road segment after all then was there?" I asked him. "Maybe the Dakar action suits were warranted after all?"

Henry laughed. "Not quite... but you remember how that road got the better of Sebastian during one of our first ever rides!" He found the video reel on his phone and played it again. We all cackled loudly. It was a classic now.

"Nah it was more like gravel in the middle of the road on a tight bend, front went, foot down, check underwear, carry on." Darren summarised his near miss for my benefit. He finished his pint and slammed the glass down on the table.

The pub was filling up nicely. I was glad I booked ahead. I deliberately requested a table in the corner, out of the way, knowing that the crew often spoke too loudly and without a family-friendly filter. Henry returned from the bar with another round of drinks. It was another non-alcoholic beer for me. I was looking forward to a bit of a ride home afterwards. Depending on what time we were going to leave the pub, even if in the dark, the roads would be quieter. With one single headlight beam on these dark country roads, riding a bike at night was like playing some weird, trance-inducing computer game. You could see the bugs in the small beam ahead of you, but not much more than that. If only I could ride my bike every day. I sighed. Olivia would likely divorce me, and I'd be a drifter forever. The idea was strangely appealing just then. Thoughts of Loud Pipes Lisa came to mind. Would she understand this itch to just leave it all behind and head off on two wheels into the sunset? It was all nonsense of course. I was a couple of years away from forty and there was nothing sadder than heading into middle age, alone, and living on the road. In the UK most of the year the weather was too crap to enjoy motorcycling and it was so damn expensive too. Where would I work? How would I afford to eat? My bubble burst like the tempting thoughts of messaging Lisa. A different, and altogether more sensible thought entered my mind.

"Boys, we should go touring. You know, get away for a week. Somewhere like the Yorkshire Dales, or the Peak District, or even North Wales! What do you think?" I was very excited by this epiphany. I was sure Olivia could keep herself busy with her pals or get her mum round for the week and I reckoned the others didn't have responsibilities that meant they couldn't enjoy a few nights away of drinking and debauchery.

"I'm in. Yes!" replied Henry instantly.

"Don't you need to check with Pippa first?" I asked.

"It will be fine. I'll just tell her. She'll have to accept it." He turned away and crossed his arms. I looked at the others. They thought it was a good idea in principle. Before long, phones were back out, and we looked at viable dates. After a few more drinks, with varying quantities of alcohol now, we decided on the Peak District. Tyrone was not messing about and booked a house in a little village called New Mills, a few miles north of Buxton, famous for its natural and fresh spring water.

"I reckon two hundred miles a day, not more." I knew what the crew was like, stopping for photos, faffing, Henry being late. 200 miles would be plenty each day if we wanted to get back before dark and enjoy an evening in the local pubs too. No one questioned my logic. I saw I had some new notifications on the Gram. "Boys, you've all seen my latest treat to myself? New genuine leather seat. Not a freebie because I'm not on the scrounge like Henry but Maurice did give me some discount." I shoved a photo series of my new Motoz Modz seat in their faces.

"Whatever mate," replied Henry. "Do you have a thousand followers yet? Oh wait, no you don't."

We all laughed loudly. A few tables, even far away, looked over at us, disapprovingly.

"Nice one mate," said Tyrone, nodding at what he saw on the phone screen, giving his endorsement. "I told Maurice he needed to up the quality on the seats. Compete with some of the luxury brands I've reviewed. Glad he went for real leather. He'll sell a bucket load."

Looking at my photos, I really liked the small embossed @MotozModz logo subtly placed on the rear right hand corner of the seat. The leather was criss-crossed in a diamond pattern, hand stitched. All the lads were glued to their phones again now.

Darren started laughing. "Mate of mine just bought a CCM. Fuck me, looks like a dog's dinner!"

We all craned our necks to take a look. I thought it looked alright. This was a CCM Spitfire. For a single cylinder 600cc engine, it was lightweight and made decent power for a B-road blast. They were made in the UK and were often limited in number. They were quite rare motorcycles, often built in a limited production run for a feel-good ownership experience. The bikes were decked out with premium parts too.

"I can't tell him that, mind," he added, chuckling some more.

"Yeah I saw one on the road in town the other day. Nice single seat but small. They have a loyal fan-base. Turns heads," declared Tyrone.

"Looks like my nan got the welder out the garage for the frame, mind," commented Darren, further laying into his mate's motorcycle.

"Has he put fucking white wall tyres on it and all?" asked Tyrone, examining the photo more closely. "Fucking state of it."

"Best of all he spunked a ton of coin on full Ohlins for it... on a fucking Bobber!" added Darren, before getting up to go the bar, likely the demolition job of his mate's bike now complete.

"Um, me and Justin have spent a pretty penny on good rear suspension too, don't forget, and we're on Bonnevilles. Hardly super naked track-focussed machines," I interjected, grinning at the hypocrisy.

"Yeah but you ride it like you stole it, and those Bonnevilles can at least handle ok. That CCM is an abomination." Darren shouted back from the bar.

"You can't buy taste," said Justin.

I returned to my phone again and started to go through the DMs. The top message was from @LoudPipesLisa.

"I like your new seat. I bet it's nice to sit on and ride," it read.

My face went red. Was she flirting? Was I reading too much into it? Was she being sarcastic? I felt like replying with something just as potentially flirtatious, something like, "are you talking about the seat or something else?" I cringed. I reckoned that was too crass, remembering the last time the crew went down this path with messages that got out of hand. I thought about adding a laughing face emoji too. That would be ok, surely? I paused. Conversations continued but I wasn't paying attention. Screw it, I thought. I wrote the message and hit send.

There's an old truism that you know when you've spent too much time with someone when you start to look the same as the other person. Today all the boys were wearing Braap and Burn T-shirts or hoodies. Tyrone was just wearing a hoodie, with his white trainers. He had decided that it was just a little, chilled out ride in the afternoon sun. Darren was wearing some really neat under-armour from Knox. This was the Urbane Pro Mk II, he informed me. He reckoned he looked like Batman, with its figure-hugging fit, thick armour pieces on the shoulders, elbows and back, that bulked him up, and with it being jet-black, it did look good. On a warm day like today, he simply wore a Braap and Burn T-shirt over the top of it. His chosen graphic was an eagle wearing an open face helmet swooping down and grabbing a lightning bolt. The design on my tee was the Wild Wrenching Customs lion print that I ordered for my garage photo set a while ago. It was covered up whilst on the bike though under my leather jacket. Justin and Henry followed suit but with different designs for their T-shirts. This #motostyle conscious crew of #braapandburn influencers were ready to wreck the Cotswolds roads! In truth, the demographic for this fashion was about half my age, but I didn't care today. Maybe it was the alcohol and good vibes, maybe it was the sunshine, or a combination of all of it and the confidence that came when riding as the five of us. With Justin behind the camera lens, and Tyrone knowing some tricks with optimising online engagement, this was going to be a good ride.

We rolled out of the car park, meandering down a tiny path that circled the beer garden. The pub patrons enjoying the sunshine, turned their heads, instinctively wary at the cacophony of thunder disturbing their lazy pints. I was at the back of the pack as usual. The lads in front of me looked up for it. We were about to embark on a little thirty mile pilgrimage to Piston Place Motor and Bean. We huddled up, all close together, before turning left out of the pub and onto the main road. No one wanted to be left behind should a car driving from our right interrupt all five of us leaving together. The engines thrummed, and burbled, waiting. A gap opened up, then one to five, we were off. I was left to wave goodbye to the patrons before the normal hubbub of chatter and birdsong filled the air once more. I hit the revs hard, the induction roar so satisfying to my ears. I could have banged up through the gears quickly at any time, but I wanted to rev the engine, hitting the limiter, Bonnie telling me to change gear in protest, nay frustration, that she needed to go faster. Up another gear, Bonnie was happy again, gaining speed each second that passed. I was in fourth now, the ideal gear for this lovely winding road, the A429. The warm wind was on my face, and I was grinning ear to ear. Henry was setting quite a pace. The odd car along the route was a mild inconvenience as we all blipped past it. We zoomed past Cotswold Airport on our left. Looking over at the rows of old Boeing and Airbus behemoths parked up, sadly there were no British Airways jets there today. A little gravel pull-in area outside the fence line was often a great photo spot, with the Union flag tail art the perfect patriotic backdrop for our British Twins. Not today though. The fence line disappeared from my rear view mirrors in a flash. I felt like I was piloting a jet. The adrenaline was up, and I was focused on following Tyrone's lines in front me, who no doubt was doing the same for the rider in front of him. Henry barely slowed down as the 30 mph sign appeared to signal our arrival to Kemble, a very picturesque little village with white picket fences and beautifully decorated flower boxes to welcome visitors. "Please drive slowly through our village," I read the words aloud to myself, before that too was a blur left behind during our fleeting passage through the grassy verge adorned single main road. Henry was a man possessed and we all followed his lead without thinking. After a few more miles, a queue of cars backed up made us slow down finally. They were all waiting to turn right onto the A433 and towards the Cirencester bypass. Henry led us to the front of the line without even thinking twice, blipping his throttle arrogantly, to let the drivers know that the crew was coming past them. There would be no queuing today. Our two wheels and outlaw attitude earned us the odd indignant, loud beep from the horns of the stopped cars. We ignored this. Huddled up again at the junction, we wanted to get onto the next road as a crew. No rider left behind. A gap appeared. Henry went for it, revving hard. I saw his front wheel come up suddenly before bashing down again on the tarmac. He nearly steered into oncoming traffic but after a wobble, gained control of his Street Twin, and all was well.

"What the hell just happened?" I said to myself. We were going through the gears again. Henry was shaking his head. Stopping at some traffic lights in Cirencester I shuffled my bike alongside his. Justin was already side by side too. He lifted his visor and leant towards me.

"I could see the fear in Henry's eyes, even through his mirrored visor!" He was laughing.

I still needed some clarification as to what had happened.

Henry shouted over to me. "Did you see that?! It wasn't just a wheelie! It was a massive fucking wheelie!"

Before I had a chance to comment, the lights turned green, and we were off again. We escaped the busy traffic that was heading into Cirencester town and looped onto the A435. It wasn't the most direct route but on two wheels it was not about that. This road had fewer cars than the bigger A417 and that meant more fun for the five of us. There were some epic corners, joined together by long and fast straights, with tall trees on either side looping over the road to provide a kaleidoscope of shimmering greens and yellows, a natural tunnel all around us. It was heaven. Henry was really pulling us along. My speedo was hitting 90 mph, then 95 mph, my eyes were starting to stream with water as the wind crept under my Hedon Epicurist visor. An open face helmet was not ideal at these speeds. I kept up, hugging the fuel tank, getting my head lower to reduce the wind drag. All of a sudden, "BRAAAAAP!" A sound whooshed past my right ear. It was easily heard over the aircraft levels of wind noise in my helmet. I swore to myself out of surprise. I could barely check my mirrors at this speed. Everything behind me was a buzzing blur due to the handlebar vibrations. It was Darren, he was hooning it. He must have been riding 110 mph or more. Within seconds he was in front of Tyrone too and gaining on Justin. This was the game then, I thought to myself. I said a silent prayer to the motorcycling gods of speed, rubbed Bonnie's right grip with my thumb and twisted the throttle, asking for more. She responded, eager, 98... 100 mph. That was the tonne. "Tonne up!" I managed to squeak, the wind resistance trying to keep my mouth clamped shut. 103... 105 mph. The front wheel was starting to wobble, but I held Bonnie straight. I was catching the others. I dared not imagine the mess if something went wrong now, #holdfast #ridefastdontdie. I was laser-focussed on the road and the lads in front of me. As if tempting fate, a row of red brake lights signalled as an alert, one after another. Justin swerved like a lunatic, into the other lane. Thankfully there was no traffic coming the other way. I gently squeezed my front brake, but it barely slowed me at all, not at this speed. The basic callipers were designed for the lazy Sunday cruise, not a hell-raising sprint through the Cotswolds with the crew. "I have to get a new front brake!" I yelled out loud, desperately trying to slow down and not lock up the wheel. A single thought of arguing with Olivia about spending more money entered my head. Bonnie didn't have ABS though! I couldn't argue with her in my head right now. It was either my ability to slow the bike, or my face on the asphalt and Bonnie in the ditch that would come next, the immediate thoughts of not dying focussing my mind thankfully. I cursed, concentrated, and managed to slow down enough before crashing into Tyrone's backside. Why had Justin swerved like that and what made everyone brake so suddenly I wondered? Within a few minutes, I saw Darren's left indicator was flashing. He was at the front now. We all followed and turned into a layby. Something was up. We shut down our engines.

Justin walked over to me. "That stretch of road is pure MotoGP!" He was shaking, his voice trembling with adrenaline. "Darren's rear wheel bobbin spindle fell out! I nearly died!"

"Did it fling up, then?" I asked him.

"More like Mad Max, spear out from the side of the wheel I think!"

I looked around. Darren was inspecting his bike, giving the rear wheel and his chain the once over. He was swearing to himself, muttering something about cheap parts.

"I thought Darren had lost his whole chain!" added Justin, reflecting on the part of the Scrambler he thought he had expertly dodged.

"Classic eBay buy, made in China," said Tyrone, cackling.

"Tyrone your rear shocks are an eBay cheap job too," I reminded him. "I've seen horror stories on Insta of those same ones collapsing on a ride. Deadly! Get them off and splash some cash."

"I would do. But I live life on the edge. No fucks given." He shot me a cheeky grin and then looked back at his bike, wincing. "Stiff as old arseholes, mind."

I shook my head, laughing.

"Fuck! Won't be seeing that lot again. Lost in some hedge miles back. I need some tools to check the bolts are ok." Darren interrupted the banter.

None of us had anything suitable to hand. This was meant to be a simple pub ride-out. We weren't carrying for emergencies.

I had a thought. "We can detour to my house in Cheltenham. It's only a few miles."

It was starting to get dark when we turned into the safety of Tivoli Avenue, the boys blipping their throttles as they slowed to a stop and found somewhere to park on my driveway, neatly in a line.

"Old habits die hard, eh!" I looked at them, nodding proudly.

Space was limited due to wheelie bins and pot plants in the way. There was nothing Instagram-worthy about this suburban cul-de-sac backdrop. Engines quiet, jackets and helmets peeled off, it was a sticky evening now. I ruffled my hair and stretched. That fast riding made my back ache. My thighs were sore too from gripping the fuel tank. No lights were on in the house, so I assumed Olivia was likely still out with friends. I opened up the garage to grab some tools. One of the neighbour's dogs was barking madly, no doubt alerting the whole neighbourhood to our presence. Not that my neighbours needed the alert. The five of us and our exhausts did that just fine. Darren got to work. His Scram seemed fine, and nothing was loose. He looked up, the strain on his face from the last few miles of jeopardy now gone.

He looked over at Henry. "How did you manage that stunt earlier? Must have dumped the shit out of the clutch because you ain't power-wheelieing these tanks!"

We laughed loudly, making the dogs bark again. A few lights went on in nearby houses.

"I don't know mate. The whole event was just frightening, and my life flashed before my eyes. All I know is that one minute I was challenging Justin to a drag race from that junction, and the next I was nearly vertical in space and time and crying out for my mum!"

More chatter ensued about the fast ride and the lucky escapes so far. I closed up the garage.

"You hooligans can get lost!! Go on, shoo! I'm calling the police!!"

We all stopped chatting and looked around. I couldn't quite believe it.

"Colin?" I asked.

"John, are you ok? Should I call the police!? Did they rob anything!?" Colin's voice was straining to remain calm and confident, but I could hear he was nervous. "Hold on, I have a camera... for evidence."

Before I could say anything, he had taken a photo of all of us, the flash blinding us for a second. That one was likely not for the Gram.

"What the fuck old man!?" responded Tyrone, blinking away the light.

"You thugs were here and robbed poor Brian a while back!" said Colin, wagging his finger in front of Tyrone. "Those biker gang T-shirts!!"

Justin and Henry looked at each other and shrugged. It dawned on me finally. I laughed loudly. Everyone was now looking at me like I had lost the plot.

"Alright old man, you've said your piece, we've no idea what you're on about!" blurted out Darren.

Colin looked petrified. I knew what would come next.

"Colin, it's ok. Look." I pointed to the design on my own T-shirt. "It's just a brand. These are my friends. We've just come to my house to fix one of our bikes. It's all ok."

He looked at the design, looked up at my face, back to the T-shirt, and then stared at the others. I could read from his face that he could not process this collective image in front of him, the five Triumphs parked up in a row, and a motorcycle gang disturbing the peace.

"But why are you dressed like a yob?"

The boys lost it at this, cackling loudly. The dog was at it once more. Colin jumped back in surprise. I noticed that a few more of the neighbours were peering through half closed curtains. I hoped no one had actually called the police. Colin steadied himself, leaning on my wheelie bin. He gawked at me once more as if my explanation made no sense.

"This is my biking gear, Colin," I stated, trying again, slowly and clearly. I was tugging at my T-shirt now. The others were silent.

Finally, Colin said something. "Well what nonsense! You should all grow up!"

I winced and looked at the crew. Everyone managed to hide their annoyance at his lack of respect for such a popular brand amongst the custom motorcycle Instagram community. Even Darren had lost interest now. I didn't have the energy to explain further. I doubted Colin even knew what Instagram was, let alone had ever written a hashtag.

"You should go back inside, Colin. It's getting dark. I'm going to close up here and then the lads are leaving."

He nodded, turned, and walked back to his house. He was muttering as he left. "Loud, noisy, reckless machines those bikes!" He shut the door.

We all looked at each other. Tyrone spoke first, straight faced. "John, why are you dressed like a yob?"

"Nob more like," added Darren.

I shoved him and laughed. The crew fell about laughing. The Tivoli Avenue alarm dog started barking again.

10. Collaboration

Olivia enjoyed my re-telling of the saga with Colin and the crew. She enjoyed it a bit too much.

"Well, if you will buy clothes bought and worn by teenagers with an anti-social behaviour order."

I had to face Colin and the other neighbours at some point, and I was not looking forward to that prospect. I reckoned after a few days the whole avenue would know that I was mixing in the same circles as yobs, hooligans, and the Hells Angels.

"It was just a few T-shirts. Christ Colin, how judgemental and wound up you were," I muttered to myself whilst peering out from the living room curtains at the quiet, neat lawns and driveways around me. I wondered if I would have caused the same fuss if I had seen a gang of unknown and loud bikers roll in like the crew yesterday, before I met them. The past few months had been the most controversial I could remember regarding near fights and causing general annoyance to the great British public. What happened to me just going for a ride and leaving it there? I sipped my morning cuppa, brooding.

Olivia walked down the stairs and saw me twitching the drapes. "Bloody hell, John stop staring out of that window and make me a cup of tea, will you!"

I wanted to ignore her, but she was right. I was imagining the neighbours spying back at me, waiting for the outlaw to show his face and move out of town, so they could all leave their front doors, safely. It was just a T-shirt. I forced myself away from the window and poured water into the kettle. I checked the Gram, again. I wondered what I used to do whilst waiting for the kettle to boil?

There were new notifications. "@LoudPipesLisa has tagged you in a post."

Suddenly my morning melancholy disappeared. I opened the messages and smiled. Lisa had snapped some great shots of me in mid-conversation with the crew, having a laugh, the lads were just generally larking about too. The final photo she posted was of me, Darren, and Tyrone leaving Piston Place Motor and Bean in our little convoy on the Royal Enfields. We looked good. The blazer-wearing rider in front of me was also tagged.

"No way?!" Blazer rider was the @AlwaysParallelTwinning guy. I never would have recognised him from his staged and heavily filtered photos. I chuckled to myself. I poured out Olivia's tea, having learned the hard way previously not to let it get cold, and visited his Instagram page again. He had saved snippets of his InstaLive vlog in Broadway. I quickly sat down on the sofa next to Olivia to watch them.

"You've cheered up?" she said, a wry smile on her face as she enjoyed a warm cuppa. I just nodded, eager to start the video. The reel started with him sipping his espresso and leaning back on the seat of the Interceptor, trying to look cool. He was not looking at the camera. This went on for thirty seconds or so. The scene then flicked to a vertical camera pan, down and up, of the outside of the Lygon Arms Hotel, Union flags flying. "Very British hotel," read a caption. Next reel, and finally he started talking.

"Hi guys, um, today I'm super pumped, um, super stoked to invite you on my very British Royal Enfield experience, um, super VIP event exclusive." He panned the camera to get a view of the bike behind his head. "I'm all traditional today, have put on my best suit to show respect to what is an epic bike; the Royal Enfield Interceptor!"

I paused the reel. It was strange to think that only minutes earlier on that day he nearly got his head punched in by Darren. I kept watching.

"Just have a look at it, yeah... um, it's a total freedom machine, total retro, vibes."

I started chuckling quietly to myself but pressed on. The next shot must have been filmed with another camera, likely mounted to a stabiliser. The shooting quality was good, I gave him that.

"The tank is so cool. It's... orange, and the headlight... old school chrome look. It's simple, um and that's the appeal, that's the vibe. The bike has spoked wheels and, um twin clocks... like an old bike of the past. But this is not an old bike. It's a new bike."

I put my hand to my mouth, stifling a guffaw. Olivia tutted at me and gave me a shove, knowing what was going on. I walked to the kitchen to avoid getting pushed again.

"I reckon you could have some uber chilled times on this steed. I'm so blessed to have been invited. Royal Enfield, guys, you are rocking it with this one! It looks really good next to this old hotel in the Cotswolds, here in Stow-on-the-Water."

I couldn't contain myself any longer and lost it completely, laughing loudly. Olivia sighed and shook her head. Tears started to roll down my cheeks. He couldn't even get the location right! I looked at the view count of his reels, the number stopping my laugher instantly. "Jesus, two hundred views already!" The really depressing realisation hit me that I counted as one of those views. I remembered to thank Lisa for her posts before putting my phone away.

"If you want the full resolution copies, give me your email and I'll send them to you. Here's my number if you ever want a ride out." Lisa replied a few hours later. I passed her my email address. For the photos, I told myself.

"Did you see, @AlwaysParallelTwinning blew his Bonnie up?" That afternoon, Justin had been enjoying going through the back catalogue of some of the posts on Blazer rider's page. "I can't believe it! He now starts the bike by shoving a screwdriver into the ignition barrel!" Look at those sparks! One thousand likes on that reel too!"

I had never seen Justin so animated online. I looked at the video. It made me wince. That poor Bonnie deserved better.

"It's the lack of respect for his bike that gets me," I stated, and I meant it. "Justin, he's got as many followers as you, makes me so angry!" Influencers were meant to be champions for their interests, whether that was showcasing new stuff, providing advice, guidance, or expertise, or being inspirational to others wanting to get into the same thing, or go to the same places. This was just pure stupidity mixed with narcissistic self-obsession. I was also annoyed at myself for spending time watching his content too.

"That bellend wouldn't know a chain tensioner from a spark plug. Shit bike reviews and all!" added Darren.

"Let me guess, you're currently in the hot tub with a Thatchers cider?" asked Justin.

"I've had a few, aye."

I was frustrated by recent events and needed a quick blast on the road. As soon as I fired up Bonnie, straddled the soft Motoz Modz leather seat, and felt the thrum of the rhythmic parallel twin between my legs, all was right with the world again. I thought of Lisa and her comments about the seat, before pushing them away quickly, kicking the gear down to first and rolling out of the garage. The avenue was quiet, so I gave Bonnie some revs to wake up the neighbours. Olivia was right. I needed to get a grip. The raspy sound of the Arrow exhausts cleared any lingering worries about their judgement. I would speak to Colin at some point, and I would not shy away from proudly vocalising my love for this bike. Turning onto the main road, I was feeling great again. Even the recent vacuous Instagram nonsense all blew away like the exhaust smoke behind me. The ride to the Piston Place Motor and Bean was short but I was able to let rip on the fast A40 dual carriageway to the business park on the outskirts of Gloucester. I was looking forward to a pain au chocolat, a strong coffee, and some good old fashioned in-real-life conversation with the crew. The lads arrived shortly afterwards. It was a warm morning, and lovely to sit outside, taking advantage of the fresh air. I breathed it in deeply. Darren brought his laptop with him and moved the table parasol so that the screen was viewable in the shade. We gathered around.

"Need some pics of you guys. Maybe an intro page," he explained.

"Cool. Happy to work on something. What software are you using?" asked Justin.

"Big Cartel. Using one of their templates. Feels like it needs some substance. Know what I mean?" Darren looked around at all of us.

I nodded. I didn't know what he meant but I felt it was the right response.

"Nice mate. Feels a bit busy on the design front though. For me, as a consumer, less is always more. There also needs to be an element of timelessness to it, to have longevity. Equally I like to feel like there's a narrative there," replied Tyrone.

I raised an eyebrow at his first impressions. We were all silent, just looking at him. He moved to a better position nearer the laptop. He started pointing away as if conducting an orchestra.

"For example, this place, Piston Place Motor and Bean," he continued and loaded up their website on the laptop. "It's not perfect by any means, but it feels like it's for moto culture rather than making money from merch." He took a step back and loaded up Darren's designs again. "So, my question would be straight away, what is the actual objective of the website and where does it want to be in two years' time?"

None of us had an answer. What did we want the Cotswolds Wrecking Crew to become? To use Tyrone's language, what was our objective?

He wasn't done. "I'm being ultra critical but some of it feels like Braap and Burn six years ago, and while I think some of it looks great... the logo for example... fantastic as a T-shirt, but on a website, I'm not sure it will stand-up in a year or two's time just because it's on-trend now."

There was that brand again. I pushed away any fleeting guilt about Colin quickly. It was just a T-shirt. I focussed again on what Tyrone was saying.

"As for the website logistics, it's a good start, but when you say the customer clicks on the product and size, presumably they aren't actually directed to that third party print press website? Because if they are, that's a huge barrier to entry in my opinion."

We were all still staring at him, silent. Suddenly a loud exhaust broke us out of Tyrone's professional feedback session and reminded us that we were still at a biker cafe. A beautiful fully chromed Harley Davidson Fat Boy rolled in. The exhaust sounded lovely. I wondered if the rider had modified it with a Screamin' Eagle kit or similar. I met the rider's gaze and gave him a nod. He nodded back. Justin got his camera out and casually walked over to the new rider.

Darren grabbed the laptop and moved it back in front of himself. "Just a bit of fun mate at the moment for me. Mrs watching shite on TV, and I'm doing it all for an hour or so as I find it relaxes me."

This really was becoming a Sunday working brunch, I thought. I looked around. The Fat Boy rider was now chatting to Jane and Justin as he ordered a coffee, gesturing back to his lovely bike. Jane was listening intently whilst keeping one eye out in case any bikers needed a caffeine refill. A few others were milling about in the shop area, taking T-shirts from hangers, holding them up to the mirror for size. I imagined what they were thinking. "Does this design look yobbish? Am I too old to wear this juvenile logo?" It was just a T-shirt. I pushed the thoughts of the other evening aside once more and looked at the laptop again.

Darren's words returned me back to the CWC boardroom. "I'm not in it to make money, just wanted to see if I could do it. Taking my artwork digital and that. I read somewhere that print on demand is the future of this industry. If in six years' time we're as big as Braap and Burn, I'll buy you a pint, mate." He winked at Tyrone and grinned.

"I'm happy to invest upfront as needed," voiced Henry.

Darren laughed. "I'll send you my hourly rate and expenses then! I bought the domain so it can be content-managed. Fill yer boots, lads!" He shut down the laptop lid and looked around. "Now let's look at some bikes! I need a bacon sarnie too. Am fucking famished."

"They don't sell bacon sandwiches here," replied Justin.

I was home by lunchtime. As I parked up Bonnie on the driveway, I could see Colin mowing his lawn. He looked up and waved. That was a good sign. I waved back and smiled. He continued forming his perfectly straight rows without breaking stride. That was also a good sign. This was his happy place. Maybe it really was only just a T-shirt. "Worrying over nothing," I muttered to myself. That would be the end of it. I checked the Gram whilst waiting for the kettle to boil.

"Hi John, my name's Freya and together with my husband, we are trying to birth into the world a new ethical and sustainable clothing brand. We're inspired my moto culture and the spirit of this amazing life. We are looking for cool people to represent us and share our journey."

I grinned excitedly at the compliment in Freya's DM.

"We would love to send you a T-shirt in exchange for a post featuring our brand and a few photos from you. Would you be interested?"

I laughed out loud. "Damn T-shirts." I wondered sarcastically if I should interrupt Colin's lawn mowing and announce to the whole avenue that I was now getting free, yobbish motorcycle culture clothing in exchange for work. It was not just a T-shirt now, it was all about the T-shirt once again. I was such a hypocrite. I checked out the company's Instagram account. The company was called The Highway to Zen. They only had a few hundred followers. I guessed they couldn't afford the top influencers. I doubted Justin checked his DMs hoping for these guys to reach out to him. Still, for me, this was perfect.

The T-shirt arrived within the next few days. The outer packaging was a paper bag and the inner wrapping for the garment was some biodegradable plastic/non-plastic stuff. Apparently I could put the wrapping in the food bin. I wondered if I should update Cheltenham Borough Council's website on such things when back in the office on Monday, to move with the times and these new, modern, sustainable brands. The T-shirt looked decent. The size was perfect, and it was long enough that I could use it as another biking tee. The style of the cafe racer jacket, including my Belstaff Mojave, was deliberately short in length to be comfortable without excess fabric when hunched forward over the handlebars, focussing on racing to the next caffeine hit. A long top was useful underneath the short jacket to keep the lower back out of the wind. So far so good. They sent me a white tee with a print of a dove, clutching some bike keys, flying towards a sunset. There was a silhouette of some generic cruiser in the background. The implied meaning was obvious. I thought about the photo shoot. Should I redo the garage montage, akin to my Braap and Burn set the other week, or something different?

"What would the bearded saviour of moto influencing do?" I said to myself. I quickly scanned Justin's recent photos on the Gram for inspiration.

There was a busy conversation in mid-flow in the group chat. I scrolled to the start.

"Not much of a range yet but these tees are good quality. Ethically sourced organic cotton thing going on too," said Henry.

Had Henry been offered a T-shirt too, I wondered?

"Yeah I'm not a fan of it to be honest. It's the name... feels a bit weird for an unestablished brand. You would think maybe some cool illustrations or messaging that's relevant to the community they're targeting. I get the whole sustainability thing, but it's not a unique selling point these days."

I read on, considering Tyrone's criticism. I hoped I was representing a brand that met with his approval.

"The quality on our CWC samples is better than that The Highway to Zen stuff. Probably because theirs is ethical and made from virgin pubes or something," voiced Darren.

"Yeah why would you want to save the planet, eh!" retorted Henry.

We'd have to stick together, the two brand ambassadors, chosen from the crew. Haters would always hate.

"Mate, I'm not joking. They sent me four tees. One for the whole family, the dog and all!" responded Darren again.

I couldn't believe this. How many others had they reached out to?

"Yeah they got batted away and all!" added Tyrone.

This was getting silly now. I hoped Tyrone was polite when declining their offer at least. Not that The Highway to Zen had anywhere near the clout as Triumph to ruin his Motos of the Gram reputation further. I hoped he had learned from the Babs saga. At least The Highway to Zen hadn't asked Justin too, I thought.

"Oh, I ignored them. I probably should have been more polite," chipped in Justin, right on cue. I sighed, very much aware of the bubble bursting around my own self hype.

"You rude bastard," quipped Tyrone, adding a winky face emoji.

It was my turn to play my own devil's hand in the group. "Yeah, so I took a free tee."

The laughing emoji replies came thick and fast from the crew.

Darren had taken all of his photos with his family. He shared the ones he had given to Freya with us. He actually had a keen eye for photography in my view. His daughter looked like she enjoyed it too, just messing around in the garage on her BMX bike, Darren's Scram in the background. The concept of father and daughter sharing quality time together on two wheels, whether pedals or engines, was genuinely heart-warming. Darren looked happy too, in a way that didn't really show itself with the crew. I would have to take my own photos soon but without the theme of family to provide a natural muse. Henry and I would just have to style it out like a pair of bottom rung influencer lemons. With zero modelling experience, if I could even call it that, my plan was to let Bonnie do the talking. She would be front and centre, with the T-shirt just being what I happened to be wearing.

Freya sent me a message. "Hi John, just checking you haven't forgotten about our deal? Sorry to bother you but if you could let us know when you might upload your posts, we'll know to repost and market them accordingly."

They were chasing me. Maybe they had seen the quality set of photos that Darren recently sent. Suddenly this T-shirt felt less free.

The day came. Olivia waved me off, laughing. I was glad my first proper influencing gig entertained her so much. I packed my stylish baker-boy cap too. No one wanted to see my helmet hair. Regardless of how silly I felt doing this, the ride to Bath was always pleasant. I rolled into the usual meeting spot at eleven on the dot. Ten minutes later, Henry roared up the cobbled streets, giving me some revs to say hi. This turned a few heads. It was a warm sunny day again and folks were enjoying a picnic in the park in front of the iconic buildings. Where better than the Royal Crescent, I thought to myself. Henry had at least brought along a decent camera, wearing it over his shoulder, on a leather strap, just like Justin. I Laughed. "Nice camera mate. Looks expensive!"

He took off his helmet and ruffled his hair. "Thanks bud. Yeah it's not cheap. It's actually the next model up from Justin's camera. Only just come out, so I paid full price... or wedge. Is that the term? No idea what I'm doing with it, but you know, needs must for the Gram. I bought all these extra lenses too." He pointed to his rucksack. I had yet to commit to the professional camera stage of influencing. The phone camera would suffice for now. The bike needed more upgrades first and Olivia was just about cool regarding my spending. God only knew how much money Henry had poured into this pursuit. He opened his bag, the new expensive lenses, tumbling to the hard cobbled floor. He scrambled around grabbing them and giving them a cursory wipe. I winced, reckoning that several were likely damaged. He fished around for a minute or so inside the bag again and pulled out a crinkled paper bag wrapper.

"Fucking hell, Henry, you've not even opened yours yet?" I was wearing my tee and was ready to go. He shot me a burdened look and stuck up his middle finger. Eventually he ripped open the packaging and pulled out a creased up, sorry looking tee. He held it up against himself. He looked disappointed with what he was holding. I raised an eyebrow. The design was of a generic cruiser silhouette again, coloured in shades of grey. There were drawn-on butterfly wings on either side. These were in rainbow colours.

"Dream the ride." Henry read the caption on the front of the tee. He looked deflated.

"It might look good on you, mate." I was glad I wasn't wearing that.

He pulled the crumbled eco cotton garment over his head. "Won't fit!" His words were muffled as the tee got stuck over his face. He took it off again and found his way to the sizing label. "It's a medium. Feels like a fucking small!"

"Maybe they size up small?"

"I've always been a medium! What size is yours?"

"Large. Fits really well actually." I was nearly a foot taller than Henry and had broader shoulders. I reckoned the large would have made him look like he was wearing a dress. It was medium or nothing for him. "Maybe they sent you a duff size?" I tried to cheer him up. "Should have tried it on at home first, mate."

We began the photoshoot. Henry began snapping away, sighing and muttering under his breath. This was not how Justin did it. I hoped that from the dozen or so clicks from the new camera that I heard, a couple photos would be useable. I stood tall, and looked over to the right, as if spotting something interesting in the park but trying to keep myself looking moody. I flung my leather jacket over a shoulder, looking nonchalant and care-free. I wore my hat at a jaunty angle. I always ensured I was stood behind Bonnie. The Highway to Zen didn't want my legs. They needed my bike. Finally, I straddled the bike, grabbed the bars, and again looked right. I kept the baker-boy cap on. No helmet. I was about to ride off into the sunset, without head protection, wearing this badass tee, #rebel. "Ok mate, we can stop now." It had only been about twenty minutes. "Don't worry about editing them either, just email or DM the raw snaps. I'll edit them myself." Anyone enjoying a sandwich in the park with even the tiniest of interest in what these two guys were doing around their bikes, posing and taking photos, would have assumed it was the saddest fashion event ever.

A few days later The Highway to Zen had all the photos for their big online marketing push. I cropped two of them, added a grainy filter from Instagram, and emailed them over. Darren's photos were already live on their Instagram page with captions.

"This has to be the most confused, mixed message brand I have ever come across!" he stated. "Yeah we're a badass bike brand... by the way, we have some vegan melts in store too! They actually said, as a caption, 'ride slow'!"

I hadn't seen Darren's photos on the Gram yet. Henry and Tyrone had already posted laughing face emojis.

"I made them change it," added Darren, ignoring the banter.

I wished I had been a fly on the digital wall for that conversation.

"Kill your speed, not our vegan children!" responded Henry, revelling in Darren's frustration.

I received a notification that my photos were live too. I opened up the Gram and read the captions. "John is wearing our peace on the open highway dove tee," it read. I scrolled to the next photo. "Disclaimer: The Highway to Zen does not advocate riding your motorcycle without a helmet. Be safe out there. Namaste." I couldn't believe it. I never even started the engine for that photo! I laughed, imagining myself now messaging Freya and demanding a change of wording. At least I gained a smattering of likes, mostly from my current followers.

@LoudPipesLisa also left a comment. "Looking good." She added a winky face emoji too.

I liked the comment. I also gained a handful of followers from non-bikers. I checked out their Instagram accounts. Most of them were young women who seemed to be into yoga. I saw that one ran a story protesting against the use of fossil fuels. Another one used the hashtag, #juststopoil and posted a photo of herself glued to the road somewhere.

"Mixed message brand indeed!" I said to myself. I had one final thing to do. "Lads, The Highway to Zen asked Henry for their tee back. They basically accused him of stealing!"

"LOL Henry, is that true!?" wrote Darren.

"No way! They asked for it back??" chipped in Tyrone too. I put my phone down and sat back on the sofa, tired from this whole experience. I grinned at the mocking Henry was on the receiving end of currently. No photo, no freebie, no collaboration. These were the rules of the influencer jungle.

11. Just business

It had been a warm and dry summer. There were the usual warnings from the local water company, telling us to preserve water and not use hose pipes. Looking around at the neighbours' front lawns, I reckoned this advice was ignored. Colin had been watering his flowers and vegetables with gusto. He was very proud of his grass too, cut in neat rows. I smiled to myself. I reckoned Darren would make short work of that grass, remembering the unplanned doughnut he did on the Royal Enfield, desecrating the unspoilt grassy verges in the quaint village of Broadway. I chuckled to myself. He had nearly whiskey throttled the mechanical beast into a few unsuspecting tourists. Those were good times. The easy, warm weather had gone, and I was missing hanging out on two wheels, wrecking the Cotswolds roads. I had spent more time with Olivia the past few weekends. She knew straight away what I was doing. She was a clever one. I told her that was why I married her.

She laughed and shook her head. "Because it's raining, you have no one to play with."

It was true. We were all far too precious to take our badass steeds out in the rain, as if the steel, plastic and rubber would melt away like snow. It was however legitimately less fun riding on British roads this time of year, with leaves starting to fall on the ground and turning into mulch, always right on a sharp corner during maximum lean. Tyres were less grippy on wet roads. I grabbed a notepad and pen and moved to the dining room table. If I couldn't ride my bike, then I would plan our Peaks trip instead. My Best Biking Roads of Britain book contained some excellent routes that I was able to naturally link together. We figured we would ride about 100 miles before lunch, and the same again after lunch. There were several quaint tourist towns in between for a lazy beer along the way. The lads from the crew weren't really fussed with the specific details. Only Justin really chipped in, often giving his view that his many, many followers on the Gram recommended this place or that place. It was useful that he had such a vast online network. A heavy hammering on the roof distracted me from my research. Damn this weather, I thought. I picked up my phone and went to the Gram. There was no new content. I should have been treated to a kaleidoscope of modern classic bikes, surrounded by reds, oranges and yellows, the leaves from the changing trees providing amazing autumnal backdrops. This was my first autumn on the Gram and I still hoped for a day or two to head out and find those colours in the next month or so, the leaves still clinging on to the trees before winter stripped them bare, making for a perfect Instagram backdrop. The next time the sun comes out, I thought to myself, I'll ride again. For now, I was impressing no one, with zero online engagement. #fairweatherrider.

I scrolled and scrolled, desperate to find any content that was cool or inspiring. From following a good number of the @BabsGoRide girls now, the algorithm recommended more female bikers. A photo of a woman straddling the bike with skin-tight leather trousers and just a bra caught my eye. I checked Olivia wasn't looking.

"Felt cute... might delete later," she wrote with a heart emoji.

I was shocked. The post had two thousand likes! I liked it too. I didn't even like her motorcycle. It was just a standard Harley Davidson Sportster. I kept scrolling and paused at a chap stood behind a Ducati Scrambler, peering into the distance looking over his right shoulder. The all too familiar pose.

"Riding a motorcycle is a simple way to reconnect with your inner self," the caption read.

True words, I thought. It got a like. I sipped some of my tea and browsed further. An older fella, dark sunglasses, long grey hair and beard. He was leaning on his BMW GS adventure bike.

His facial expression said it all. "Across southwest France to lunch in Biarritz, over the Pyrenees to the Camino statues at Alto del Perdon."

He got a like too. I was envious of his long road trip. It looked like an epic adventure. We made the right decision to go on this Peaks trip, if I ever finished the route planning. I kept scanning the followers. Some guy was riding a Kawasaki W800. I paused on the photo. This was a lovely parallel twin motorcycle that sadly Kawasaki stopped making in 2016. For many people the W800 actually looked more like the Meriden Bonnies of the 1960s than the modern Hinckley Bonnies of today, with its skinnier lines and less bulky proportions. You didn't see many of these about. He was parked in front of an old, corrugated iron shed, helmet on with goggles.

"The rusted patina of iron. I absolutely love the mood and composition of the shed's lines, blending with the W800's vibes," boasted the rider.

I had no idea what he was talking about. It was just a shed. A shame really as I liked his bike. He did not get a like. I was getting bored but out of habit continued perusing the feed. There was Henry but it was an old post. Why was that in my feed, I wondered? I noticed the post was sponsored, and it had a thousand likes. "Has he paid to get a post noticed?" That was cheating, I thought.

"I wanted to see if it would do anything. Only paid about six quid." Henry was on the defensive after I told the other boys. The rain had not let up for a good week now and I needed to get out of the house for an evening. We met in Nailsworth for a beer. It was cold too, as if winter had arrived early. It was cosy and warm inside, with a log fire blazing away. Otherwise, it felt more like January than September. Justin got there a bit early and claimed the little corner chairs in front of the warm orange flames. He was wearing a Navy blue fisherman's jumper. With the dark shadows cast by the fire jumping about, he looked like he was in some old, dark lighthouse, with his big beard and muted, solemn expression. He looked good in everything. If the motorcycle modelling didn't work out, then selling fish fingers in Cornwall might be an option, I thought to myself. It was a Thursday, and the place was busy. Everyone wanted to warm themselves up out of the rain. The Britannia pub, or Brit, was in the heart of the Cotswolds. On a day like today, it was the perfect location to spend an afternoon. The boys were shaking their heads sardonically at Henry now.

"Turns out, it does not, apart from appearing on your mates' profiles and providing fodder for abuse". Henry finished his tale and sipped his diet cola.

The rest of us laughed. I looked again at the post. Another version of Henry's sponsored photo appeared. It was from @MotozModz. Good old Maurice, I thought. He didn't miss a trick. Maurice promoted the parts on Henry's bike as "back in stock" or "stock drop soon!"

I laughed out loud, reading his latest caption.

"What is it?" asked Henry.

I looked at him, smiling, and read Maurice's words to the crew.

"Hashtag Little Red Riding Gloves!"

"For fucks sake," responded Henry.

"That's going to stick now mate," added Justin.

Tyrone disappeared to the bar to get the drinks in. Justin was snapping away on his phone to capture that perfect, yet raw, somehow spontaneous, candid shot of the crew just being mates.

He tagged us all in a story. "Crew vibes #cotswoldswreckingcrew"

Followers needed to see the lads behind the bikes. To give Justin credit, he didn't need to add a filter. The fire and deep shadows bouncing off the walls provided the dramatic refinement that the shot warranted. I reckoned there would be haters and trolls, claiming it was staged. We were guilty of that at times, but this was a rare capture. That was the trouble with the Internet. People mostly only posted the good stuff, and it invariably made others jealous or cynical. I ignored the hubbub around me and just took in the details of the shot, now posted to a simple 3:4 Instagram-pleasing aspect ratio. Henry was mid-story about some random topic, Darren was sipping his beer and grinning, listening but waiting to take the piss, Tyrone was making some kind of rap music sign with his hands looking at the camera all the way from the bar, and I was laughing loudly with my eyes shut. Justin of course just looked cool with his typical muted expression, the big beard taking centre stage in the selfie.

"Anyway, I'm a big baller now online so six quid is nothing." Henry wasn't done with the sponsored post saga. "Small change, right. I give more to homeless charities."

I nodded, rolled my eyes, and sipped at my beer.

"At least you're not an egocentric narcissist like that @AlwaysParallelTwinning guy we met, filming himself giving money to some homeless guy on the street. You lot see that the other day? Fuckin' 'ell," added Darren.

I had not seen that. What was the world coming to staging a charity thing for likes, I wondered?

"I did that too, but then I saw your abuse, and deleted my post," responded Henry.

We all burst out laughing.

Olivia and I got a takeaway for dinner as it was too grim to head outside, the rain drops thudding heavily on the windows. I felt sorry for the delivery rider, braving the elements on his little scooter to bring us our food. I tipped him well. He thanked me with a faint smile. I could tell he was cold. He would have thought me a right idiot had he seen my Instagram posts, giving it all the tough biker chat. He was the badass one working a shift on two wheels in this shitty weather, I reflected. I pushed the thought away quickly. I had dopamine hits to savour. I checked the Gram. Henry shared an Instagram link of a biker on a Ducati Scrambler thanking a company for some free gloves. I looked at the brand. Bennedict Franklin was the name. All the gear looked hand-made, in England, by this one guy called Bennedict. There were some close-up photos of him sewing buttons to wax jackets and punching studs into leather. This was biker hipster influencer gold, I thought. I gave him a follow.

"Maybe he's open to collaboration," I joked, sipping my tea. The rain no longer featured in my mind. Bennedict's artisanal wares were the total opposite of the printed tees made by The Highway to Zen.

"That's crazy awkward. They're called Bennedict Franklin, but he called them Benjamin Franklin, said Henry, "when the influencer life gets too much for you, eh!"

I laughed so much, I had to show Olivia.

"What an idiot," she said, "that'll be you if you're not careful. This influencing nonsense is the devil."

I stuck my tongue out at her and replied to the message. "I bet he treats a free T-shirt with contempt too!"

"Actually, I sent it back yesterday," retorted Henry.

He must have held onto that tee for just over a month, I thought. The Highway to Zen guys must have been furious at him.

"I paid postage and packaging to send back a free T-shirt that didn't fit me," he added.

"I'm pretty sure they're supposed to pay you. I think you're doing it wrong," responded Justin, adding a face palm emoji.

"To be fair to Henry, The Highway to Zen are odd! The stories they put up about shit craft fairs isn't exactly conducive to a cool moto lifestyle brand now is it? I mean, what the fuck? Just stop it, ya vegan melt!" chipped in Darren.

I guffawed a bit too loudly, and instinctively moved away from Olivia, expecting the customary shove. It didn't come. I looked at her.

"John, I really mean it. Be careful. This online motorcycle gang, club, crew... whatever you call it, does not bring out the best in you. Remember what is real, yeah?"

After dinner, with full bellies, I went to the kitchen to wash up.

"Oh my god!" blurted out Olivia. She looked over at me standing at the sink.

"What is it?"

"I don't believe it. You lot! Have a look at this!"

I dried my hands and walked over to her. Olivia turned her laptop screen so I could look at it.

"And you were lecturing me about social media," I said to her, staring at her open Facebook page. I didn't know what she was trying to show me. It was just random posts from her friends gossiping about other friends. I had no interest in that.

Olivia tutted. "Look, here!" She scrolled down and pointed.

"That's so funny. Why are you getting motorcycle ads on your page?" I laughed.

"Well, I had to research your birthday gift and I guess I'm on some marketing lists."

A million miles away from the little Instagram nook where the crew lurked, was Justin's expressionless face, beard looking glorious under an open face helmet, sunglasses on, peering over his right shoulder. He was sitting majestically on a Royal Enfield Interceptor. I remembered that specific photo from the Piston Place Motor and Bean day, months ago. The ad was trying to entice Olivia with a finance offer for her own bike, of just four percent interest if she paid a thousand pounds deposit, over three years. Justin's cool demeanour was doing the hard selling.

"There's a lesson there, Olivia." I couldn't contain my smug smirk. "You can't escape the crew!"

Olivia punched me on the arm. I couldn't dodge out of the way quick enough that time.

"Yeah those Piston Place Motor and Bean photos have blown up big," said Justin replying to my many questions. "Royal Enfield contacted me a few weeks ago. They asked to use them. I reckon I might be in a few more ads yet!"

"I hope you got some proper wedge for those," replied Tyrone. "I got a fat slice for my review. Not like that @AlwaysParallelTwinning geezer and his amateur fumbled vlog. I recorded the audio on a voice note and posted it online later, with some edits back at the house, all whilst doing a shit."

I winced at that mental image. "Have Triumph had got back in contact? Did they see the Enfield gig?"

"No mate, haven't heard a peep."

That was awkward, I thought. I didn't push it further.

"I'll be doing a commuter series though on Motos of the Gram. I got a free Commotocate intercom kit. Will write a review of that. Trying to keep the smaller brands on side and that."

"I'm sorry mate," said Justin. "I'm sure Triumph will come back to you. They got some sick new bikes launching soon. Chrome fuel tanks and limited editions."

"Whatever... for now, it's all about the wedge, you little lycan bearded poser."

The rain had finally stopped and after a few days the roads had dried out enough for me to release Bonnie from her garage cage. I was itching to go for a ride after work, daydreaming about smooth, warm asphalt. A chap called Dave had moved to my department in the office recently. I had seen him walk to his desk a few times carrying a motorcycle helmet and wearing a leather jacket. He rode a Harley Davidson V Rod. This was a cool motorcycle. It had a classic muscle bike stance. Dave's machine was finished in chrome all over and it shone like a mirror in the sun. We chatted about motorcycles a bit, in between dealing with spreadsheets. One day he invited me out for a ride. After the drab and miserable first few weeks of September, his bike, gleaming in the dull, concrete office carpark, was a sight for sore eyes. I got my camera out and started snapping away after we both finished work. As everyone else was leaving work in their steel cages, Dave looked at me like I was mad, circling his machine trying to get the best angles, my bike parked next to his. He raised an eyebrow when I asked him to move out of the shot as he was ruining it, stood too close to the beautiful machines, putting his Bluetooth headphones in his ears.

"It's for the Gram," I told him.

He shrugged his shoulders. "I don't have an account." He stepped back to his bike.

"You've not heard of the Cotswolds Wrecking Crew, then?"

He paused, staring at me, looking confused. "Sounds like some extreme local landscape gardening business?"

I sighed. "Never mind." I fired up Bonnie and put my helmet on. Maybe it would be liberating to not worry about social media image for once. I had been cooped up for far too long. #justgoforaride I thought to myself. I couldn't help it. Dave was happy to follow today. I almost didn't know what to do. With the crew, my place was at the back. Rider number five. I suggested going for a pub dinner at the Cross Hands Hotel in Old Sodbury.

"I need some petrol first," said Dave. Memories of Sebastian trying to find fuel in rush hour Bath traffic flooded back to me. At least this time, I would lead Dave to the petrol station that I knew. We filtered our way out of Cheltenham town centre, my exhaust giving a satisfying rasp in low gear. Dave had an aftermarket pipe too. God only knew what brand it was, or from which corner of hell it was conjured, but that zorst was loud! I thought the crew were ASBO material with our exhaust setups, however this V Rod deserved to be locked up with the key thrown away. It was bordering on unpleasant with its low booming rumble reverberating off the townhouse walls. I was glad to be in front of it. The bike would not have been out of place in the American Midwest. I imagined Dave wearing a bandana, short sleeve T-shirt and leather vest. Here in the UK, with his sensible modular helmet and nylon adventure jacket, it looked like he was on the wrong bike. He was using an audio feed from his satnav to his helmet with turn by turn directions too. So much for the spirit of the open road, I reflected. "John you pretentious Instagram wanker," I muttered to myself whilst waiting for him to fill up at the forecourt.

Traffic was busy what with it being home time for everyone after a day at work. A small gap opened up. Dave went for it, exhaust booming in my ears. Fair enough. He was off. I had not seen his riding style on fast roads yet. Maybe he was an unassuming speed demon and would teach me a thing or two? One did not buy a V

Rod just to sit in traffic. With its huge engine, over 1000cc, the bike had bags of torque and was like a rocket in a straight line. It was a heavy beast though. A good fifty kilograms more than Bonnie, and she was a weighty girl too. I couldn't allow him zooming off into the Cotswolds wilderness, leaving me in his dust, not on this road that I knew so well. I had the crew's reputation to uphold. #gotfastdontdie. I pulled out onto the road from the petrol station and gave the old girl the beans. Throttle pulled back, the induction roar was music to my ears. Second gear, more revs, third gear and then into the sweet, sweet optimum power band around the 3500-rpm mark. The bike surged and I overtook three cars at warp speed. I'd catch Dave soon enough, I knew. I leant over my clip-on bars, seeking his rear taillight like a falcon after a hare. A few hundred meters ahead I saw a rider pulled over off the road. It was Dave. Why had he done that, I wondered? I was accelerating still and looking forward to the chase. I shot past him like a bullet and twisted my head back, threw up my left hand in a confused gesture and half hit the brakes. Luckily there wasn't a car behind me or I might have been rear-ended. Now Dave had to get back on the road and find me! I had no desire to play slingshot overtaking games on our ride this evening. I reckoned I needed to find somewhere safe to pull in as something about his recent manoeuvre told me he was not going to try to catch me. That was a shame as this part of the road was open and was lovely and twisty. Perfect in third gear all the way. It was a lovely evening too. The leaves were golden yellow now. I pulled over at a layby. I did the hard part overtaking the commuter traffic leaving Brockworth. Now the line of cars that I overtook only minutes earlier all drove past again. I wondered if they thought I was mad for undoing all my good progress.

A few minutes later, I heard that massive low boon and there Dave was, indicating left to join me. I waved him on, to stay on the road this time. I'd join him. No point us both stopping. He understood my gesture, turned off his indicator and sped up again. I pulled out in front of him and just hooned it. My adrenaline was up but it wasn't healthy to ride in this grumpy state.

"Calm down," I told myself. "It's not his fault that he doesn't know how you ride." I wondered if this was also a bit of a wake-up call for me. Maybe Dave was the typical rider and I was the reckless one? Maybe I was desensitised due to riding with the crew? Did we all bring out bad, fast, habits in each other? That was likely. I smiled. I liked it though. I soon caught up with the row of cars again. They were slowing down, arriving to Painswick. I overtook them, ignoring the 30 mph speed limit, just to be at the front of the queue. I knew that the speed would pick up again after the slow amble through the very pretty, yet tiny village. I waved as I went past the cars. "Yes, it's me again. Hi folks!" Not that they could hear me. Waiting at some traffic lights, after two or three minutes Dave's headlight appeared in my rear-view mirror finally. He was sat at the back of the line of cars. "For fuck sake!" I muttered to myself. He had lots of room to filter and join me. The lights were about to turn green and I wasn't going to hang around. I let rip once again, grinning ear to ear, enjoying an open set of corners towards Stroud. Dave would just have to ride his own ride. I wondered if there was a #rideyourway hashtag to use at the end of this.

I didn't see Dave until I arrived to some traffic lights just outside of Nailsworth. He pulled up behind me. The road had plenty of room for two bikes side by side. I gestured to him to pull forward. When he duck paddled his bike next to mine, I lifted my visor to check he was ok.

"Yeah it's great," he bellowed, "just nice to be out and away from the missus and kid."

That was reassuring. "You happy with the pace? Sorry I've just been enjoying the corners myself and with all the traffic, it's not easy to find opportunities for us both to overtake together much." The last fast stretch of open road was the therapy that I craved. I was not going to miss out.

"No, no it's fine. This time of year, the roads are a bit greasy for me to go much faster anyway." He pointed and nodded at Bonnie. "That thing can really fly, eh!"

I smiled at the compliment. The lights changed to green and we were off, this time together. We were now on the wide and open stretch affectionately referred to by the crew as MotoGP. This very fast twelve mile stretch crossed through little villages on the outskirts of Bath. I held back and decided to take it easy. Dave was happy and relaxed and maybe I should take something from that attitude this evening. The crew was not here. I chuckled to myself thinking that I should have been wearing my The Highway to Zen T-shirt. Instead of leaning forward, head pressed towards the fuel tank, I sat upright and just looked left and right at the fields of wheat husks, or whatever crop had been reaped over the summer. Flocks of birds were dancing in the air before descending together onto the now muddy land, exposed after the harvest had been collected. No doubt some good worms down there to eat for the swallows, I thought. Hedgerows were full of ripe berries, and the few trees that dotted the road had a rusty iron patina about them. I hoped for such a vista from the pub car park for the #autumnride Instagram post to come. The sign welcoming us to Old Sodbury met us at another set of lights. We turned left, off the glorious A46 and parked up at the pub. We were both smiling. I reckoned that Dave liked it that we rode that last bit together. He actually twisted the throttle a bit quicker. MotoGP was mostly straight and that really suited the V Rod's cruiser stance. I parked up deliberately parallel next to his bike and killed the engine. I got my camera out instinctively and danced around the bikes as if dancing the Hokey Cokey. He had parked near a skip. I sighed, wondering why I hadn't led him into the carpark, so I could pick our backdrop for the motorcycles. The closest thing to golden leaves here were old beer glasses half full of stale yellow and amber ale, yet to be cleared away.

"You love a bit of bike posing, eh John!?" he said, laughing and shaking his head.

I laughed back at him, pulled out of my silly photo dilemma suddenly. "Yes mate, yes I do."

I gained a few dozen followers from the Harley Davidson camp. I read some comments.

"Hardly Ableson," wrote Maurice.

I gave it a like and laughed. Motoz Modz made plenty of custom parts for the that crowd too. The well-known play on the brand name, and performance of their motorcycles was likely to trigger some riders. I wondered if an argument, a Triumph versus Harley Davidson scuffle, would break out on my comments section now. I scrolled down.

"Looked a nice night for it. Where was my invite? You're now dead to the crew," wrote Henry. I shook my head, gave him a like, and replied back. "He invited me. Guy from the office. Only wanted to ride with the most popular rider in the #cotswoldswreckingcrew."

"We are live!" blurted out Darren. He shared a link to our Cotswolds Wrecking Crew website. It was impressive upon initial glance, I thought. He had seemingly been very busy during the recent wet weather spell.

"If you have any better ideas, then go for it. I put three postage prices... UK, US, and everywhere else. We might win some and lose some but I can't be arsed to work it out for every country. The idea is to get as many pre-orders as possible then use the profit to cover the cost of the first batch of stock."

I was smiling. This was a good plan. Our very own merch.

"I'd just make the descriptions a bit more inclusive, mate. Say, 'can be worn on any bike'. That sort of thing. Not just us hipster Insta nob heads." Tyrone was in straight away with his critical eye. "Get that tacky background off too."

"Everyone's a fucking critic!" retorted Darren. "Happy to hand it over, boys!"

"Fuck me, says he!" replied Tyrone, with a laughing emoji.

We met for our regular Sunday morning coffee at Piston Place Motor and Bean. I walked around their merch section, checking out their own designs. I was imagining our own motifs, patterns, and sketches on garments also hanging on rails in a cool biker place like this one day. Justin was chatting to Jane again. I wondered what other influencer gig he was working on next. Henry, Darren, and Tyrone were sitting on the old, scuffed leather sofa in the corner. It had a patina and look that we could appreciate. There was a custom BMW R100 that was propped up, pride of place, on a wooden plinth above our heads. Altogether, the old bikes turned into decor and furniture must have been worth thousands. I took it all in, sipping a tasty brew, lovingly made with some beans from Brazil, from the deepest regions of Minas Gerais.

"How much do you reckon the baseball cap should sell for?" Darren's question brought me out of my reverie. It was marketing time. I joined the others, perching on the arm of the old leather and craned my neck to get a view of the website.

"I can only add five products unless we upgrade. See how it goes, yeah?" he asked.

We all nodded. Better to sell a few things, but do it well, I thought.

"Very cool mate. I think you've done a great job. The logos look sick!" said Henry. "But I noticed on the home page, none of the products have names or prices until you click on them."

"Yeah that's the template, mate. I'm not sure how to tweak that. I'm happy to order off the PrintTeeBenefit4U printing site but that means all orders will come to me. If you want to order off the site direct then I can give you a few quid back when I see you... the profit I mean. It's not much but if we sold a few hundred, we'd have a few beer tokens I reckon!"

"I'm not worried about profit. I don't need money from this. Just want to see people enjoying a tee from the crew here and there. Escape the humdrum of their home lives." Henry looked away and glum suddenly.

"Alright money bags." Darren was smirking. He sat back away from the laptop to swig his mug of tea. "My lass has learnt some new swear words over the past few week, whilst I've been getting the web forwarding and credit card working," he continued.

Justin walked over and looked at the screen, then to the table and sofa, his normal passive demeanour changing to a thin smile of approval. We were sat around a see-through Perspex slab mounted on the top of a repurposed Harley Davidson knucklehead engine.

Tyrone nudged Darren out of the way. "I think an 'About Us' would be good. Link it to the crew's Instagram too. Am thinking a grid. We post a product shot, then a bike image, then a product shot, and so on. Make it black and white then colour and repeat."

I nodded. Even I could handle a black and white Instagram filter.

"You can tell when a photo is shit on the Gram when people use a black and white filter to mask the poor quality of it, like they're cynically trying to give it gravitas," said Justin suddenly.

"But our photos will be sick," replied Tyrone, a glint in his eye. "Trust me, that grid idea, like a chequered flag, will stand out once we've got a dozen or so on the page. Cheap and easy moto blogger trick."

"I'm going to order a tee when I get home later," I said.

There were more questions to Darren on profit margins and some website functionality specifics amongst others.

"What's the sizing like, mate?" asked Henry.

"Not sure. I'll get a guide up. Fucking web guru, me," responded Darren.

"The medium tee is the same size as the medium tee made by The Highway to Zen," I added, laughing.

The postman knocked at the door. There it was, the first Cotswolds Wrecking Crew T-shirt. It was a black tee, with a light grey, badass skull, wearing a 1970s vibe helmet. An orange visor contrasted the black and grey nicely. I tried it on. It fit really well.

"Very tough!" said Olivia, grinning. "You'll upset poor Colin again wearing that around the neighbourhood."

I asked her to take a photo for the crew.

"Sick! How long did it take to arrive?" asked Justin. "Can't wait to go out on a ride with all of us wearing one."

A few hours later, Henry appeared online. He also ordered a tee. "Now to see what the returns process is like, as this is definitely not a medium, or maybe I have been kidding myself recently. Any of you lot want this tee?"

"Ha-ha, no I'm a Small," replied Justin.

"You muppet! Don't know why you keep doing that!" chipped in Tyrone.

"What about Maurice?" responded Darren. "I said I'd sent him one. Trade it in for some free indicators or something?"

"Pfft don't think so. I'll get Maurice to just send me new parts for free anyway."

I couldn't tell if Henry was joking or not. "Actually, we need it back due to stock demands. Please return it ensuring you pay full postage and packaging." I couldn't help myself. The others laughed.

"Yeah good one, John. On a serious note, who makes our tees? The ink on the label is not clear."

I hadn't actually looked, being too busy to get an inaugural photo ready. I checked the label.

"Made in Bangladesh," I read out loud to myself. I informed the group. Bangladesh wasn't exactly known for its organic, ethically sourced, eco-friendly cotton.

"Small children make them then," replied Justin.

"But which company manufactures them, I mean?" asked Henry.

I wasn't sure that Darren would have the exact name and address of our particular sweatshop.

"PrintTeeBenefit4U. You lot were happy about that at Piston Place Motor and Bean the other day. Fuckin' 'ell!"

"It's ok, it's not small children, it's robots who make them," quipped Justin.

I sensed he was trying to keep the chat light-hearted. I tried to help him. "The small children oil the robots when they break down."

12. Fame

The site had been up a week. Darren's personal therapy, channelling his thoughts and ideas via his talent for drawing, showcased the crew, each one of us and our #motorcyclelife. The Cotswolds Wrecking Crew Instagram page had already gained more followers than my own personal account after only two weeks. The boys were tagging the page at every opportunity. I enjoyed playing at marketing management too. "Here's Henry rocking our new #cwc cap. In stock now."

We all purchased a few of the garments and went for a little ride out to Tetbury to take photos and generally lark around. The Great British weather felt more like August again. We sat outside. There were some fallen apples already on the ground, turning to mulch with the brown leaves, but the warm sun today was more suited to a cool, refreshing apple cider. I put the drinks tray on the table with some crisps. It was no surprise that the crew were on their phones when I returned. I took a sip of my crisp, sweet cider. Damn it was refreshing. I had chosen well, I reflected smugly. We had sold about a dozen items already.

Darren took it upon himself to be the Cotswolds Wrecking Crew customer service rep today. "I've looked at the returns policy on the PrintTeeBenefit4U site and if there's a defect, then they will sort it," he explained before looking at Henry. "If it's buyer's remorse or some stupid numpty buys a medium when he's a large, then that comes out of our pockets, or we can tell 'em to get fucked at our discretion."

Henry stuck his middle finger up at Darren and sipped his diet cola. The rest of us laughed.

"That @KickAzTriumph dude bought one in the States! That's crazy!" Justin was scrolling through and saw a post. It already had several hundred likes. "International shipping is working then," he added.

"Quick, get a repost of him up on the CWC page. Tag him back... and do a story thanking him. Which one did he buy?" asked Darren.

Darren's designs were cool. He had created a "Sunday Service" long sleeve tee, as a tribute to our Sunday coffee trips to Piston Place Motor and Bean. "Kneel at the altar of speed" was the witty tagline. It had the potential to annoy the church-going religious types, but Darren didn't worry about that sort of thing. He had also drawn a snake, stabbed by a dagger, with the caption, "Send it". Tyrone was wearing that today. I made a note to remember to add #sendit to my posts in reference to sending the motorcycle fast down the road, if I understood that correctly. Henry was wearing the popular CWC baseball cap. Darren and Justin wore a Motocross style MX jumper with black and white striped sleeves. This design was iconic for off-road bikers in reverence to the black and white chequered flag used at races. This style was made famous by the classic prison stripe worn by Chino, the badass antagonist in The Wild One. The words "Roaring Thunder" were written across the shoulder blades. With my CWC tee that I bought the other week, we looked like we had just walked straight out of a custom motorcycle catalogue.

"He bought the 'Send it' tee," replied Tyrone.

I took another sip of cider and looked around, taking in the hubbub, all of us here today, awesome machines parked up. Parallel twins in parallel lines. This was our turf, the green and pleasant Cotswolds, and now its digital version too. Dog walkers and families were out enjoying the unseasonal weather. Wellington boots and wax jackets were worn still. It looked like the fields and footpaths were muddy despite today being so warm with the sun out.

"Uh oh!" gasped Henry. We all looked up at him. He took our attention as a sign to continue. "Didn't you park at that bridge the other day, Justin?"

Henry showed us the link and the post on the Gram he had spotted. Some biker had parked his Ducati Monster in front of the stunning backdrop of the Severn Bridge. Justin had parked his T120 there only two days prior to that. The photo got him two thousand likes.

"Everyone on the bandwagon nowadays eh," I said.

"Imitation is the sincerest form of flattery," replied Justin, before casually looking away over his right shoulder. "Although my shot was more hardcore. I stopped on the hard shoulder. He looks like he parked at the pedestrian viewpoint at the start of the bridge."

I laughed and shook my head. Biker gang turf indeed, I thought.

Online motorcycle gang life was 24/7 in this digital era, I reflected. The chat was in full flow about our merch, even as I got home.

"Some matey on his R nineT has been whining that his new tee wasn't made in England!" exclaimed Darren.

I knew this was coming to bite us in the backsides. The beer tokens had finally started to roll in, but that meant the chances of someone actually checking the location of manufacture became higher every time another item was sold. We had better remove #artisan and #handmade from the product descriptions, I thought. I checked out the R nineT owner's name. I shook my head. His complaint didn't stop him from posting a photo.

I read the accompanying caption to myself. "Looking west and thinking about the curvy roads on Sunday. Loving my new Sunday Service shirt." He was staring off towards the distance whilst the Beemer was parked in front of a quaint church. He was looking at the beautiful fields behind it.

"Another one boys... this young lady has been complaining to me, saying the cotton feels cheap and thin." Henry posted a screenshot of the DM he received from her.

"Fuckin' 'ell!" replied Darren.

I checked her out online too. It was the same thing. I called Olivia over to show her, whilst I read the caption. "I love the right side view of my #Triumph Scram. Took it offroad today with my #cwc MX jersey. Roaring Thunder for the win!"

We were all tagged in the post. I scrolled through the comments and everyone had left either a hot emoji or comments telling her how good she looked. She even directed her followers who asked about the tees to our CWC page.

The next day, after leaving work, I checked my phone. I had a new DM. "Mate, your cap is shit," It read.

I had not checked my phone all day, being busy drafting a new policy on the green kitchen food waste bins provided to residents with central Cheltenham postcodes.

There was a second message a few hours later. "You there?"

I felt my face flush red. Did he think I was at his beck and call just waiting by the phone to answer messages?

My phone beeped again. A third message. "The dye from the cap stained my forehead and won't wash out. I want a refund!"

I was now part of the customer service team, and chief of the complaints department today by the looks of things. I checked out his Instagram page. "Unbelievable!" I exclaimed loudly. There he was, smug as you like, riding his Honda Africa Twin with Mount Kilimanjaro in the background.

The caption summed it up. "My only regret is not seeing the trip meter hit 10k miles on my epic trip around Africa. Huge vibes to the #cwc for my baseball cap keeping me cool in the savanna."

It had three thousand likes! I told the crew all about it. It seemed I was not the only one fielding comments from unhappy customers that day.

"That @AlwaysParallelTwinning guy, he fucking messaged me saying the MX jersey we did was ripping him off! Can you believe it?!" said Darren.

"He looks like Pepe Le Pew in his shirt," quipped Tyrone in reply.

I expressed my delight at this with several laughing face emojis. What the hell was Blazer rider doing? Everyone knew the black and white stripes were legendary in motorcycle culture and no one individual owned that pattern.

"I'll end up getting cidered up and dropping the nut, I reckon. Ruin it for everyone," added Darren.

That was very nearly the outcome in Broadway on the Royal Enfield day, I thought.

"Count me in. Loves a scrap, mind," chipped in Tyrone.

"Proper carnage... loves a tear-up," continued Darren. "Such a holier-than-thou punchable face."

I laughed. "You really don't like him, do you?"

Darren did not answer.

A few days later and @AlwaysParallelTwinning appeared in my Instagram feed. "Because it's more than unnecessary consumerism. Being part of the #cotswoldswreckingcrew scene is about nailing the ethos."

He was wearing the very same MX shirt that he complained to Darren about previously in his photo. I shook my head and rolled my eyes at the caption.

"CWC! It's Saturday morning. Who are we gonna terrorise today?"

Olivia was away and this was an opportunity to test out a new front brake calliper that I had purchased. I was in. I owed it to the motorcycling weather gods for keeping this spell of unseasonably warm air for another week too. It would be sacrilegious to waste it, certainly if Darren was keen to ride, as it appeared from his message. He had been quiet since the complaints about our merch. A day riding hell for leather was needed for all, I reckoned.

"I need half an hour or so to pick up the bike from the MOT at Powerhouse Triumph. Will have to change my old stock peashooter exhausts," replied Justin. He was in too. That meant good photos. The day was going to be good.

Darren agreed. "Got some new parts on the Scram and I want Justin to take some proper lush photos to continue my influencer rise to proper dickhead status."

Tyrone just sent a simple thumbs up emoji.

Henry was last to reply. "Can one of my office colleagues come along?"

"So long as he rides a Triumph," I jested. No one else objected.

"So long as he's not an asshole," added Darren, helpfully.

"He mentioned he rides a Scrambler, so he's definitely an asshole," replied Henry.

That got a few laughing face emojis and a thumbs up from Darren.

"I'm a bit embarrassed to say, chaps. But he's from one of our London offices and is visiting the area on holiday. Doing some touring. Visited my office whilst here and we got talking about bikes. He's quite senior and I'd do well to impress him. My girlfriend... Pippa, I mean, is keen I do so," explained Henry.

I let that information sink in. No one else replied. I assumed they were digesting the detail too. I found it amusing that Henry was trying to leverage the crew to influence in the real world as well as on the Gram. I wasn't sure this would be the best tactic. We could at least present the image we wanted to project online. There were no edits, witty captions, nor filters to hide behind on the actual open road.

Maurice at @MotozModz didn't build brake callipers... yet, but he recommended a company called Pretech. They made an awesome beefy six-pot calliper for my Bonnie that would mean she would stop on a dime. I didn't think too hard about the expense and didn't even blink when clicking the 'buy now' button on the website. I also ordered a steel-braided brake cable and got to work in the garage. Thankfully, my online video oracle, Gary from Gary's Garage, was on hand to help. He had never installed this specific calliper but the principles were the same.

"Be slow, relaxed, and methodical..." he stated simply, whilst sucking on his cigarette. "Do not touch the front brake lever before attaching the calliper to the disc," he added, exhaling smoke into the camera.

I had to rewatch this part three times, his own demonstration blurry from the vapour.

He coughed. "Or opening it again will be a right nightmare if it clamps shut."

I scribbled down this sage advice.

"Then with the lever still depressed, go ahead and close the bleeder valve, then release the brake lever, and repeat... pump, crack, close... repeat."

Before long I had removed all of the air bubbles in the brake cable, and all the spongy feel had disappeared. The new brake pads were sports sintered, which meant they were made from a mixture of metallic particles and thus far more durable than the cheap, stock pads that came with Bonnie when she was new. I was looking forward to riding into the corners harder with the confidence that I'd actually be able to stop now. I took a close-up photo of the shiny new calliper for the Gram and tagged Pretech. They reposted it and I gained another five followers. All was going well. The same could not be said for Justin, however. He messaged to say there were some MOT garage issues and he'd meet us at the halfway point if we hung around there to grab a coffee. MOTs could be the bane of a would-be custom motorcycle builder. Bonnie would not need to suffer that inspection for another month. I was sweating just thinking about it, knowing the clipboard list of tests that awaited her. I had made a number of modifications since she passed last year. I was confident that the indicators worked just fine, and I had tightened all the bolts to the correct torque specifications on my new shocks, but my newly fitted front brake needed to pass too, and I had not tested these in anger yet. I didn't need old tyres to add to the burden of my potential #shedbuilt #wrenching woes either. I therefore got the local garage to fit some new Michelin Road Classics to Bonnie a few days earlier.

Reflecting on the upgrades to Bonnie's grip, handling, and stopping power, I was smiling cheek to cheek just cruising along the A40. I took it steady to allow the brand new rubber to settle in, this being the first long ride out since fitting the Road Classics. I was gingerly testing my new brake set-up too. So far, so good. The sun was out and it was warm. If it wasn't for the lack of leaves on the trees, one would be forgiven for thinking it was a summer's day. After the annoying town traffic leaving Cheltenham, and negotiating my way past slow cars, Bonnie weaving in and out of parked cars in the village of Charlton Kings, the road became a delight. I increased speed past the Dunkertons cider shop, confident that I had connected the new front brake line correctly now. My mouth watered. Today would be a perfect cider day again, sat outside as the yellow glow of the sun, lower in the sky this time of year, provided some late warmth to bask in. It was the perfect weather for biking and wearing my open face Hedon helmet, catching the pleasant rays on my face. I overtook the remnants of the slow line of cars and turned left onto the A436. Most traffic stayed on the A40 heading east, as it was straighter and faster, all the way to Burford and then to Oxford. That meant the more picturesque and curvier A436 was often empty of cars, perfect for the discerning motorcyclist with a craving for corners. I was meeting the crew, who were all riding north, at the Bourton-on-the-Water junction where the road met the A429. The loose plan was to ride further north and meet Justin in Chipping Campden, taking in the splendid Cotswolds villages of Lower Slaughter, Stow-on-the-Wold, and Moreton-in-Marsh.

The lads were already there by the time I arrived. There was one bike I did not recognise. It looked brand new. I pulled up to the neat row of bikes that were parked in the standard formation. Even the new guy, who must have been Henry's work mate, was parked up like his steed had always belonged. I laughed to myself that the normally late Henry was also here before I was. "Trying to impress someone, are we, Henry?" I said to him with a smile whilst waddling Bonnie backwards to park next to his cherry red machine. His bike was looking cleaner than I had ever seen it, as if a real-world filter had been applied. I killed the engine and removed my helmet. Henry introduced me to Christian as I got off the bike, ignoring my mockery. I ruffled my hair and nodded to the newcomer. I glanced at his bike, deliberately giving it exaggerated praise. I would do my bit to help Henry today. "Nice Scrambler mate! The XE version of the 1200, yeah?" I gave Christian a big smile too. From my initial inspection, I could see it was an all-black model but otherwise, I hadn't really noticed other details. Tyrone would appreciate it, what with his penchant for barbeque spray, I thought.

"Thank you, fella!" the outsider replied. "Nice to ride over from London to the Cotswolds and check in with the provinces and all that." He looked over at his bike. "Yes, the Triumph... it's the James Bond limited edition. Only two hundred and fifty models released worldwide." He paused and stared at me, letting those facts sink in.

Triumph made easy money by making a few production runs of these types of limited edition motorcycles at inflated prices as part of a movie collaboration or similar.

I wondered if this guy thought of himself as James Bond with this motorcycle? "Ah yes, er... very nice. I see the Bond branding etched into the side panels now. Neat." I tried hard to keep the cynicism out of my voice.

"Yeah only got into riding recently. Thought it was a cool thing to do. Steve McQueen and all that". Christian looked off into the distance as he spoke. After a quiet few seconds, he looked back at me. I had nothing to say to him. He broke the awkward silence. "What's all that about then?" He nodded to Tyrone who was taking some photos, ducking and weaving to get good angles. He even had a tripod out and was propping up a box on his seat for a close-up shot. I reckoned this was likely for some review of some free product. Christian's demeanour looked baffled. Maybe it was a good thing Justin was late as no doubt he would have been milling around too, camera out, alongside Tyrone.

"Just capturing the ride. We take photos for our online collaborations, and for our followers. We're the Cotswolds Wrecking Crew. A motorcycle gang," I replied, this time trying to keep any defensive tone out of my voice.

Christian guffawed. "Really? You lot? That's a bit silly isn't it? I mean you're hardly the Hells Angels!" He looked around at the stoney faces in front of him. No one was laughing. I stared at Darren hoping my eyes would meet his, praying that he would not start a fight with this Johnny-come-lately. I could tell he looked ready to launch at Christian, but something stopped him. He also knew that today was about helping Henry win favour with him, I judged.

"Well, you wanted to ride with us, mate," retorted Darren finally, before snorting and pulling on his helmet. He fired-up his own Scram and gave it some revs, the awesome Vance and Hines aftermarket exhaust roaring away. I guessed he didn't want to hear any more from Christian. We all followed suit. I noticed that Tyrone was wearing his new Commotocate intercom system on his helmet, and was talking into it, likely recording a review or testing the kit.

Henry rode in front with Christian following him. I was at the back of the pack as usual. I settled into the rhythm of the road and the ebb and flow of the corners. Henry took us on a B-road rather than the more direct A-road. The lane was quite narrow but we could see far into the distance in case of oncoming traffic. On a typical muddy autumn day, we would have got filthy, but today the tarmac was as dry as a bone. There was also no traffic. The pace was slower than normal. Not that I minded, as I was still testing my brakes. I wondered if Henry was going easy on Christian? "We can't have James Bond riding into a ditch now," I said out loud. Without having to concentrate so much on not dying if I messed up a corner, I simply took in the scenery. Beautiful Cotswolds dry stone walls dotted the fields to my left and right. Most were in a state of disrepair sadly, either half tumbled over by animals, or years of tough wind and rain. It was cheaper and easier to install an electric fence instead, but it meant the landscape was losing some of its charm. We rode past old fashioned road signs, pointing out Stow-on-the-Wold and other tiny villages. It would have been silly to ride into Stow on a Saturday morning. We would leave those traffic jams to the day tripping tourists. Around another bend, and over a junction, onto another B-road we rolled in together, the line of bikes like a lazy mechanical giant snake. I would have been lost if it wasn't for my Google Maps on my phone. Henry did not need such things, seemingly sensing the squiggly line northwards, and towards Chipping Campden. A flock of peasants flew out and away from us in a panic from a low hedgerow, thankfully not close enough to cause any of us to change tac or ruin the hypnotic rhythm of the bikes dancing in the corners. I wondered if those birds would be on the menu in the local pubs around these villages. This was rural England at its finest. Henry was riding a bit quicker now. That was good. I noticed that so far Christian was still keeping up. I sensed Darren was itching for a few cheeky overtakes on the outside and was keeping himself in check too.

We arrived to Chipping Campden, slowing down to cruise past timeless thatched cottages, with hard oak doors and lead-lined windows. It was picture postcard perfect. We had agreed to meet Justin outside a little bakery. He was already there and on his phone, casually leaning on his bike, sunglasses on. He looked up at us riding towards him in convoy, and like a cowboy drawing his pistol in a standoff, he whipped up his proper camera and started snapping away as we swept in. I revved my engine to say hello. It was a tight squeeze fitting the various Bonnevilles around his T120 but we managed it. Miss Miggins Bakery looked like it was stuck in the 1960s. There was even an old red phone box next door.

"Sorry boys, had one hell of a time at the MOT. They were going to fail the bike as they knew about my slash cuts, even after I dropped it round with the peashooters fitted. They wanted to see the slash cuts on the bike for the test though. How cynical and spiteful is that!?"

"That's mad Justin! Is that even a legal thing for them to do? Surely what you bring fitted to the bike is what they have to test?" responded Henry.

"They wanted to put the slash cuts on my bike to take a photo too!"

Henry laughed. "What for their Instagram page?"

"You should have done it mate, and then sued them for letting you ride away on an unroadworthy bike," added Darren.

"I won't be taking my Street Twin to them, man," chipped in Tyrone. He removed the Commotocate intercom earpiece and microphone from his helmet as he spoke. He looked like he was kitted out to fly to the moon. "I only go to Powerhouse Triumph once a year, with Henry, just to eat free sausage baps at their cafe."

"I never keep a car, and likely this bike, long enough to worry about a MOT," said Christian, pointing at his limited edition XE. "That's what leasing at zero percent interest is for, am I right?" He looked around, grinning, hoping to find any form of agreement amongst the crew. I nodded at him, just for Henry's benefit. I wondered who would be owning James Bond's bike in a few months' time.

"Just glad I changed the number plate back to the legal one." Justin continued with his MOT saga, pointing at the rear of his T120. "One of the old mechanic dudes there told me off previously because of my black eBay special plate. 'That'll be a hundred quid fine if you get caught', he said."

I nodded, sympathetically. The crew could relate to that worry. A black and silver number plate meant your vehicle was essentially historic and was the privilege reserved for vehicles registered before 1980. The original Meriden Bonnevilles all had these plates. We tried to copy that look with cheap plates that were much smaller than the standard barn door number plates that came with our modern machines as standard.

"I don't understand," replied Christian.

A few days later we were in our normal corner hideout in the Potting Shed.

"That Christian guy who rode with us the other day has messaged me about a million times asking if I took any photos of him. How do I say, 'pay me', politely?" said Justin.

"That's funny. He didn't seem so keen when we were out. He barely took a photo as he was above the whole thing," I replied.

"Yeah... and now he's creeping into my DMs," he continued.

It was cosy in the pub, and the perfect place to be after a day in the office. The evenings were getting cold now. I was glad I took the car. Darren was on his phone, concentrating. I peered over. He was trying to find Christian on Instagram.

Suddenly he laughed out loud. "Why has he called himself Lord Cuckwinston?! Henry, is he actually a Lord?? Surely that's not his real name too?"

That hook was too good to miss. I jumped on my phone to check him out too. Yes, that was him, straddling his 007 James Bond limited edition Scrambler XE, using a black and white filter on his avatar photo.

Tyrone returned from the bar carrying a round of drinks. "My take on it is that I'm not impressed by people whose tone of voice changes when they tell you what they do for a living. It's usually a sign someone is a little pompous. Gets my back right up!" He placed the drinks on the table, a bit too firmly.

"Oi, careful!" exclaimed Darren, seeing some of his beer spill onto the floor. We grabbed our drinks.

"Yeah he's a bit much I guess," responded Henry. "His father is the Lord, but yeah, that's his surname." He sipped his cola. We all watched him, expecting him to say more, to finish the joke that we started.

"You alright, Henry?" I asked, seeing that he was not smiling, let alone laughing along with us.

"If I took a promotion I would be working for him, in London. Pippa is very keen. She worships his wife. Apparently he met her at a party in New York a few years ago. Pippa thinks she is well-connected and is pushing me at every opportunity to hang out with Christian and his missus, and that includes London too."

London? That couldn't be good, I thought. "Mate, I had no idea."

"Does that mean you might be moving then?" asked Tyrone, "and with a promotion? Earn even more money?"

"I don't know. There are options... Christian told me about it all the other day. Pippa wants me to go. She pushes me every day. It's been bringing me down. I don't actually want to do it. My life is here, and now having met the crew... this year is only the beginning. I don't actually like my job either. The influencer stuff has been an amazing escape. It won't pay for the lifestyle that Pippa wants though." He finished the dregs of his cola, now diluted and weak from the ice cubes, melting away, just like the jovial mood of earlier.

Tyrone finished his beer. "I just hate the absolute cattiness of the Insta shit sometimes, and what we talk about in here." He slammed his glass down on the table. "There's so much hypocrisy about it all! Have you seen some of our stuff lately? Fuck me! I make myself sick!" He paused, looking at each of us before pointing at Henry. "You're one of the normal ones, what with your actual proper real job and house buying plans and all that. Don't throw that away for the Gram! There's fuck all wedge there mate! Trust me!"

I found myself nodding. Justin shot Tyrone an annoyed look.

He noticed it. "Except for you, Justin." He slapped him on the back, nearly sending Justin flying off his chair. "Can't get away from your skinny little bearded pelt popping up on my socials."

That at least made Henry smile.

13. Grand tour

Orders for our Cotswolds Wrecking Crew merch were rolling in, despite the complaints aimed at the crew in one-to-one DMs, publicly, customers seemed happy. The #custommotorcycle #modernclassic community was fickle. The CWC Instagram page benefitted from all the tags, hype, and plaudits. It had over ten thousand followers now. It was about to get even bigger. The weather for the end of September looked cloudy, but more importantly, no rain was forecast. Our road trip to the Peaks was close by and I was excited for the surge in social media content the five of us would be able to post by the end of this trip. Justin had managed to blag us some free intercoms for the trip. Many of the brands had ignored his DMs but during a trip to Piston Place Motor and Bean recently, he mentioned the idea of bike comms to Jane. Being in the biking apparel business, she knew someone from Helmet Chat UK, and voila, we were hooked up, quite literally. I had rarely seen the usually demure Justin so happy to give us this news during another coffee run, this time to Powerhouse Triumph.

"They better be good ones, mind. No shite," said Darren.

Justin ignored him, sipping his espresso. "Why did we come here again? This coffee is awful."

"Only place I can get a bacon sarnie," retorted Darren.

Piston Place Motor and Bean this was not. It was my first time visiting Powerhouse Triumph, and after hearing of Justin's MOT issues the other week, I was surprised the crew decided to spend money here. The garage smelt of fresh rubber and cooked bacon. It was a good smell to get your motor running, I'd give them that. Slick sales assistants with computer tablets were chasing potential motorcycle buyers, offering finance deals, and parts upgrades. The bikes were new and expensive. There were no slash cuts, ribbed panels, or barbeque paint custom parts here.

"What helmets are you lot taking?" asked Tyrone.

"The Hedon open face," I replied.

"You managed to fit the Bluetooth for that brand without a chin bar on your Hedon?" he asked me.

I reckoned Tyrone had done his research on comms systems whilst doing his journalistic write-up with Commotocate. "Will sort it on the day when we travel. Unless you know if it will all connect together already?"

"It comes with an extended mic for that," he replied.

"For a Britney Spears sing song job," added Darren taking a bite from his sandwich. He dropped ketchup in his mug. The tea bag was stewing in it still.

Tyrone ignored him. "I need to check my Commotocate can link with what you lot got though."

I raised an eyebrow. "Surely you would have looked into that?"

"The instruction manual was massive. Written in Spanish too."

I shook my head. "Remind me again, how did Motos of the Gram get so many followers? Unbelievable."

Tyrone winked at me. Darren spat out some of his sandwich, laughing.

"I still need luggage for the trip," said Henry.

"Fuckin' 'ell," mumbled Darren, nearly choking on what was left in his mouth.

The day arrived. Piston Place Motor and Bean was the official launch location for the trip. I heard the others before I saw them. They gave me some revs to say hi, blipping their throttles, and beeping their horns excitedly. Henry had some luggage thankfully but it was half falling off the back of his seat. We would need to fix that and tie it down properly or god only knew what accidents it might cause if it fell onto the road. Darren and Justin looked sorted with neat holdalls strapped to the seats. Tyrone's bike was decked out in brand new modular bags. I nodded in appreciation of it as he pulled in next to me. There were straps all over the place, with little side bags hanging from medium sized bags, which were on top of larger bags. I reckoned you would need a qualification in buckle connectivity management just to know how it all fitted together.

Removing his helmet, he saw me drooling over the gear. "Kriega mate. Another review. That's just how I roll. You should see me when I go fishing. Bring a bathtub with me and all."

"You didn't book a house with a hot tub though," said Darren, parking up next to Tyrone.

I inspected Henry next. He was frantically trying to adjust his luggage. Maybe he nearly lost it on MotoGP road on the way over, I wondered.

"What are you carrying, mate?" I asked him. The pack was bulky and seemed far larger than our gear.

"Full of condoms, mate." He patted me on the back. "Has anyone bought a tool kit with them?"

"I have one," responded Justin, as he handed out everyone's box-fresh Helmet Chat communications systems.

For the next hour, Jane kept the coffee coming as we unboxed, plugged in, adjusted, and tested our new toys.

"This will make group rides a lot easier!" beamed Henry. "And will help when Darren and Justin go the wrong way and fuck off at one hundred miles an hour!" He was laughing.

"Pleased to be getting away are we?" I asked him, already knowing the answer.

"Wonder if we can record the sound? Be good to capture some of our banter along the way," considered Darren. "For the Gram and reels."

He had recently purchased an Insta360 camera and wanted to test it. Henry had his old GoPro with him too. The crew was moving from simple photos to full on movie production. Biker gang debauchery filmed in 4K High Definition. I was not going to volunteer to wear the chest harness this time though after Cheddar Gorge all those many months ago.

"I need to test my Commotocate with your Helmet Chat. You reckon it will work?" asked Tyrone.

"Pretty sure it will. Does it let you choose channels when you use mesh?" Justin walked over to him and picked up Tyrone's bit of free kit, turning it over in his hands and examining it.

"Fuck knows. I never used it to chat," he responded, shrugging his shoulders.

"Should be like cb radio... channels are open and you can join if nearby," continued Justin.

"Why did you not get a freebie with the rest of us then, Tyrone?" asked Henry.

Tyrone snorted and walked away, lighting a cigarette.

"Sold his soul to Commotocate. Made them one thousand followers in twenty-four hours or something like that. That's before he's published his review on Motos of the Gram too." Justin spoke for him.

"What was your deal with Helmet Chat UK then, Justin?" I asked.

"I told them we'd make them a lovely video of us using the kit. No swearing though." He looked around at Darren.

An hour later than we had planned, we finally set off. We filtered and weaved our way out of Gloucester, and finally made it to the fast and open A417 towards Leominster. The notable absence was

Tyrone who couldn't get involved with the hijinks via the intercoms. He really looked pissed off. We laughed whilst on the road, annoying him further, but every now and then he gestured back, sticking up two fingers. The picturesque market town of Ludlow was the first stop, and we got there quickly. We were on time for a decent break and some lunch. This stretch of road was fast. Tyrone was often leading the way, at the front. He had the route on his phone, rigged to his handlebars via a Quad Lock system. He had mentioned earlier this was another freebie, the price of a few hundred words in a positive online review, no doubt. He knew where we were heading and so even without voice comms, he wasn't going to get lost. I knew Tyrone was mainly dragging us forward at warp speed due to his frustration at not joining in the banter. I hoped he wouldn't be grumpy for the whole week.

Ludlow was buzzing this Saturday morning, with folks out and about buying and sampling pastries and sipping coffees at the array of artisan coffee houses. We could get on board with that. Henry was now back at the front of the pack, scouting for a decent little food place. He led us past impatient car drivers, stuck trying to find the same thing, likely hungry and angry. A few of the drivers beeped at us as we filtered past.

"Sorry fella, but it's not our problem," I remarked to one, feeling smug as I waddled Bonnie past his right-wing mirror. The noise from our exhausts wound them up too. I had little time to reflect on that further as the road opened up to reveal a vibrant flagstone square, called Castle Square. Day-trippers started to stare at the bikes in shock now, engines still thrumming, the monstrous bass reverberating around the whole area. Looking at their faces, the majority did not look happy. I did not care. I was with the crew and we were outlaws rolling into town. I wanted a locally sourced beef burger, and we found just the place. Ego Cafe bar. The name was apt. The trouble was we couldn't just park outside the restaurant. I hadn't seen a hi-vis traffic warden yet, and I had no desire to get a ticket this early on in the trip. Henry must have read my mind, for he then signalled for us to follow him, through a tiny stone arch, too small for cars, and only open to pedestrians. We all buzzed through, making the locals jump out of the way. Someone hit the rev limiter behind me. "VAAROOROOROOROOMM!!"

It was a classic move for the biker under the bridge or in a tunnel. The loud bark tore the air apart in the tight space. I heard a few locals cry out in surprise. I shook my head, grinning. I looked around. It was Tyrone. He was smirking too. Hopefully that was all the morning's frustration gone. We were in a tiny, trendy square called Quality Square. The name was apt. We parked up in our usual line. Now the locals approached the bikes tentatively and with admiration on their faces. Our five Triumphs, loaded with bags, presented the image of adventure in a bygone era. Helmets off, we all looked at each other, beaming. This was a new town for us and we were on our way. The journey had properly begun. It was burger time.

"Can I get the Baconnaise burger please," Henry asked the waiter. "But... erm, without the sauce... and no gherkins." The waiter made a note, raising an eyebrow. "Um, could you also remove the cheese... and no slaw. Just the fries, but no paprika... do you have plain chips, not fries?" he continued. The waiter pursed his lips, and scribbled away, before finally disappearing to the kitchen.

"Hiya, I know this sounds crazy, but if I pay you for a normal burger and chips, do you think it would be ok to bring me nothing, and just act like you're giving me food? Like, mime it maybe? That would be great, cheers."

We fell about laughing at Tyrone's impression of Henry.

We pushed on with full bellies before we got too sleepy and comfortable. Heading north again via the A49, another fast road with autumnal views of woods and fields to the left and right of us, we turned slightly east towards the A53, towards another quaint town, Market Drayton. Carving up the corners, adrenaline keeping us sharp and focussed, all notions of a food coma had disappeared. Suddenly Tyrone zoomed to the front, indicating for us to turn off the road, and waving frantically with his arm, flapping like a chicken desperately trying to fly.

"What's up with he?" asked Darren via the intercom.

"No idea, let's pull over," replied Henry.

We stopped on a wide bit of kerb, off the busy road heading into Market Drayton. Tyrone didn't even make it to a carpark. On the kerb, we blocked off the pedestrians who were tutting and pushing through our herd of metal steeds.

"What's up mate?" asked Justin.

"It's the Kriega bags mate." Tyrone was examining his tail packs and pulling on straps, unclipping and refastening buckles, as if about to rely on the kit before a skydive.

"Did you actually read the instructions to assemble them?" I asked.

Tyrone stuck his middle finger up at me, still fiddling with a buckle. "I need to figure out a way to strap this down better. I think it should fit on the subframe and the other bags fit to the main bag."

Darren grabbed the bags and gave them a shake. "Fuckin' 'ell mate, they're looser than a prostitute's chaff!"

The rest of us laughed. No wonder Tyrone was keen to get off the road. If that whole luggage ensemble had fallen off the back of his bike, there would have been carnage.

That would have been an interesting review on @motosofthegram. Good bags but didn't survive an 80-mph crash with the traffic behind me, I mused as if writing my own review.

After a good thirty minutes of faffery, Justin managed to help Tyrone fit the straps to the subframe correctly. Tyrone had only looped the straps under the seat.

"Fuckin' 'ell," reiterated Darren, via the intercom this time, all of us enjoying a laugh at Tyrone's expense, oblivious to the banter. We hit the road again.

"Only thirty miles towards Longnor, now boys. It's all beautiful twisty B-roads in the Peaks from there, right to our front door," I revealed. I was keen to just get there now. The A-roads had been good, but it was already a long day, and the route, just with the practicalities of getting to the north of England in the time frame we allocated, necessitated big, long, and fast roads. On our bikes, typically not ideal for all-day touring, it was fatiguing, certainly on my cafe racer, with its sporty, uncomfortable riding position.

"Yeah, from there it will be sick," replied Justin. "I've ridden some of them before."

We shortly turned off the A53 before Upper Hulme and onto a B-road. The road was going up and up, twisting and turning, hand-railed by dry stone walls. I smiled. It was like the Cotswolds but just more monumental. The stone was darker and certainly the local houses built from it that we passed reflected that different look too. Slate on the rooftops was a common sight up here. These tell-tale signs that we were in such a different part of the country told me that we had arrived. The next few days offered such promise. I had included a viewpoint on the route, for photos for the Gram, just before we'd crest a hill and roll in through Buxton, towards the final victory location of the B&B in New Mills. The Paul Rey viewpoint was named after an inspiring rambler who died back in the 1970s. Certainly I could understand why he was energised living in this part of the world back then, with the epic scenery that we were now starting to ride into. We parked up in formation. The boys were in awe. Cameras were out and photos and videos were being created. It was dead quiet apart from a gentle wind that was blowing all around us. We had an amazing 360-degree panoramic view of stunning dry stone walls, fields, quaint villages in the distance, marked only by the tall steeples of old churches. Looking at the lads, the irony had already hit me. All of England's green and pleasant land was here, yet they were looking down at their phones. The Instagram stories were being posted already.

"#cotswoldswreckingcrew in the #peaks."

Justin looked over at Tyrone, who was nodding in satisfaction that his Kriega packs had not budged on his bike since Market Drayton.

"Tyrone, when you booked this place in New Mills did you say a biker gang was coming?" he asked.

"Well, I said that we were a group of lads coming to explore the Peaks on our bikes," he replied, grinning. "If the owner is expecting Lyra-wearing blokes on pedal bikes, we'll be a shock for them!"

Justin's mouth turned upwards into a hint of a smile.

One final leg on the road to go. Henry was at the front, weaving and fist pumping as we crested a hill, taking in the views, before racing down at high speeds, slowing down only when he rolled into the town of Buxton, famous for its bottled spring water. The tourists on the busy pavements turned to look at the five Triumph Twins rumbling through. Darren gave them a rev-bomb, hitting the limiter to tell everyone that the Cotswolds Wrecking Crew had arrived. It turned out that Peak District stone was just as effective as Cotswold stone for amplifying the roar of our engines. We would come back here to explore another day. Just before it got dark, we arrived to our B&B, on the other side of Buxton, heading up and into the wilderness again. New Mills, in the borough of High Peak, was aptly named. Tired and satisfied after an epic day, having ridden 172 miles, we had arrived. Justin was already snapping the bikes parked up, surrounded by this glorious landscape.

He checked the Gram regarding the engagement from his earlier stories. "I've already had four people asking if they can join us on our trip."

I looked at him, nodding, enjoying the envy of the followers.

"I said no," he added, his smile showing cheerily through his unkempt beard, dusty after the long motorcycle journey. "One of them was that Lord Cuckwinston. He was very persistent." Justin looked at Henry.

"The Peaks is just for us, the crew," he replied, patting the cherry red fuel tank of his Street Twin.

"This geezer, mind." Darren held up his phone, drawing attention to a comment on one of his Instagram feeds.

It was the morning of our first full day in the Peak District and we were looking forward to what the roads and scenery had to offer us. Staying in this one location, we could leave our bulky luggage behind for the ride each day. There would be no near misses of bags nearly sliding off the bikes today. Our heads were slightly fuzzy from enjoying a few too many local beers in town after we arrived yesterday afternoon and now I was looking forward to awesome roads to clear away the fog. We checked out what Darren was showing us. It was a back and forth set of comments for a recent photo set he had posted. Maurice had sorted Darren out with some hard-wearing replacement parts to protect some of the original Scrambler parts from scratching, preserving the condition of the bike.

"Kombat Kit? For this? This is the bike you buy when you're more of a car driver than a biker!" stated a random follower.

I laughed at the trolling attempt.

"Wow, you must be so cool," Darren had responded.

I could sense this conversation was going to get good. I scrolled down.

"Yeah, goes without saying, well at least cooler than the sort of prick who buys a car driver bike!"

That escalated quickly, I thought. The irony was that Darren had the ability and talent to ride his Scrambler like a sports bike.

"That's it lad, let it all out."

Darren's calm response likely annoyed the troll even more. I looked up from my phone. The other lads were smirking and shaking their heads, clearly amused having read the post too.

"Seems like he rides a small penis bike," quipped Justin.

"I dunno. Seems more creative than the usual bunch of flame emojis," replied Darren. "And I am a prick, so he's not wrong."

With that online motorcycle drama out of the way, we fired up the engines of each of our car drivers' bikes and hit the road. This morning I had planned a route of 54 miles. The village of New Mills was waking up. Tourists with small kids were already out, wearing raincoats and wellington boots, no doubt ready to explore the hills and woods. It was a cold, damp morning, but no rain was forecast. We took it easy meandering through the picturesque high street. The B5470 was our target, south through the village of Whaley Bridge. If any locals were staying in bed a bit longer, our Triumphs would have been their alarm clocks. Heads were turning and looking at us and I was smiling, anticipating the fun to come. Once we passed our first national speed limit sign, we were off. It was like the rolling start at Daytona. Henry cheered loudly but otherwise It was quiet on the intercom, either due to tiredness from the night before or more likely, as we needed to concentrate on the technical twisty roads whilst taking in the amazing hills, half covered by dramatic fast-moving clouds in the distance.

"This is what I was needing!" I said to myself, riding past the broodingly dark waters of Toddbrook Reservoir on my right. The air, hitting my open face was so fresh and clean. I inhaled a lung full as I carved up the corners at big speeds.

We took a left at the Brookhouse junction and headed slightly east on the bigger A537, known as the Buxton New Road. The moors loomed before us. We could see the smooth grey ribbon of tarmac twisting and turning, teasing us with good things to come. The adrenaline kicked in and I twisted the throttle wide open. Bonnie responded as I knew she would and the induction roar was music to my ears.

"John, woah, slow down, fifty here!" Henry's voice appeared in the intercom.

I looked up. I spotted a tiny yellow speed camera a few yards ahead. I hit the brakes. Thanks to my new Pretech calliper, I slowed nicely. You ain't gonna catch me out today, I thought. "Thanks for the warning!" I replied.

Once past the evil yellow box, I opened up the pace again but then, looking further ahead I saw another camera only a mile or so down the road, and then what looked like another further in the distance.

"Fucking cameras!" I muttered.

"Yeah shame that," replied Darren, "on a peach of a road and all."

I had read somewhere that this road was one of Britain's most dangerous, certainly the stretch that we were going to ride this morning, past the famous biker pub, The Cat and Fiddle. Seeing it in the distance, it looked like a lonely beacon of hope in this vast and bleak wilderness. A place for the weary two-wheeled adventurer to rest and warm up. This was not on our itinerary today, however. Our first caffeine stop was still many miles away in the village of Monyash. We had distance to make up, and if we wanted to avoid speeding tickets, the crew would be constrained to this depressingly slow average speed for now. We still had fun. Past one camera, Darren and Justin drag-raced as fast as possible to the next, before hitting the brakes hard, the victor of the two fist-pumping the air in delight. The slower speed meant we were able to take in the scenery and warm up our tyres. There were faster roads to come. Right on cue, the satnav told me to take the junction, zigzagging southwest onto the A54, before our route turned east again. This was perfect. We opened up the throttles, pushing our heavy Triumph Twins to their limits on this now smaller, yet quieter road, with no speed cameras in sight.

"Coming through, boy," warned Darren over the intercom.

Before I had a chance to check my right-hand mirror, his burbling Scrambler was side by side with me. He had a good lean angle on. It was impressive. He rode around me on a corner, looking like he was trying to get his knee down. Top skills, I thought. He rounded Justin just as easily, and Henry was in his sights up ahead, currently leading the way.

"Absolute nutter," said Justin.

"Woah, Fuckin' 'ell!" I heard Darren shout suddenly, his voice crackly via the intercom. Three sets of red brake lights came on instantly. I slowed down too but had more time than they did to react.

"Gravel, gravel, gravel!" shouted Henry, warning the rest of us.

I saw the bikes up ahead weave and wallow a bit but they all seemed under control. The road was being resurfaced and even going slower now, I could hear gravel bouncing off Bonnie. I hoped she was not getting scratched. I was not the only one.

"Fuckin' 'ell, Henry, your rear tyre is kicking up all sorts of shit into my bike! I better not a get a scratch on he!" yelled Darren.

"Mate, ride further back then," he replied.

"Jet ski bike," added Justin.

The gravel ended after a few miles and the B5055 road that we were now riding on was just delightful. Fast downhill straights, led to tight blind corners, which led to more fast stretches. I was quite nervous on some corners, praising my previous decisions of up-grading Bonnie's suspension and brakes. If I survived the week, I'd remind Olivia of their life-saving value. The gravel had freaked me out a bit, and I was watching for loose patches on these corners. I dreaded to think what would happen if I slid into these picturesque dry-stone walls in this rural community.

Before long we arrived at another quintessentially English village called Monyash. There were already several bikes parked up outside The Bull's Head. The riders nodded at us as we rolled into the old pub and found somewhere to park. There was a nice mix of motorcycles here. Adventure touring bikes, sports touring bikes, a few modern naked bikes. It was time for a pint, and a breather, and this place was perfect. I didn't need any caffeine as the roads so far had me wide awake. Justin already had his camera out, taking panning videos of the bikes parked up here.

Tyrone walked over to him. "Get me one will you." He tapped the side of his helmet. "So I can actually join you degenerates."

"I'll give you the Helmet Chat UK guy's email. You can do a review and stick it on Motos of the Gram. You'll get the latest one or something I reckon," responded Justin.

"Yeah go on then. I'll get in trouble with Commotocate but fuck it."

Tyrone saw me laughing and walked over to me next. "Yeah I signed all sorts of stuff with them…. to be exclusive with that brand." He shrugged and took off his helmet finally.

"Amateur," joked Justin.

"Nothing amateur about some fat wedge, mate," retorted Tyrone, and walked inside the pub.

After our quick pit stop, we continued east, before skirting around the town of Bakewell, famous for its tarts and puddings. The A6 beckoned us south shortly afterwards. I was getting hungry now, and lunch was planned in the market town of Matlock Bath. We found ourselves on the B5056, surrounded by beautiful woods, the sun peeking through the clouds with streaks of white light hitting the road through gaps in the treeline every now and then. I was so glad it wasn't raining. We didn't have to worry about slippery roads today. Sadly the number of big and lethargic trucks was a problem. Slow trucks meant queues of backed-up cars, and on this twisty road, overtaking opportunities were scarce.

"Go Justin, go!" shouted Henry through his mic.

My heart was pounding as I watched Justin attempt a blind overtake, literally his life in Henry's hands, who had already gone round and was past the sluggish juggernaut in front of us.

"Yep, yep, I'm through," replied Justin, his voice slightly shaky. "There's a gap now, Darren, go for it mate!"

I saw Darren drop it down a gear and accelerate hard, riding into the oncoming lane to commence his overtake run.

"No, no, don't! Stay, stay mate, car, car!! Justin suddenly screamed into his mic.

Darren quickly hit the brakes and swerved back into his own lane just before an oncoming BMW hit him. The Beemer beeped furiously at him as if to say, "are you fucking mad?!" The driver wouldn't have known we had voice guides, but regardless, it must have looked a suicidal manoeuvre.

"Fuckin' 'ell!" responded Darren.

Eventually there was a window and Darren was through too. It was just me and Tyrone to go now. He was next in line but hadn't any voice comms. The lads were telling me there were wide open windows to get us both through with no ongoing traffic but I had no way of telling Tyrone that news. He sat, and sat, and sat behind the lorry for miles. I told the other boys just to get to the town and find somewhere to eat. After a few minutes their voices disappeared as they rode out of range of the intercoms. It was infuriating but at least we'd arrive safely. Eventually Tyrone could visibly see a gap himself and he overtook the truck. There was even room for me too. I banged the gearshift lever down one, and stuck to Tyrone's rear tyre, determined not to miss this overtake.

Matlock Bath was buzzing with tourists, all trying to get a seat for lunch with a view overlooking the River Derwent. There was bike specific parking opposite the river, and I saw Henry waving us down and guiding us to park next to the other bikes. We had survived. That was a thrilling morning of riding, I reflected. Arriving to this tourist spot at a busy lunchtime without a booking meant options were limited. We had to eat outside but the cold weather didn't bother us as it was still warmer than being on the bikes. The fresh air was welcome and I could hear the sound of the river, flowing fast now this time of year. The boys were on their phones, checking their stories, comments, and messages.

"I see that Braap and Burn have their Winter collection out. Don't think much of their designs," said Justin, holding up his phone for us to see. "Darren could do a better job with a box of crayons in his garage."

I was only listening with one ear, too busy enjoying the picturesque scenery in front of me. We were lucky to get a space right on the river.

"Just lazy and unoriginal for such a big brand. I've seen better designs by Harley Davidson, that I've reviewed, and that's saying something," added Tyrone.

He seemed oblivious to us nearly dying on the blind bends earlier. Maybe that was the advantage of not being connected to the voice intercoms. He had to pick his overtaking moments on his own terms, when he could see it was all clear.

"Yeah probably." Darren sipped his pint. "I've been tagging them in everything I post and all recently."

"Good for you, mate," I responded, whilst trying to flag down a waiter.

Tyrone was still scrolling through the designs. He turned his phone towards us next. "For try-hard hipsters that haven't got the bottle to get their hands tatted up!" He showed us an image of Braap and Burn's new gloves, a cartoon tiger roaring just below the knuckles.

The waiter noticed my gesture and was walking over to us finally.

"Also, talking of tattoos." Darren pointed to more sketches he found on their Instagram page. "It's like the designs that the fat birds walking around Weston-Super-Mare have on their massive bingo wings."

We burst out laughing as Darren gestured to the shocked waiter for another pint.

The afternoon involved a fast ride northwest on the bigger A515. I had planned about 80 miles and we were running late. There were some exceptionally fast sections, with the boys doing the tonne a few times. With my open face helmet, at that speed, my eyes were watering but I held on for dear life, front wheel wobbling. I was praying to the motorcycle gods of speed as we arrived to Buxton again... safely. We filtered through the busy traffic, before coming out the north side of the town on the A6. We rode through the village of Glossop on the B6105 and alongside dramatic, dark green forest blocks and the three reservoirs of Valehouse, Rhodeswood, and Torside. There was even a sailing club up here.

"What a place to live in," I said into the mic, speaking my thoughts.

"Bit spenny mind," replied Darren. "Only Henry can afford a nice place here I reckon".

We were going to do a loop into the wilderness. As we turned off, the heavens opened and we saw our first rain of the trip. No one cared though. This was motorcycling at its purest. There wasn't another car on the road as the tarmac disappeared into the treeline. Darren and Justin were off. They were quick. I was not confident to keep up with them. Henry tried but lost ground mile after mile. So long as I focussed on keeping his red taillight in view, I was happy to arrive in fourth place. Tyrone disappeared in my rear-view mirror and my dust. That was fine, he knew the route. Halfway round, I saw two bikes, pulled in at a layby, the orange of their indicators illuminating where to roll in. I could even see the gravel patches to avoid. Henry pulled in just before I did and through a deep puddle, his rear wheel flicking up water that just missed my face.

"That rear tyre has to go when we get home," I said into the intercom.

Darren's and Justin's engines were still rumbling patiently.

"Well, Justin did say my Little Red was a jet ski," he replied.

The others killed their engines finally and we followed suit. The atmosphere changed instantly. Without the growling motors, it was quiet except for the pitter patter of rain on our helmets, and the satisfying sizzle of droplets hitting the very hot engine parts. It was peaceful and dark. It was a moment of pure bliss, pulled over for a minute, the motorcycles waiting patiently for it to all go again. No one said anything.

We got back to the B&B an hour later. I was knackered. Eventually Tyrone rode in.

"Everything alright, mate?" I asked.

"Yeah man, just didn't want to rush it. In that rain, I might have fucked it, and without being able to speak to you lot on your intercoms, I would have been stuck."

I nodded and looked up to the sky, pitch black.

"And besides, I was listening to my playlist and leaving voice notes for the Commotocate review. Mixing work and play," he added.

It rained overnight but fired-up engines soon turned the heavy Peaks rain into steam, rising like the mists in the beautiful valleys below our accommodation. We cruised the same route out of New Mills again, today a lot quieter due to the weather. The rain was lessening thankfully and I hoped for a dry spell. This morning the Cotswolds Wrecking Crew was taking on the famous Snake Pass. This road was on the bucket list for many UK bikers. 50 miles of winding bends on the A57 that cut across the hills between the market town of Glossop and the Ladybower Reservoir. The road, even wet, was smooth and our rubber gripped the ribbon of asphalt nicely. It was a road to be appreciated and not rushed. There were no cars out and about this morning to disturb our flow, and that meant no frustrating slowing down, nor life or death blind overtakes. It was zen on two wheels. Even Tyrone looked happy from his body language, casually letting his Street Twin rip forward, overtaking Henry, leading the pack, just for fun. We all stayed together, very much a long serpent of five motorcycles, slithering around the corners in perfect form, carving perfect lines. We all knew each other's riding styles and this road demonstrated that. We stopped at Hope Valley for a break and a few photos, surrounded by majestic hills. Justin already had his phone out and was filming a panning video of the mighty Triumphs, dry stone walls and hills, the backdrop. He posted it, tagging us all, even before I took off my helmet. By the time I checked the Gram from my phone, I had twenty new followers. I reposted it.

Tyrone was on his phone too, laughing. "Justin mate, how furious are you going to be when I tell you that you didn't add a thumbnail to that reel?"

Justin's mouth dropped wide open. He checked his phone, rushing to unlock it, and shook his head, suddenly less interested in the beautiful surroundings. I had no idea what they were talking about.

"I did but it dropped off for some reason. Must be because I saved it as a draft first. There's an annoying bug." Justin typed away furiously, presumably to correct some social media influencer faux pas.

"My Insta grid looks like dog shit since I've been doing more reels and all that bollocks too," chipped in Darren. He was adjusting the angle of the arm mount of his Insta360 recording device. "Dunno how I get noticed like you two, with your lush, fancy pages." He nodded towards Tyrone and Justin.

"Mate, it's the devil," replied Tyrone.

The sun finally burst through the clouds and I removed my waterproof trousers finally. They did not look cool. We headed further south on even more twisty roads. The A625, A623, and B6012 all ran parallel to the river Derwent. We made an impromptu stop at the beautiful little village of Rowsley, before looping back westwards again, hitting the tonne once more on the very fast and open A6. We raced each other on this lightning-fast stretch, my eyes streaming again in the wind. Arriving to Buxton, this time we stopped in the town for a drink, but not for its famous namesake water, and instead to sample an ale or two at the trendy Buxton Brewery. It was busy there, with the pop-up food caravans doing a good trade sating the hunger of drunk customers. Locals and tourists were taking advantage of the sun coming out. We joined them. The first pint of a very hoppy craft ale went down very well. I didn't check the strength but it was refreshing. We ordered another round. This time Darren came back from the bar, grinning, carrying a tray of some fruit beers.

"You've changed, mate," I told him. The atmosphere was buzzing and conversation was free flowing wherever you looked.

"No cider, mind," he replied, placing the tray down on the table.

"Trouble is," stated Tyrone, wiping froth from his mouth, "Insta's algorithm is absolutely fucked at the moment." He took another swig.

"What makes you say that?" Justin was intrigued what the professional moto journalist had to say on this topic.

"Just the big pages. They are suffering like mad. There are lots of variables, but the main thing is of course the forced cap on engagement to encourage paid campaigns."

I had no idea what he was talking about but I suddenly remembered Henry's amusing attempt at a paid post months ago. I sipped my blackcurrant beer. I nodded in appreciation at the surprising taste.

Tyrone downed the rest of his second pint. "I'm working my way around it, but it's a piss take. Insta is turning into TikTok, it is!"

I laughed. I guessed that when your actual work depended on these algorithms and trends, real income was at stake.

"Fifteen second videos of girls with their little titties pointing through their T-shirts," blurted out Darren. There was no follow-up joke. He was serious. "Frightens the life out of me, this social media and kids." He returned to his drink.

"Yeah those posts are everywhere," added Henry, finishing his cola.

"Keep all that shit on TikTok, it's not welcome on Insta, Jesus!" responded Tyrone, getting up from his seat and walking to the bar, swaying slightly. Justin joined him. Within a few minutes they were back with another round.

"What the hell is that?" asked Darren, pointing towards Justin's glass. It looked like some sour milk curdled in an otherwise decent looking ale.

"Ice cream beer," he replied coolly, taking a sip, leaving milky white froth on his moustache.

"That's the most Justin thing you've ever said... ice cream beer, fuck sake!" retorted Darren. We all fell about laughing. Justin simply shrugged and drank. We eventually put our jackets on and walked towards the bikes. A drunk group of lads with their girlfriends stumbled and fell over right in front of us, cackling and shouting, but almost tripping up Tyrone.

"Jesus!" he yelled and shot the pissed-up gaggle a pissed off look as he stepped over them. "Lads, I can't be fucked with the jacket!" He looked down at their vomit on the grass. It just missed his boots by inches. "Sun is out, I'm hot and bothered! I just want to ride back slowly, yeah, no hundred miles an hour hero stuff, just a chill one... skins."

The A5004 was a lovely, zigzagging road and perfect for motorcycles. It was also often empty due to the straighter and quicker A6 just to the east of it. We didn't take that perfect motorcycle road, however. For us, right now, it was the direct route, riding north on the A6, with the wind and late autumnal sunshine in our faces. No one was talking. Personally, I was happy with both those choices right now. The straight road meant it was easy and the lack of banter on the voice comms helped me concentrate. I was a bit drunk. I think we all were, except Henry. But then it was likely he had a sugar high from all the cola he drank. It felt like a scene from Easy Rider. Just a straight highway, no cares in the world, and knees in the breeze. We were in a close diamond formation. Pals sharing the bond of the highway. Seeing Tyrone to my right and slightly in front of me, as the A6 turned into a dual carriageway, he looked relaxed. His tattoos on his arms in full view, T-shirt flapping in the wind. Maybe there was something in just letting it all hang out on two wheels. I was feeling hazy and grinning lazily but was vaguely aware we were due to turn off the road soon, near Chapel Milton. Darren was in front of me and Tyrone was leading the easy riders. The 'get in lane' and 'keep left' blue and white sign appeared up ahead. Surely we should turn off here, I thought. Tyrone continued straight on, and Darren followed. Ok, I thought, I'll follow... but it didn't feel right. Before I knew it, we had flown past our junction exit.

Justin was behind me. "Err, lads, we were meant to have turned off there!" he said, the first words uttered on the voice intercoms for a while.

I came to my senses all of a sudden, the blurry, foggy feelings disappearing as adrenaline-forced clarity hit me. "Boys, we're gonna be on the wrong side of the dual carriageway!!"

Up ahead the oncoming cars were flashing their lights at us.

"Fuckin' 'ell!" shouted Darren.

Cars swerved out of our way and beeped at us, likely as panicked and confused as to what we were doing as we were.

"Quick, pull over left, move left and slow down!" I added, trying to get us all out of harm's way.

We stopped, in a line, hugging the central metal dividing barrier as best we could. Thankfully the oncoming traffic moved out of what was the fast lane for them, noticing the idiots on their motorcycles there. More beeping cars zoomed past us.

"Blimmin' heck, Tyrone!" I shouted to him. "Did you not see the exit left sign back there?"

"Sorry mate, was just in the zone."

The road wasn't too busy and that was lucky. We might have been in serious trouble otherwise. We waited for our moment and as one, swung round and accelerated hard, now riding back the way we came but on the correct side of the road. One, two, three, four... we were safe. But where was number five? Henry was missing.

"Yeah he was at the back of the pack and saw us muppets turn into oncoming traffic. He peeled off the road where we should've. I'm sure we'll see him back at the house," clarified Justin.

Leaving the A6, and riding on the smaller, slower, yet more interesting B-roads back to the B&B, we were laughing to ourselves, incredulous that four grown men could somehow ride our steeds into oncoming traffic like that. Henry greeted us, shaking his head yet grinning. We turned off our engines and the banter ensued. I could see Henry was relieved we all made it back safely. It must have looked mad from his point of view, as the crew embarked on a crazy stunt directly into 70 mph traffic.

"Just going for a chill one, eh Tyrone!" he quipped.

14. Realisations

Two weeks passed. October arrived with solid rain for most of that time. Like the gloomy weather outside, the mood of the crew seemed to be grey and miserable too. Tyrone had finished his review for his free intercom system.

"Commotocate, your voice system is fucking diabolical," he had written by way of introduction.

I remembered when I read it, the day after we got back from the Peaks. I didn't know if he was drunk when he wrote it but I remembered my reaction.

"Oh Tyrone, what have you done now?!" I had said, loudly enough for Olivia to hear me from the living room. Before that, I was riding the euphoric wave of dopamine, having gained a thousand followers from the content we uploaded from our grand tour alone. I came crashing back down to earth quickly. We hadn't heard from Tyrone since his infamous review. His words were noticed on Motos of the Gram and re-posted by his followers, going viral amongst the custom motorcycle community, but more seriously, Commotocate had seen it and decided not to collaborate with him, basically severing their contract with him. It was a shame as his actual review, beyond that headline statement, was very well written. I hoped he could salvage this. None of the other lads knew what he was up to currently. I noticed that over the past two weeks Motos of the Gram had lost over ten thousand followers. Instagram was a fickle beast. To cheer myself up, I read some of the trolling and flaming that went down on Tyrone's motorcycle journalism page. He had posted a great photo of himself sitting on his Street Twin, looking very cool, forearm tattoos out, holding a pint aloft when we were at Buxton Brewery.

"Cheers!" he was saying when Justin took the snap, I remembered. The photo went viral as Tyrone looked badass, wearing our original CWC tee, with #nofucksgiven. This was what everyone wanted their #motorcyclelife to really be like. It nearly got us killed. I chuckled to myself. No one else needed to know about that beyond the five of us though. The Peaks trip was #goodvibesonly. I scrolled down, reading the comments for that photo.

"You're a professional in the business, with thousands of young and new riders, who follow your reviews!" Someone had lectured Tyrone on how irresponsible he was.

"All the gear, all the time, ATGATT!!" commented another anonymous face.

There were many crying face emojis and spark emojis too, depending on if you were for 'Team Tyrone' or against him. @motosofthegram had a fiercely loyal fan base.

"You are dangerous and should be ashamed of himself," expressed another hater. His account name was @stu_safe_rides. I chuckled at Tyrone's reply to that last one.

"You probably put condoms on your dildo. Ride your own bike and stfu, Karen!"

There were several other comments adding fuel to the fire from both sides. I moved on and glanced at some stories.

"Stolen. Help get it back. Pride and joy, Triumph Street Triple, 2013, black," it read along with a photo of the stolen bike. At least another half dozen of the riders I followed re-posted that story. This was one of the positive things about social media and this custom motorcycle community, they helped out strangers in times of need.

I shared it too and also sent the victim a DM. "I hope you find it, mate."

I felt sick just thinking how I might react if Bonnie was stolen.

A few days later the Street Triple owner posted again. Thanks to the efforts of the community raising awareness, the bike was spotted and he got it back. The thieves must have thought it was too hot to handle. That cheered me up. I turned to the chat to share this positivity with the crew. There were a few messages already waiting for me to read.

"Do I accept a thousand-pound hospitality ticket as part of a corporate package that Christian has offered me for the British Touring Championship on Sunday at Silverstone?" asked Henry.

"Who's Christian?" replied Darren.

"He's that Lord Cuckwinston chap that is pulling Henry away from us and towards the big city life. You met him!" said Justin.

I winced. It wasn't that long ago that Henry had poured his heart out to us all in the pub on how much of a dilemma this was for him.

"Ah yes, that prick." Darren was seemingly now up to speed again. "Is that what it costs these days? That a seat or standing?"

"It's VIP. Unlike you, I won't be standing."

Sunday came around. I rolled into the Piston Place Motor and Bean car park, still wet from many days of rain. Justin was crouching down, camera out, snapping his T120, perfectly reflected in a puddle. The still water played the part of an artistic mirror superbly. I parked up to the left of Darren's Scrambler. His bike was covered in mud splatter. It actually looked like it had seen some good off-road action this morning, but then all the roads were filthy with mud after the weeks of torrential rain we had. He usually washed the Scram after every ride though, I thought. I was relieved to enjoy blue sky and some sunshine again. It was still cold out, but the thought of an artisan coffee and ginger cake warmed me up.

"No bacon sarnie at this place still," said Darren.

I didn't know if it was a question or a comment about my cake. It was only the three of us today. There was still no word from Tyrone.

"Has Henry taken those corporate tickets then?" I hadn't heard from Henry either.

"Yeah seems that way," replied Justin.

On this nice morning, Henry would have liked to have ridden with us, I knew. If the allure of seeing Christian and his mates was stronger than that, things did not bode well. I sipped my coffee and opened up the Gram as a distraction. Darren just sat there whilst Justin resumed his clicking. My T100 was being included in the shots now. I smiled at that in anticipation of the photos I could post later. I needed to increase my followers after a drought of posts these past few weeks. There was plenty of content there for engagement, mainly dozens of unedited photos from the Peaks, but replaying old hits was getting stale. The online trend now was puddles and mud. The shots of autumnal leaves had ended, and the trees were becoming bare. I saved my remaining Peaks photos for Thursdays and the #throwbackthursday hashtag. I relied on that as a free win on a week without much content. I looked at Darren. He was still silent, just staring off into the distance. He had barely touched his tea, now dark brown and stewed. I wasn't going to tell him he should take the teabag out.

"New camera?" I shouted over to Justin instead.

"Yeah mate." He walked over to me. Justin wasn't one for shouting. "Fujifilm X Pro2 with thirty-five-millimetre lens. That @KickAzTriumph dude recommended it."

I nodded and smirked. Well, if it was good enough for an influencer in America, with hundreds of thousands of followers, it was good enough for our very own influencer-in-the-making here in the Cotswolds. I ate a mouthful of ginger cake. It was moist and hit the spot.

Darren sighed loudly.

I tried to cheer him up. "Have you seen that @AlwaysParallelTwinning guy in his new Braap and Burn jacket? You remember him? That blazer-wearing rider from months ago."

Darren didn't reply.

I shrugged and returned to my phone, desperate to find something to break the silence. I scrolled through a few more posts. "He's announced that Braap and Burn have made him an official brand ambassador?" I was surprised.

Justin walked over and took a look too. He laughed. "That doesn't look comfortable at all! That new little Royal Enfield Meteor 350 looks alright though. Can't believe that they lent him that bike for the shoot. Jacket is tight as a nun's chuff though, as Darren might say." Justin looked over at him, looking pleased with himself for using the crass analogy. There was still no reaction. Justin frowned and was about to return to his photography.

"I'm never tagging those assholes in any of my photos, or videos ever again, those Braap and Burn wankers!" Darren stood up suddenly, facing us. I was stunned and looked around. A large, bearded Harley Davidson FXR rider across the car park looked up at us, and then quickly looked away, avoiding eye contact. On any other day, the Harley rider looked like he could snap my neck just for looking at him the wrong way.

"The amount of fucking photos and videos I've tagged with them dickheads in," he continued, his voice getting louder. He started doing a high-pitched voice, mimicking his followers asking questions online. "Oooh, what jacket's that? What fucking jacket's that?!"

Jane looked over from serving coffee and gave us a death stare. Loud pipes were fine, but shouty, angry customers were not. I could only look back at her with sincerely apologetic eyes.

"Fucking get this blazer button-popping new rider, just passed his CBT, with his twenty horsepower leaf blower of a bike, fully kitted out in Braap and Burn kit... they can kiss my fucking ass! I'm gonna get a CWC patch and stick it over all my Braap and Burn badges, and when any fat lad on a twenty horsepower bike asks me, 'what fucking jacket's that?' I'm gonna tell them, it's Cotswolds Wrecking Crew and not Braap and Burn... they're shit!" He was panting by the time he finished.

There was a silence, not just at our table but all around the cafe and the car park. Even the big Harley rider was looking anywhere but towards us, suddenly looking like he had important chain maintenance to do. Back at our table, Justin burst out laughing. It was a big belly laugh. I had never seen him so loud. I joined in too, we couldn't stop ourselves. The customers at Piston Place Motor and Bean continued their conversations and finally Darren sat down.

He looked a relieved man for getting that off his chest. "Still no bacon sarnies though," he said, laughing too.

I had no idea Darren was angling for an official role with Braap and Burn. He always seemed above it all. Olivia was right and had told me months ago to be careful with this mad influencer world. It had gripped us subtly. The devil, she had called it. My mind suddenly flicked to Lisa and her loud pipes, straddling her Street Twin suggestively, in some photos that I remembered. I looked at her Instagram account saved in my search history. I put my phone down, grimacing. I thought about unfollowing her but stopped myself. The problem was with me, not with her. She could sit on her motorcycle however she wanted. I had seen how the online motorcycle scene had got to Tyrone, and then Darren, in different ways recently. I was not going to let it get me too. I checked the crew's chat.

"Would do in my swede if you were sucking them off on socials anyway," wrote Tyrone. News of Darren's epic rant had reached him and the gossip had got him talking again. "They're getting fairly reckless when it comes to copyright too the past few months, best leave them alone," he added.

We hadn't heard from Henry since our ride to Piston Place Motor and Bean on Sunday either. I assumed he had enjoyed a fun day out, sipping champagne, and mixing with the corporate shills in the VIP room at Silverstone, working out his inevitable move to London. Or maybe the normally teetotal lad just had a massive hangover, I wondered?

It was Monday night when the message arrived to my phone.

"Boys, I've been in a crash," it read. It was from Henry.

My blood ran cold and my heart stopped for a few seconds.

"Went for a ride Sunday after Silverstone and hit a car. I'm in hospital."

We all knew the risks involved in what was our passion. Everyone knew someone who had been in a crash, or if you didn't, then likely you would be that victim. The others saw the messages. Sympathetic questions came thick and fast.

"What happened? Are you ok? How's Little Red??" asked Justin.

Darren managed a few swear words that we all knew meant he was very concerned. Out of all of us, with his experience of racing on two wheels, he had been involved in more crashes than he could count. That was on a track though, wearing full racing leathers, and likely not involving a stone wall, or hitting a heavy, metal, moving four-wheeled object coming the other way at speed too.

"My own stupid fault. I was wearing the tinted visor. The one that looks sick on the Gram, but it was dark. Couldn't see a thing through it. Then on a corner on that road out of Tetbury, must have been on the wrong side, just as an old lady in her car was driving the other way."

"Mate, so sorry. Yeah I know the road, sketchy as fuck. Nearly binned it myself a few times," replied Tyrone.

"I was so lucky. I think I hit her front wheel and my head bounced off her wing mirror. Little Red went down and somehow I was surfing on top of her, on her side, before rolling to a stop in a ditch. I should be dead!" stated Henry bluntly, finishing the re-enactment of the horrible incident. No one replied for a minute or two. I shuddered at Henry's last words. He was a lucky lad indeed, I thought.

"How's the bike then? How's the old dear that you hit?" asked Tyrone.

"Yeah she was shaken up. I think she thought she had killed me. My helmet took her wing mirror clean off. She called the police and they closed the road. Little Red was taken away. I doubt she'll be rideable again. Am more gutted for that to be honest."

I wondered how I would feel if I crashed Bonnie. I felt sick at the thought. It was strange how we valued these inanimate objects, a form of transportation really, beyond our own broken bones, cuts and bruises. I asked Henry if he had broken anything.

"No, thankfully, just a huge bruise on my right thigh and shin and am sore all over. Was so lucky."

That was good. Hopefully he would be out of hospital soon.

"Oh and boys, it's true what they say, get good proper biking gear. I'm sure that saved me too. Not the visor though. Never wearing a mirrored visor again. Stupid hubris," he added.

"But at least your school shoes are safe and intact at home," joked Justin.

The next day I visited him in hospital. He was in good spirits. I took a few photos of a smiling Henry giving a thumbs up for the Gram and his followers, along with a warning about riding at night with a visor designed to stop sun glare. He got some hate for that in the comments. He ignored it all and focussed on the well-wishers.

Back at home a day later, he posted a series of stories on the Gram, including chilling photos of his damaged gear with the very important reminder to "wear proper motorcycle gear all the time". He lined up his helmet, jacket, gloves, boots, and trousers on his bed. The once beautiful paint on his Biltwell Gringo helmet was scratched as if mauled by a gorilla in a cage. The offending visor was nowhere to be seen. His trusted and well-used Merlin jacket was scuffed all over, with small holes where the fabric did not survive the abrasion of his slide on the tarmac. No motorcycle rider really knows how their gear will hold up in a crash, and no one ever wanted to find out really. I was reassured that Henry's gear did a decent job of protecting him, and doubly so as our gear tended to be purchased with the priority of looking cool in photos on Instagram, rather than being the absolute toughest gear available, #motorcyclestyle and #caferacerstyle taking priority. Henry's wounds and ego would heal and he would ride again, but Little Red would grace the twisty roads of the Cotswolds no more. A few weeks later the garage replied giving Henry the bad news that no rider wanted to hear. She was a write-off. The news hit Henry hard. He managed to salvage some of the parts that he added to the bike himself. The good quality CNC-machined aluminium parts from Maurice at Motoz Modz were mostly unscathed. They would live on, fulfilling their purpose of making a future modern classic Triumph look cool. A tale of motorcycle reincarnation. Like the phoenix from the flames, Henry and an evolution of Little Red would ride with the Cotswolds Wrecking Crew again. Not now though. Now was a time for healing, for reflection, and staying indoors.

November arrived with sleet and very cold weather. That meant the salt spreaders were out to keep Britain's gloriously unequipped roads open.

"Sally salt is out. Fuck me, I miss going for a ride," said Darren in the group.

It had been over a week of miserable ice on the roads now. Salt was the grim reaper to our precious machines. Rust did not look good on Instagram. If a photo of a rusty motorcycle did well regarding the likes and follows, it was no doubt posted in the context of #patina to try to convince the custom motorcycling faithful that the machine had character by being well-ridden through all weathers, or it was actually a genuine classic old bike. Our steeds were neither. #fairweatherrider came to mind again. Darren would agree. He kept his Scram in pristine condition. Sally was therefore to be avoided at all costs. He hated her nearly as much as he despised Melvin the mildew.

"Give a fuck!" replied Tyrone. "I'll be riding in that."

He received some winter products to test. For a motorcycle journalist who depended on companies paying him to review gear, this meant riding all year round, even in deepest, darkest winter.

"Your latest photos are sick!" I said. A warm and waterproof Tyrone, straddling his jet-black Street Twin looked moody, gritty, and confident. I read the title of a lead story he posted to the Gram.

"The Winter Rider? What's that then?" Tyrone had posted a dozen or so photos showing off different jackets, helmets, and trousers, with an urban backdrop hammered by sleet and rain. Unlike Justin, the model and muse of own his photos, Tyrone was not centre stage. The focus was on the details of the products, the zips, buttons, and fabric quality.

"Yeah man. The Winter Rider, it's some play on the Marvel superhero character. Thought it sounded cool. You know, we're all heroes on two wheels, doing the commute, especially in winter, battling cars and the elements. I think the vibe works."

"Chaps, me and Pippa are having a break." Henry dropped that message out of the blue.

We had been enjoying some banter about Justin being invited to the Wrench Masters Motorcycle Show as a special guest and new official influencer on behalf of Michelin tyres. It was his first paid gig too.

I saw Henry's message first. "Mate, I'm so sorry. We're here for you… anything you need."

"Thanks mate, I appreciate that. I'll need it," he replied.

It was an incredibly brave thing to do, I thought. There was some back and forth on his reasons and who might live where. No one wanted to ask about the job in London. Selfishly I wanted Henry to stay in the west country and keep riding his motorcycle.... his new motorcycle with us. We were the Cotswolds Wrecking Crew.

"It was the Peaks trip, just having time away," said Henry. The concerned brothers on two wheels asked more questions and he answered straightforwardly. "That four days away, not returning home each evening to Pippa, it was just… such a freeing experience. I didn't miss her one bit either. I wanted that trip to never end. It gave me time to think each night before going to sleep. You lot were drunk and snoring away."

I didn't write anything. He needed to pour this all out.

"And then I went to that Silverstone event… and Christian was there, and his mates, and other people I had to network, sipping champagne… that I don't really like anyway. I just thought to myself, this is not what I want and these are not my people. You lot are my people."

I smiled reading that message.

"I left Silverstone after the race had finished, but instead of heading home back to Pippa, I just took off on Little Red to clear my head."

No one interrupted him still. I read the detail he had written several times. He hadn't told us that part when he recalled the events of his crash the other week.

"And the rest… is history. It taught me that life is too short, and it could have all been over for me on that nasty corner… and so I decided that I don't want Christian's job offer, and I don't want to move to London."

Tyrone replied first. "Wow mate, good for you. Much love, yeah."
We all echoed the sentiment.

"Well you can't be in the Cotswolds Wrecking Crew without a motorcycle… a Triumph motorcycle," I added, trying to bring some light relief back to the chat.

"Fuckin' ell, John," replied Darren. "Bit harsh mate, too soon!"
Henry wrote a laughing face emoji and a heart.

The sun was out, on a crisp and cold sunny day. I owed it to Bonnie to go for one final December ride before Sally and Melvin ruined it for everyone, possibly until early spring next year. She was a different girl from that sad, dust-covered, rusty, neglected motorcycle under a sheet in my garage at the start of the year. Bonnie was looking trim and fit for the road, several thousand miles of good road tarmac had been the health kick she had needed. I was talking about myself too, I realised. I kissed Olivia on the forehead before heading out.

"Have a safe trip. It's icy! No racing!" she said.
I looked at her and winked.

Damn it was cold. I was wearing my thermal merino lambswool base layers but the icy chill cut through to the skin. My nose was streaming, snot collecting on my woollen buff under the open face Hedon helmet. That at least kept my mouth and neck from freezing.

"Who's smart idea was this then, girl?" I said to Bonnie, teeth chattering. Her pistons were firing away beautifully though. I was glad she was warm. The only warming thought as consolation to keep me going was that I knew I'd regret not seizing the moment to ride on this dry day in a few months' time. I had to feed my followers new content. They were a hungry mob. I had been losing more and more over the past few weeks due to my drought. I told myself I didn't care about that, but I did. I was also reflecting on Justin's invitation to Wrench Masters. That bike show also ran an amateur shed build exhibition. It was too late for this year, but next year, if I customised and modified Bonnie even more, I could enter the competition. The thought was tantalising and made me giddy with dopamine. I had already found several custom motorcycle parts to change.

The devil was whispering to me over my shoulder. "Chop the subframe," he was saying. Motoz Modz bolt on and plug-and-play parts were one thing, but to chop metal parts off the bike, was akin to surgery. It was irreversible. I'd need an angle grinder too. Sparks did make for good reels on the Gram though, especially in slow motion, I thought. I winced seconds later. That was the hipster cliche that I mocked in that BMW R nineT advert previously. I didn't have the beard nor skill for that.

I was riding higher and higher towards MotoGP road, past Nailsworth now. My inner dilemma of spending more money had at least distracted me from the biting cold. I was on autopilot until the motorcycling angels reminded me to focus on these icy roads, the back wheel slipping suddenly.

"Fuck! Focus, concentrate!" I said to myself. I managed to dab the rear break, conscious that grabbing a handful of the front might lock up the front wheel and throw us both to the ground. A bit of steering to keep her upright, and we were safe again. Mental note to self, I thought. Watch for black ice.

I was riding to Powerhouse Triumph, near Bristol, to meet Darren for a warm, hearty brunch... or a late breakfast as he called it. Sally and Melvin were everywhere on the fast and twisty country A-roads now and Darren's Scram was tucked up in his garage. He was happy to join me in town though at the biker cafe, only a stone's throw from his house.

I saw a bright, white light gaining on me quickly in my right-hand mirror.

"VARRROOOOOOOMM!" the bike went past me like a smooth bullet, the rider kicking out his left leg as he did so, another greeting sign on two wheels.

"Jesus!" I exclaimed. I looked at my speedometer. I was riding between seventy and eighty myself. This was our road. I couldn't let that guy humiliate me like that. I checked myself before the red mist and adrenaline descended. "Steady. These roads are slippery..." I ignored the chase. I thought of Olivia, #arrivealive more than #ridefastdontdie this time.

I finished my warm eggs, bacon, hashbrowns and a double serving of toast. I was still cold. The food quality was not worth the hypothermia risk, but on the plus side, I managed to get Darren to take a few snaps of the intrepid pair, Bonnie and I, pulling into the carpark looking like arctic explorers.

"Some absolute nutter flew past me on MotoGP. He was on an old Goldwing, I think, six cylinders from the sound," I said to him, sipping my second cup of hot coffee now. I was gripping the mug trying to coax the warmth back into my hands. "Looked like one of those late eighties GL1500s."

Darren laughed. "I used to have one of them. I'd ride mine like that to fuck with all the wobbling Power Rangers."

I nodded. Darren gave up his sports bike full leathers, matching fluorescent colours jacket and trousers, years ago but he'd hang with the fastest of them on MotoGP still.

"Took me and the missus around America on it, after I sold my Fire Blade. Can take the man out of racing..." he trailed off, grinning. "Couldn't get the kid on the bike, so the other Honda got sold too." He finished his mug of tea and wiped his mouth.

"But a Goldwing destroyed me. That's embarrassing?"

"Don't knock it, mate. Hundred horses and torque for days, even on one of they old ones."

I nodded but didn't listen. "I'm going to upgrade the engine. Big Bore Kit. That will give her 904cc rather than her current 865... should provide about thirty percent more torque and horsepower from looking at some graphs." I got out my phone. "Look... I also found this parts company that does a rear loop, to bolt to the sub-frame after its cut away. Bonnie will look even more like a cafe racer then." I grinned, looking for Darren's approval.

He laughed again. "Fuckin' 'ell mate, it's not an S1000RR, leave her be! Your bike is lush."

Darren's words might as well have been in Greek. I had made up my mind. The devil had won. If the crew couldn't or wouldn't ride over winter, then I'd at least do some #winterwrenching.

15. Bike show

The Wrench Master's Motorcycle Show marked the unofficial end to the riding year. It was an exhibition that took place in London at a huge country estate. For one weekend only it was transformed into the centre of the universe for the custom motorcycling community paying homage to our passion. The vast and open space was needed to house and show off hundreds of fantastic custom motorcycles, designed and built by talented and creative garage mechanics from up and down the country. Never were #shedbuilt, #builtnotbought, and #wrenching more overused than at this annual event. Having a ticket to view the eclectic mix of cafe racers, scramblers, flat trackers, brat bikes, cruisers was the hottest ticket in town. "You meant to be brown-nosing at Wrench Master's on Saturday, Justin, or just going for the banter?" asked Darren in the group chat.

Justin had mentioned something about that a few weeks ago but with Henry's big personal life news, the details had passed the crew by. The race was on for us to buy any remaining tickets to attend and try to arrange all going on the same day. I was keen not to miss this, certainly noting my intentions for the following year. There was research to be done regarding the standards of novice exhibitors. I hadn't parted with my cash just yet for those parts I wanted. An engine upgrade would cost about two grand. Putting Bonnie under the knife also made me feel queasy. If Olivia found out about the money, she'd no doubt take the angle grinder intended to chop the subframe to parts of my anatomy instead.

"I'll be heading up Friday night actually. There's some private party. Michelin invited me. They're one of the main sponsors. Tyrone is coming with me," replied Justin, casual as anything for such a big deal in this community.

"Fuckin' 'ell," replied Darren. "Tyrone got a gig too then? I must have missed that."

"Yeah man, doing a piece on new tyres for the new year. Michelin loved my stuff on the Winter Rider. What works in the wet and all that. The only issue is I'll be using photos for my article with the bearded capybara in all the photos, straddling beautiful bikes that you lot can only dream of touching."

"The funny thing is, I don't even have Michelin tyres on my T120. Never have. It all makes no sense," added Justin.

I felt slightly bitter at that. They both deserved their moment to shine at such a big event, but I was the only one who actually rode on Michelin rubber. I even tagged them on the Gram when I had them fitted. The Road Classics were a great tyre for my T100. They looked like old-fashioned rubber too, adding to the heritage aesthetic of Bonnie. I blinked away the jealousy. I had a plan. Bonnie would be here next year, fast, sleek, a true cafe racer.

Henry, Darren, and I arrived mid-morning into London on the train. Darren bought a six pack of Thatchers cider on board with him, and as Henry didn't drink, it was three tins each for the two of us. That loosened us up nicely for joining the huge, yet fast-moving queue to show our tickets at the venue. The place was buzzing. These were my people. I didn't know any of them, but I felt a connection via the power of our custom motorcycle culture. This day and this show was all about celebrating #goodvibesonly. It was also refreshing that neither Henry nor Darren got their camera phones out for the usual stories of the crew entering such an iconic show. There was no selfie in front of the main stage, showcasing the custom bike of the year. This year the motorcycle was an expertly and pristinely modified 1998 Triumph Thunderbird TT Legend. This limited-edition Thunderbird was built for three years and was a nod to the Isle of

Man time trial races. The 885cc engine was a relatively smooth triple that made about 69 bhp. Plenty enough for our Cotswolds roads. Even though this version of the bike had a cool name it was actually cheaper than some of the original bikes, owing to the fact it was more blacked out with fewer expensive chrome parts on show. I thought this made the bike look and feel more modern and I liked that. Clearly this talented bike builder thought the same, using the beautiful engine as the centrepiece to build around. He had beefed-up the power using a NOS, Nitrous Oxide kit. The owner claimed it made over 200 bhp now. That was crazy, I thought. The front forks, brakes, rear shocks had been upgraded too. Top-end Stylema Brembo callipers and Ohlins forks kept the rider safe now. The swingarm was a custom job and was longer than the stock bike too. This was done to stop the bike doing an insane wheelie off the line and gave the bike more straight-line stability at top speed. He had hand-stitched a beautiful soft deer leather seat, which was embossed with his initials to give it a lovely, personalised touch. A sleek and retro 1950s era custom racing cowl was added to the front, to improve aerodynamics, which was very much needed at the claimed 200 mph speed. #ridefastdontdie sprang to mind. The sexy vibrant red custom paint job and hand painted coach lines just oozed quality and gave it an expensive, exotic Ferrari vibe too. I could see why this was the centrepiece. I loved the look of this thing and struggled to hide my jealousy of the bike mechanic with the vision, talent, time, and money, to build such a wonderful motorcycle. This was the pinnacle of #caferacerstyle for me.

We were looking for one of the coffee places to meet Tyrone and Justin, no doubt grinning from ear to ear at being invited down a day early for the VIP party. I reckoned they'd need a strong, full flavoured artisanal brew about now. There were plenty of pop-up places to buy one. There was even a whiskey bar that was open at this morning hour. They were both sat at a table when we arrived. Tyrone was wearing dark sunglasses. Indoors.

"Alright lads, good night was it?" I asked, grinning expectantly at the tales of debauchery to come.

Tyrone yawned and sipped a can of Red Bull. "Mate, it was messy. I am broken now. Been doing laps of this building to clear the post-boozing anxiety," he replied.

I laughed and looked around. I could hear some buzzing. I spotted a tattoo artist plying her trade in another booth.

"What some kind of anxiety walk?" asked Henry. "Nervous about the big gig are we?" He was also smirking at the suffering pair.

"I've already been shooting this skinny hipster teen wolf since nine o'clock, before the gates even opened," responded Tyrone, looking over at Justin who cooly smiled back, sipping his coffee. He hadn't even said hello to us yet.

"Looks like someone has done a diarrhoea shit in your coffee," stated Darren, suddenly noticing the odd muddy green colour in Justin's cup.

I laughed and stared at it too. It looked disgusting.

"It's called a matcha latte. Green tea powder and steamed milk. I didn't expect you to appreciate such a novel and fine taste," retorted Justin.

Tyrone laughed at that. "Come on you Lycan-pelted bean pole, we should get back to work. I need to see you straddling that custom Moto Guzzi V7 850 over there, looking right. I should interview the builders and see what mods they've made before I feel sick again too."

He pulled out a wrinkled pamphlet, blotted with ink smudges, from his hoodie pocket and thumbed it open. "My VIP press notes tell me that this sick machine is rocking the Michelin Road Classic tyres."

The rest of us looked around whilst the professionals worked. Henry made a direct beeline to an area selling motorcycle lifestyle clothing. There were racks and racks of the stuff, leather jackets, riding jeans, trendy boots, and so many sweatshirts with racing stripes and lightning bolts everywhere. I wondered if our very own Cotswolds Wrecking Crew merch might grace these hallowed railings one day. The set-up reminded me of Piston Place Motor and Bean, but just larger, scaled up to a full stately home. Henry was browsing some motorcycling lifestyle gear, casually draped over upcycled wooden fruit crates, no doubt to give some rustic aesthetic to the display. Darren turned his nose up and disappeared to look elsewhere. I didn't need to buy any clothes. It was all about the custom motorcycles and novel build ideas for me. I had to see what worked and what looked awful, for inspiration. I started to drool over a gorgeous Ducati Sport 1000, on a plinth that separated the shelves of clothing. The bike was rocking a sleek Zard aftermarket exhaust set-up. I thought about selling Bonnie just for a second to help fund a bike such as this one. These things just grew in value, and just from the sexy and aggressive, yet classic stance of racing bikes of yesteryear, I could see why. The fuel tank of this model was in the classic Ducati orange, not like the red of the modern performance-oriented machines. I was a fan of the simple look, without the cowling too, which gave the bike a naked vibe. The Desmo V-twin air-cooled engines were well-proven from many of Ducati's bikes from the early noughties. I reckoned this thing made about 90 bhp or so, and as it was quite a lightweight machine, I knew instinctively she would be fast.

Henry was at the till and was completing his shopping spree. I noticed that Darren was looking a bit glum and was sat at a bar, sipping a beer now. We joined him. No one spoke for a while. We just listened to the general hubbub. Every now and then some awesome throaty engine kicked in, with a few revs and then the sound of cheers and whooping from happy festival goers. Some of the visitors were getting excited and wanted to show off their own machines unofficially. Looking around, there were rows and rows of old portraits on the walls, likely of some lord or lady. At least the current owners had the sense to hide the fine, antique china tea sets. The oak-panelled walls and doors added to the grandeur of the whole event, which screamed hipsters in turn-ups crossed with gentrified tweed. I breathed in deeply, contentedly getting a whiff of Castrol oil and furniture polish.

Darren spoke suddenly. "I went to this sick little warehouse the other day, before Sally Salt arrived. None of you were around so I just went, and well Henry binned his bike anyway."

I winced and looked at Henry.

"Fair comment," he said.

Darren continued. "It had some cool graffiti and I wanted some gritty urban night-time shots, for Braap and Burn… look how that all turned out. But anyway, the place wasn't tagged to fuck by little thugs, so I took the Scram for a ride out over there."

"Oh yeah, nice. Any good? Where was that then?" I asked him, sipping my beer and looking around some more. I noticed that Herald Motor Co. had a stand here at the show this year. I made a mental note to check out their bikes later. I really liked the look of their single cylinder Classic 125. I reckoned it was a fun little run around on some tiny B-roads or around town.

"Bottom of the M32. The ride was awful mate. Tiny little back-alley streets and I got lost. Was chased by some fucking dogs at one point. Had to give one of them a kick. Thought I might get fucking rabies!" continued Darren.

Both Henry and I were looking at him now, wondering how this tale might end.

"It got worse, lads. I parked up at this artsy warehouse. Stank of piss, like some dingy concrete multi-storey car park. The light was banging though. Spot on. I set up my new tripod for the camera, and fuck me, a gang of little hoody shites come around the corner, all in balaclavas. I nearly shit myself. Never packed up the bike so quickly in all my life!"

He took another swig of beer. Someone was revving the hell out of an inline four. I waited for it to stop.

"Jesus, Darren, sounds like you were lucky to get away mate!" I replied.

"Yeah mate, blimmin' nearly launched myself off the back seat with a huge wheelie to get out of there and all!" He downed the rest of his pint.

"There are loads of sick places for photos in Bristol, it's just not good for actual riding," said Henry. "We should get up early and do the suspension bridge as a crew one day... when I get another bike." He winked at Darren.

Tyrone and Justin joined us, and I got another round of beers in. Tyrone wasn't wearing his sunglasses now. I checked out the Gram on my phone. Even though I hadn't taken any photos today, it was just habit. Justin appeared all over my feed. There were half a dozen stories and several posts already. I noticed that Tyrone had been invited as a collaborator by Justin for some joint updates. The likes rolled in already for me, where I was tagged. I noticed several sponsored Michelin posts too, uploaded by the joint collaborators.

"Absolute influencing machine, eh Justin!" I said.

He nodded and smiled. "It's going well. It's actual proper money too... or wedge, thanks to him." He looked towards Tyrone, who raised a glass in return, grinning.

"What's with this bromance then?" I asked.

"I'll let Tyrone tell you," responded Justin, still smirking.

"Yeah, well, one of the reasons I got absolutely boat wobbled off my cod piece last night was Triumph got back in touch," explained Tyrone, ruffling his hair and yawning.

I waited for more detail. I heard the buzz of the tattooist's needle again. I looked over, noticing a woman sat on a chair, her top was off as the artist was finishing a giant black bat drawn across her breasts, just above her nipples. Her eyes locked on to mine. I looked away quickly, and back to Tyrone.

"And?" I asked.

"And... they've only gone and given me one of their new Chromed-out Thruxtons to review," he continued, his voice sounding gravelly.

We clinked our beer bottles together in celebration at Tyrone's news. My phone beeped. There was a new message from Olivia. I walked away from the banter for a minute to read it.

"Love you so much. Sorry I've been on at you about spending money this year. I miss you is all. I get so jealous that you have that bunch of friends doing your motorbike stuff together. Just to say... I won't nag again. You being happy is more important. Hope the show is fun... or sick xx."

I chuckled to myself at her joke but then felt the guilt hit me. She had no idea of my plans. I couldn't lie to her about this, surely? The new modification mission required me to go further than a few Motoz Modz parts that I had purchased previously.

Suddenly, Darren pushed his own chair back, making a loud creaking noise as it scraped on the hard, varnished, expensive oak floorboards. He stood up and waited until we were all looking at him.

"I haven't been back on social media... I fucking mugged it right off. I was being a right little attention-seeking prick. I feel fucking loads better for not being on it. Still go out riding and all that, but I can't be doing with all that anymore."

He sat back down. Apart from the chair dragging on the floorboards again, all was silent for a second at our table. We all looked at him, and then laughed loudly, drowning out the sounds of the humming and whirring tattoo needles across the corridor too.

He was right. Bloody hell, he was so right! I looked back at Olivia's message. One of us nearly lost his reputation and his livelihood for this shit. Twice. Heck, one of us nearly died in a crash too chasing this fakery. All for the Gram. We all had several near misses on two wheels but those thrills and near spills were the real stuff. Hanging out with the crew on the twisty, gravely, roads, with bugs and stones in the face. Pure motorcycling. Getting beeped at by angry car drivers, laughing it all off, and surviving the mad overtakes, adrenaline running as fast as the machines in the wind. It was the feeling of that parallel twin thundering away between your legs, the induction roar as the motorcycle hits its peak power band, rider and machine surging forward at warp speed. No amount of flame emojis, comments from random, anonymous fans... or new expensive custom parts and showing them off would replace that.

"Well fucking said," I replied, raising my pint again. "Cheers lads!"

After our drinks, we walked towards the Wall of Death, an awesome and spectacular carnival set piece, where the rider goes full throttle around a wooden velodrome to enable the bike to ride horizontally on the wall, the friction keeping the rider in place whilst performing stunts. This guy looked like Evel Knievel with his pristine white suit trimmed with American Stars and Stripes. He was a blurry vision of red, white, and blue as he zoomed around, letting go of the handlebars and high fiving those spectators standing at the top of the velodrome, reaching down to him, whooping and clapping. Everyone loved it. After watching that for thirty minutes or so, I needed some food to soak up the morning's beers. Smart Chesterfield full grain leather sofas were dotted about the place. I grabbed a spot on one that was the same colour as my Belstaff riding jacket. It was just as comfortable too. I could have fallen asleep there. In front of the sofa was an engine block with a glass tabletop. Again, it reminded me of Piston Place Motor and Bean. This engine block was huge, however. It took me a while to realise that it was from a bike and was not an old car engine. Had I looked closer I would have seen the subtle Triumph branding stamped into the grey metal. It could only have been an old Rocket 3 engine. I looked closer. Yes, there were only three cylinders. It was huge on full display when not tucked away inside the bike's steel cradle frame. Not as pretty as the Harley Davidson knucklehead at Piston Place Motor and Bean though. There was something pleasing about the symmetry of Harley V-twins, but that table would not have been big enough for the crew, all tucking into burgers now. I heard Tyrone laughing and looked over at him. He was mumbling something, his mouth full of chips. He was pointing to his phone. I shuffled over and had a look. It was a story posted by Maurice on @MotozModz.

"Strongest engine crash bars - don't be a Hooligan Henry," it read.

I laughed too. "Is he marketing crash bars using Henry's accident?" I asked.

"Looks that way," replied Tyrone. "Did you know about that, Henry?"

"Yeah but I thought it was a joke," he replied. I supposed it wasn't every day that a quality brand like Motoz Modz named a piece of gear after someone. I smiled and slapped Henry on the back. He needed some positive news after the past month. This was a mark of endearment and respect for him. Henry told us that Maurice had messaged him a few times after that horrible Sunday night and had offered to replace some parts if they were damaged. As it turned out, due to the build quality, most were salvaged anyway.

"Lads, check out the next story... this one's even better," said Darren. I had my phone out now and was replying to Maurice's stories with laughing face emojis. No one did advertising with captions as effectively as Maurice.

"Each set of Hooligan Henry bars will come with a signed topless photo of the man, the legend, the inspiration behind the crash bars," it read. There was an old photo of Little Red too. Henry's signature red leather motorcycle gloves were purposefully laid out on the seat. Maurice had also written #littleredridinglovesneverdies on the story. We all looked at Henry. No one spoke. I raised my beer glass again, and the others followed suit.

"Mate, I'd be rinsing that cheeky git if he was doing me like that," said Tyrone.

"Yeah but I'm not a big deal in the motorcycle world like you," replied Henry. "No wedge for me but... my free crash bars will arrive, with some other bits and pieces soon. It was the deal I struck with Maurice for using my misfortune to sell his parts." He laughed and sipped his cola. "They won't be used for a while though." He said that last part quietly then wiped his mouth with a napkin, looking down at the table.

I was intrigued where he was going with this. "What do you mean?"

The others were paying attention too. All the phones were put away.

"I'm taking some time out. I'm going to take a sabbatical from my current job. I turned down London and, with a break from Pippa, I can take time to figure out what I want. I'm going to travel around

Thailand for a bit. The new year is actually a great time for good weather over there."

There was silence. Henry looked around at our faces. Expressions of bemusement, confusion, worry, and sadness.

"I'll be back tearing up the roads with the crew in the spring, don't worry. I've already put down a deposit on next year's Speed Twin… and in red of course."

I nodded at that, already looking forward to next spring's riding season, and hearing his tales of Bangkok nights. A Speed Twin would be a nice upgrade in power and performance for him too. He'd have the fastest bike out of the whole crew, although Darren would still rinse him on MotoGP. I heard another engine roar again. I turned my head to take a look. In the distance, someone had got too excited over at the exit doors and was doing doughnuts in the car park. I remembered there was a beautiful stone fountain there. I could see the bike from where we were sitting. It was a Suzuki TL1000. It looked badass. This machine was nicknamed 'the widow maker' when it first came out in the 1990s due to some new sophisticated suspension technology, that I guessed didn't always work. The lord or lady of this manor would not be impressed with tyre marks on the neatly kept lawn out front. It was good that Darren hadn't ridden his Scram to add to the carnage too. The crowd was cheering at this spontaneous and unofficial Wrench Masters entertainment, the rider, just wearing a thick flannel chequered shirt and a hoodie, dark beard in the wind, was loving it.

I turned back again and looked at Henry. "So next year you'll change from Little Red, to Medium Red, yeah?"

The others laughed and groaned at my joke.

"Mate, I'm always a medium," he replied smiling.

We walked around some more. I spotted the Braap and Burn stand, rails of tees and hoodies on display. Loud obnoxious American hip hop was thudding out of some speakers, the loud bass making them crackle. The stand was decorated in neon spray painted colours, making the place looked like it was tagged by several rival gangs. I looked at Darren who hadn't noticed it yet. I wondered if I should try to steer him away. Suddenly I heard a voice that I recognised.

"Hi guys, um it's me, coming live from, um Wrench Masters in London, repping, that is to say, representing the sick bros, err, from Braap and Burn today..."

I spotted where it came from. The blazer-wearing rider, aka @AlwaysParallelTwinning, was here too. I needed to definitely shepherd Darren somewhere else now, and quickly, I thought.

"Fuckin' 'ell!" he gasped. I was too late. Darren was pointing towards the stand.

"Easy mate," I said, concern showing on my face. "Let's leave them be, yeah."

He just stood there, then after a minute, shrugged his shoulders. "Don't worry about me, John. I'm chill."

He walked over to the stand and browsed the garments on offer. Thankfully the InstaLive continued without interruption. Darren walked over to the children's clothes section and picked up a hoodie.

He held it up and looked at me. "For my daughter," he said, smiling. "This style is very popular at her school apparently, so being a cool dad and all that..."

I laughed, relieved. Darren paid for the hoodie and we walked away, heading to the next area. I looked around, back at the stand. The vlog was still going.

"And these hoodies, are rude man, I mean, this one... it's black, and it has a hood, right..."

I shook my head.

Tyrone and Justin had gone back to working the floor. I was now in a small corner dedicated to Indian Motorcycles. I loved these machines. If I were in the market for a cruiser I was genuinely torn between the Indian Chief or a Harley Davidson Fat Boy. I was a tall chap and the stance of these unapologetically heavy bikes would suit me. Sat back, feet forward, with some ape hangers, knees in the breeze. Maybe one day if the more aggressive cafe racer vibes of Bonnie didn't suit me anymore, I'd consider it. Maybe Olivia and I could cruise Route 66 in America, just the two of us front and pillion, I wondered. The thought made me smile. These bikes were not cheap though. For the new models the cost was around twenty thousand pounds, for either model. Both engines were around 1860cc, with bags of lumpy torque to just roll on the gas at any speed. The engines looked beautiful on both machines. Indian's liquid-cooled cruisers took a more modern silhouette, but it was still obvious you were straddling a V-twin from sight and feel. In front of me right now, I was drooling just looking at some custom Bobber Scouts that an American builder had brought to Wrench Masters. Like Triumph, Indian really tried to sell the lifestyle image too. The bikes were nearly buried in shoulder high piles of hoodies, beanie hats, and scarves, perfect for the winter.

"Yeah I hang with the Cotswolds Wrecking Crew… Cotswolds… it's an area of outstanding natural beauty in the south of England…"

I looked up. Justin was here at the Indian stand too. I knew I recognised his soft voice. He was networking, and by the sounds of it, promoting the crew. I walked up to him.

He saw me approach. "This is John. John, meet Mike. You might know him better as @KickAzTriumph on Instagram." He introduced me to a tall, well-built chap, wearing an Indian T-shirt and dark sunglasses.

He held out a hand to shake mine. "You look familiar... Bonnie fourteen days, right?"

I shook his hand. He got the name close enough. I recalled getting angry at this guy, months and months ago, when he ignored my messages commenting on his tyres. Right now, seeing the person in real life, and not the anonymous, faceless online avatar, Mike oozed confidence and charm, and was giving me a big white teeth smile.

I decided to follow Darren's example and let bygones be bygones. "I'm a huge fan of your content mate. Very cool. Your Speed Twin is one of the best I've seen. You must really love that bike, the amount of work you've put into it," I beamed at him.

He smiled back and nodded. "Aww thanks buddy. Yeah that girl has been my passion for a few years."

"So what brings you here then to Wrench Masters, and to the Indian section?" I asked.

"Well... just looking for a new steed for the stable. You know how it is, right? One bike is never enough. Got some exciting collaborations with some creatives coming up in the new year." He looked over at Justin, who was nodding and smiling through his bushy beard.

I understood the implications. I was pleased for Justin. He had the right look to make it big in America I reckoned.

"You ride that sleek little air-cooled cafe, right? The one with the Arrows, and YSS shocks. You got that beefy front brake too... and top race quality clip-ons?" asked Mike.

I was stunned. How did the owner of @KickAzTriumph, with several hundred thousand followers remember such specific and complimentary details of my little Bonnie?

I tried to remain cool. "Yeah that's her. She's my beloved machine."

Mike continued. "You wrote to me a while back. Something about the Speed Twin getting new and improved Metzeler tyres in the new year? I was going to revisit that and think about upgrading my tyres because of your message."

"Yeah, the Racetec RR K3s, I think," I responded. I tried not to smile too widely.

"Good knowledge man!" Mike laughed loudly and slapped me on the back. Justin was nodding at me too.

It was getting dark now and I could hear some live music starting up somewhere. That signalled the end of the show. I grabbed another beer and headed towards the sound of drums, guitars, and people enjoying themselves. I could see the other lads all dancing in a group together, laughing, holding beer bottles aloft. No one had their phones out. I was looking forward to joining them shortly. I passed through the BMW section on my way, making a slight detour. It was about to close up. A man sweeping the floor gave me a look, but I signalled that I would only be two minutes here. I stopped and looked around in the dim light. There were the typical customised R60s, R80s, and R100s on display. The centrepiece of those bikes was that iconic boxer-twin engine. That was the only thing these customised machines had in common with each other today. The designers and builders had done an amazing job showcasing a typical cafe racer, Scrambler, and Flat tracker. One of each. I spotted an R nineT in the corner too. The newer and modern machine looked chunky and huge compared to the genuine classic machines that served as inspiration for the modern bike. I sniggered, thinking back all those many months ago when I was inspired to ride Bonnie again, after rewatching the BMW advert produced to promote the very motorcycle in front of me. Those custom bike builders in that video, in a random shed in the middle of the desert, ratcheting away, were cool. How I wanted to be those guys back then. I placed my hand on the bike's fuel tank, and gently patted the white and blue circular logo, the colours of the spinning airplane propeller depiction representing BMW's home State of Bavaria. It was a lovely machine up close, I reflected. I had my own crew of bearded, tattooed, eclectic, badass misfits now, and we rode Triumphs. I reckoned the Cotswolds Wrecking Crew would smoke those BMW boys in a drag race, I thought to myself jokingly. At least on social media, no one could match us there. Our photos, reels, stories, and hashtags made us a biker gang to be respected. I shook my head, chuckling. "The devil it is, indeed!" I walked towards the lads, the Cotswolds Wrecking Crew, now manically jumping up and down to the music. No hashtags and no filters.

The Cotswolds Wrecking Crew will ride again…

Printed in Great Britain
by Amazon